Office 2003 For Dummies®

D0508253

Microsoft Word 2003 Tips

Moves cursor to	Keystroke
Front of line	Home
End of line	End
Beginning of document	Ctrl+Home
End of document	Ctrl+End
Right one word	Ctrl+ →
Left one word	Ctrl+ ←
Bold text	Ctrl+B

Moves cursor to	Keystroke
Italicize text	Ctrl+I
Underline text	Ctrl+U
Copy selected text	Ctrl+C
Cut selected text	Ctrl+X
Paste previously cut or copied text	Ctrl+V
Undo last action	Ctrl+Z
Redo last action	Ctrl+Y

Microsoft Excel 2003 Tips

Typing data into a worksheet

Typing data into rows or columns can be cumbersome and tedious. To simplify this task, Excel offers a special Data Form feature, which lets you type data into an easy-to-read dialog box; the dialog box automatically pastes your data into your worksheet.

To use this Data Form feature, click on a row or column label, then choose Data ⇨ Form. Excel displays a Data Form dialog box for you to type in your data.

Navigating around a worksheet

To move the cursor around the worksheet quickly, use the following shortcut keys:

Microsoft Excel 2003 Shortcut Navigation Keys	
Moves cursor to	Keystroke
Cell A1	Ctrl+Home
Last cell in bottom right-hand corner	Ctrl+End
Top cell of a column	Ctrl+Up arrow
Bottom cell of a column	Ctrl+Down arrow
Left cell of a row	Ctrl+Left arrow
Right cell of a row	Ctrl+Right arrow

For Dummies: Bestselling Book Series for Beginners

Office 2003 For Dummies®

Cheat Sheet

Displaying PowerPoint slides out of order

If you want to jump to a specific slide during a presentation, type the slide number and then press Enter. (You can get the slide number for each slide by viewing the Slides or Outline pane.)

Saving/Closing multiple files (Word, Excel, and PowerPoint)

If you have multiple files open, you can save or close them all at once if you hold down the Shift key and then click the File menu. When you hold down the Shift key, the Save and Close commands turn into the Save All and Close All commands, which save or close all open files respectively.

Microsoft Office 2003 Shortcut Keys

Function	Keystroke
Copy	Ctrl+C
Cut	Ctrl+X
Find	Ctrl+F
Go To	Ctrl+G
Help	F1
Hyperlink	Ctrl+K
New	Ctrl+N
Open	Ctrl+O
Paste	Ctrl+V
Print	Ctrl+P
Replace	Ctrl+H
Save	Ctrl+S
Select All	Ctrl+A
Spell Check	F7
Undo	Ctrl+Z
Redo	Ctrl+Y

Microsoft Internet Sites

World Wide Web site:
http://www.microsoft.com

FTP site: ftp://ftp.microsoft.com

Microsoft Newsgroups

microsoft.public.access

microsoft.public.excel

microsoft.public.office

microsoft.public.outlook.general

microsoft.public.powerpoint

microsoft.public.word

Office 2003 Mouse Button Functions

Mouse Button Used	Action	Purpose
Left mouse button	Click	Moves the cursor, highlights an object, pulls down a menu, or chooses a menu command
Left mouse button	Double-click	Highlights a word or edits an embedded object
Left mouse button	Triple-click	Highlights a paragraph
Left mouse button	Drag	Moves an object, resizes an object, highlights a text, or highlights multiple objects
Wheel mouse button	Click	Automatically scrolls a document
Right mouse button	Click	Displays a short-cut pop-up menu

Office 2003
FOR
DUMMIES®

Office 2003

FOR DUMMIES®

by Wallace Wang

Wiley Publishing, Inc.

Office 2003 For Dummies®

Published by
Wiley Publishing, Inc.
111 River Street
Hoboken, NJ 07030
www.wiley.com

Copyright © 2003 by Wiley Publishing, Inc., Indianapolis, Indiana

Published by Wiley Publishing, Inc., Indianapolis, Indiana

Published simultaneously in Canada

For general information on our other products and services or to obtain technical support, please contact our Customer Care Department within the U.S. at 800-762-2974, outside the U.S. at 317-572-3993, or fax 317-572-4002.

Wiley also publishes its books in a variety of electronic formats. Some content that appears in print may not be available in electronic books.

Library of Congress Control Number: 2003101905

ISBN: 978-0-7645-3860-5

Manufactured in the United States of America

10   9   8   7   6   5

1B/RW/QZ/QT/IN

WILEY   is a trademark of Wiley Publishing, Inc.

About the Author

Wallace Wang is a *Boardwatch* magazine columnist and standup comedian whose many bestselling books include *Beginning Programming For Dummies* and *Steal This Computer Book 2*.

Publisher's Acknowledgments

We're proud of this book; please send us your comments through our online registration form located at www.dummies.com/register/.

Some of the people who helped bring this book to market include the following:

Acquisitions, Editorial, and Media Development

Project Editor: Pat O'Brien

Acquisitions Editor: Bob Woerner

Copy Editor: Rebecca Huehls

Technical Editor: Michael Gibson

Editorial Manager: Kevin Kirschner

Media Development Manager: Laura VanWinkle

Media Development Supervisor: Richard Graves

Editorial Assistant: Amanda Foxworth

Cartoons: Rich Tennant (www.the5thwave.com)

Production

Project Coordinator: Maridee Ennis

Layout and Graphics: Amanda Carter, Jennifer Click, Seth Conley, Lauren Goddard, Stephanie D. Jumper, Michael Kruzil, Lynsey Osborn, Barry Offringa, Heather Ryan, Jacque Schneider, Julie Trippetti, Shae Wilson

Proofreaders: Laura Albert, John Greenough, Angel Perez, Carl William Pierce, TECHBOOKS Production Services

Indexer: TECHBOOKS Production Services

Publishing and Editorial for Technology Dummies

> **Richard Swadley,** Vice President and Executive Group Publisher

> **Andy Cummings,** Vice President and Publisher

> **Mary C. Corder,** Editorial Director

Publishing for Consumer Dummies

> **Diane Graves Steele,** Vice President and Publisher

> **Joyce Pepple,** Acquisitions Director

Composition Services

> **Gerry Fahey,** Vice President of Production Services

> **Debbie Stailey,** Director of Composition Services

Contents at a Glance

Table of Contents

Chapter 6: Making Your Words Look Pretty .89

Chapter 7: Creating Fancy Pages 119

Introduction

Microsoft Office 2003 consists of a word processor (Word), a spreadsheet program (Excel), a presentation graphics program (PowerPoint), a personal information organizer (Outlook), and a database program (Access). Your version of Microsoft Office 2003 may include a Web page design and management program (FrontPage). *Microsoft Office 2003 For Dummies* gently explains the basics for using each program so you can get started using them right away.

Who Should Buy This Book

Everyone should buy this book because this sentence says that you should, and you should believe everything you read. But you should especially buy this book if you have any of the following versions of Microsoft Office 2003:

- *Standard Edition:* Contains Microsoft Word, Excel, Outlook, and PowerPoint.
- *Small Business Edition:* Contains Microsoft Word, Excel, PowerPoint, Publisher, and Outlook with Business Contact Manager.
- *Professional Edition:* Contains Microsoft Word, Excel, PowerPoint, Access, Publisher, and Outlook with Business Contact Manager.

How This Book Is Organized

This book uses the time-tested method of binding pages and gluing them on one side to form a book. To help you find what you need quickly, this book is divided into six parts. Each part covers a certain topic about using Office 2003. Whenever you need help, just flip through this book, find the part that covers the topic you're looking for, and then toss this book aside and get back to work.

Part 1: Getting to Know Microsoft Office 2003

Even though Office 2003 looks like a bunch of unrelated programs thrown together by Microsoft, it is actually a bunch of unrelated programs that have been tortured over the years into working together. All Office 2003 programs provide similar menus, icons, and keystroke commands; when you know how to use one program, you'll be able to quickly figure out how to use another Office 2003 program.

Part II: Working with Word

Microsoft Word is the most popular word processor on the face of the earth. You can use Word just to write letters, proposals, or apologies, or you can create fancier documents, such as newsletters with graphics and multiple columns. If you can't type, don't like to write, or flunked spelling, you can use Word to turn your $2,000 computer into your personal secretary. With the Word spell checker, grammar checker, outliner, and foreign language translator, you can turn random thoughts into coherent words and sentences that even your boss can understand.

Part III: Playing the Numbers Game with Excel

This part shows you how to design your own spreadsheets by using Excel. You discover what the heck a spreadsheet is, how you plop numbers and labels into it, how to create formulas so that Excel automatically calculates new results, and how to format the whole thing to make it look pleasing to the eye. After you get the basics of spreadsheet creation, the next step is to convert your raw data into eye-popping graphs, charts, and other colorful images that can amuse everyone from high-powered CEOs to children roaming around in a day-care center.

Part IV: Making Presentations with PowerPoint

PowerPoint can help you create slide shows, overhead transparencies, and on-screen computer presentations that either enhance your information or hide the fact that you don't have the slightest idea what you're talking about in the first place. Any time you need to make a presentation, let PowerPoint help you develop a dynamic presentation that includes visuals, notes, and handouts.

Part V: Getting Organized with Outlook

To help manage your time while your peers wander aimlessly through the corporate landscape, Office 2003 includes Outlook, a program that combines the features of an appointment book, calendar, and to-do list in one screen. Besides organizing your appointments and tasks, Outlook can also organize all the e-mail that may flood you every day. From within Outlook, you can write, reply to, send, and receive e-mail to and from friends down the hall or on another continent.

Part VI: Storing Stuff in Access

Access is a relational database that lets you store and retrieve data, design reports, and even create your own programs. If your edition of Office 2003 doesn't have Access, you can buy Access separately and install it on your computer. If you need to save and retrieve information, use Access to do it quickly and easily. You may find Access handy for saving mailing lists and storing esoteric information, such as part numbers, Web addresses, and credit card numbers.

Part VII: The Part of Tens

For those people who just want to find keyboard shortcuts for accessing commonly used commands and tips for working more efficiently with Office 2003 (so they can take the rest of the day off), this part of the book provides common keystrokes for using all the Microsoft programs. Other tips can make Office 2003 seem a lot easier than the incomprehensible manuals may lead you to believe.

How to Use This Book

You can use this book as a reference, a tutorial, or a weapon (if you throw it hard enough). It isn't designed to read from cover to cover (although you could if you wanted). Instead, just browse through the parts that interest you and ignore the rest.

To take full advantage of Office 2003, read Part I first to acquaint yourself with common Office features. The other parts are for your reference. You may not need PowerPoint presentations today, but one day you may want to play around with it just to see what it can do. To your surprise, certain programs you thought you would never use may turn out to be more useful than you imagined.

Conventions

To get the most from this book, you need to understand the following:

- The *mouse cursor* or *pointer* appears either as an arrow or as an I-beam pointer (depending on the program you happen to be using at the time). If you lose track of the mouse cursor, start moving the mouse until you see something flashing across your screen. What you're seeing probably is the mouse cursor.

- *Clicking* refers to pressing the left mouse button once and then letting go. Clicking is how you activate buttons on the toolbar and choose commands from pull-down menus.

✔ *Double-clicking* refers to pressing the left mouse button twice in rapid succession. Double-clicking typically activates a command.

✔ *Dragging* refers to moving the mouse pointer while holding down the left mouse button. To drag an object, select the item by clicking it and then hold the left mouse button and move the item in the desired direction. When you release the mouse button, Windows places the item where you want.

✔ *Right-clicking* means clicking the button on the right side of the mouse. (Some mice have three buttons, so ignore the middle button for now.) Right-clicking usually displays a pop-up menu on the screen.

Note: If you're left-handed and you have changed your mouse settings so that you use your left hand to operate the mouse, *clicking* means pressing the right mouse button, and *right-clicking* means pressing the left mouse button.

Icons used in this book

Icons highlight useful tips, information to remember, or technical explanations that you can skip if you want. Watch for the following icons throughout the book:

This icon highlights pieces of information that can be helpful (as long as you remember them, of course).

This icon marks certain steps or procedures that can make your life a whole lot easier when using Microsoft Office 2003.

Look out! This icon tells you how to avoid trouble before it starts.

This icon highlights information that's absolutely useless to know for operating Microsoft Office 2003 but could be interesting to impress your trivia buddies.

Getting Started

By now, you're probably anxious to try out Microsoft Office 2003. Turn on your computer and get ready to jump miles ahead of the competition by using the world's most powerful and dominant programs bundled together in Microsoft Office 2003.

Part I
Getting to Know Microsoft Office

The 5th Wave By Rich Tennant

"Did you click 'HELP' on the menu bar recently? It's Mr. Gates. He wants to know if everything's alright."

In this part . . .

At first glance, Microsoft Office 2003 may seem a complicated beast that gobbles up megabytes of hard drive space and offers enough features to overwhelm even the most battle-hardened veteran of the personal computer wars. But after you get over your initial impression (or fear) of Office 2003, you can understand (and even admire) the elegant madness behind Office 2003's massive bulk.

Despite the fact that Microsoft Office 2003 contains more commands than any sane person could ever possibly use, Office 2003 can be conquered. To guide you through the multitude of commands you may need to get your work done, Office 2003 provides several ways to get help, one of which (hopefully) will actually provide you with the answers you need.

Besides showing you how to get help within Microsoft Office 2003, this part of the book also explains how to get the various programs of Office 2003 started in the first place. After you start using Office 2003, this part of the book also shows you some of the more common keystroke and menu commands that all Office 2003 programs share. That way when you learn how to use one Office 2003 program, you can quickly learn and use any other Office 2003 program with a minimum of retraining and hassle and join the ranks of the many happy people already using Microsoft Office 2003 to get their work done.

Chapter 1

Playing with Office 2003 Files

• •

• •

Microsoft Office consists of several programs, each designed to create and manipulate different types of data, such as words (Word), numbers (Excel), presentations (PowerPoint), and structured information (Access). Although the type of data each program uses may differ, the general procedure for creating and opening a file remains the same.

So this chapter teaches you how to create, save, open, and print any Office 2003 file, no matter which Office program you may be using. After you figure out the standard ways to create and use different Office 2003 files, you can focus on doing something useful with your data, rather than tearing your hair out, trying to figure out how to do something as seemingly simple as printing a file.

Creating a New Office 2003 File

When you want to create a new Office 2003 file, you have two choices:

✔ Create a completely empty file.

✔ Create a file (such as a résumé or a sales invoice) from a *template,* which provides a basic design that you can use to format and arrange your data automatically.

Creating a blank file

A blank file can be useful if you need to customize the formatting yourself, but it may take time to do so. A file created from a template can help you format your data quickly, but may not always be formatted in the way you really want it. The more you use Office 2003, the more you'll find that you probably need to create both blank files and files from a template at one time or another.

Loading a program to create a blank file

Every time you start Word, Excel, or PowerPoint, that program automatically creates a blank file for you. To load one of these programs and create a blank file, follow these steps:

1. **Click the Start button on the taskbar.**

   The Start menu appears.

2. **Click All Programs.**

   The Programs menu appears.

3. **Click the program that you want to use, such as Microsoft Word or Microsoft PowerPoint.**

   The program you choose appears with a blank file ready for you to use.

Creating a blank file within a program

If you have already loaded Word, Excel, or PowerPoint and want to create a blank file, choose one of these two methods:

- Click the New icon on the Standard toolbar
- Press Ctrl+N

The result is shown in Figure 1-1.

After you choose either of these options, your Office 2003 program creates a blank file for you to use.

If you choose File⇨New from any Office program, the Office task pane appears, which lets you create either a blank file or a file based on a template. (See the section below, "Using a template stored on your computer.")

New icon

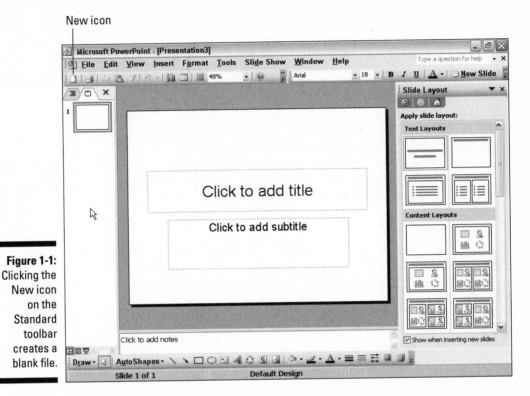

Figure 1-1:
Figure 1-1:
Clicking the
New icon
on the
Standard
toolbar
creates a
blank file.

Creating a file from a template

After you have loaded Word, Excel, PowerPoint, or Access, you can create a
new file based on a template. Templates act like cookie cutters for your data.
The template provides predefined formatting for your data in the shape of
résumés, business letters, invoice reports, or business plans so that you just
have to type in data and print out your file.

You can find templates in two locations: on your computer and on Microsoft's
template Web page.

Using a template stored on your computer

When you install Office 2003, the program stores a bunch of templates on
your computer for you automatically. The problem is finding them again.

If you have already loaded an Office 2003 program, such as Access or PowerPoint, you can load a template by following these steps:

1. **Click File⇨New.**

   The New task pane appears on the right side of the window as shown in Figure 1-2.

2. **Click the <u>On my computer</u> link under the Templates category.**

   A Templates dialog box appears as shown in Figure 1-3.

3. **Click a template to use and then click OK.**

   Office 2003 loads your chosen template. Now all you have to do is add your own data to create an instant document.

Downloading a template from the Internet

In case you can't find what you're looking for among the limited number of templates stored on your computer, you can also download templates from the Internet.

To download templates from the Microsoft template Web site, you need an Internet connection.

To download a template, follow these steps:

1. **Click File⇨New.**

   The task pane appears on the right side of the window (see Figure 1-2).

2. **Click the <u>Templates on Office Online</u> link.**

   The Microsoft Templates Web page appears as shown in Figure 1-4, listing different categories to choose from, such as Calendars and Planners or Meetings and Projects.

3. **Click a template name under a specific category, such as the Calendars and Planning category.**

   The Templates Web page lists all the available templates you can choose.

4. **Click a template that you want to use.**

   The Templates Web page displays the format for your chosen template, so that you can see how the template formats data, as shown in Figure 1-5.

5. **Click the Download Now button.**

   Office 2003 downloads your chosen template and displays it in the appropriate program, such as Word or Excel. At this point you can start typing in your own data and save your file.

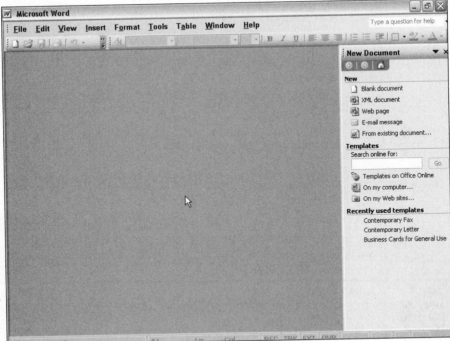

Figure 1-2:
You can
load a
template
from the
New task
pane.

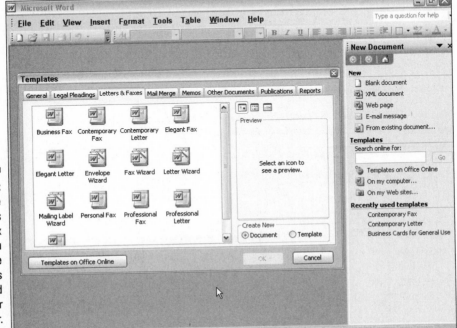

Figure 1-3:
The
Templates
dialog box
shows you
all the
templates
stored
on your
computer.

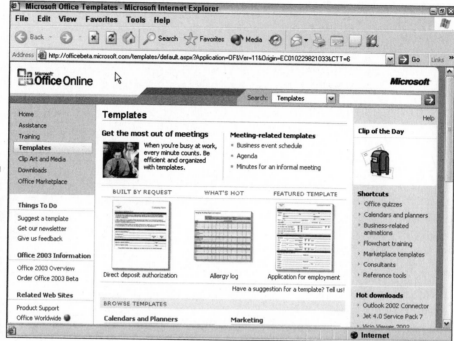

Figure 1-4:
The Templates Web page lists different templates organized into categories.

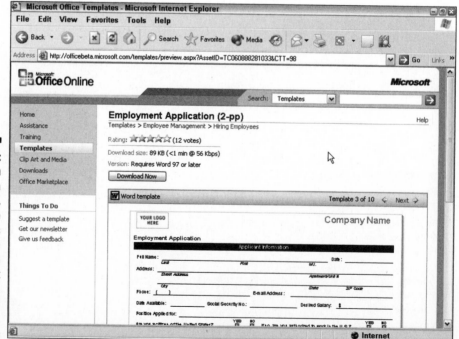

Figure 1-5:
When you choose a template, the Templates Web page shows you how that template formats data.

Opening an Existing File

You'll probably spend more time opening and editing existing files than creating brand-new files from scratch. The most common way to open a file is to load the program you want to run (such as Excel or Access) and then open the file you want to use. A second, faster way involves opening the file you want to use, which automatically loads the program needed to edit that file.

You can open multiple files within each Office 2003 program (with the exception of Outlook and Access). So if you load Microsoft Word, you can open your résumé file, your letter of resignation file, your business report file, and your love letter file all at the same time. In general, it's a good idea to only open those files you need to use at the time and then close those files you don't need right now, because the more files you have open, the less memory your computer has for working with any other programs that you may have running at the moment.

Opening an Office file right away

If you want to open a specific Office file, you must first find that particular file and then double-click on it to open both the file and the Office program that created it. To do this, follow these steps:

1. **Click the Start button on the taskbar.**

   The Start menu appears.

2. **Click All Programs➪Accessories➪Windows Explorer.**

   The Windows Explorer window appears.

3. **Double-click the file that you want to open.**

   If the file you want to open is buried in another folder or even on another drive, you may have to dig through the different folders stored on your computer. For more information about using the Windows Explorer, pick up a copy of *Windows XP For Dummies* by Andy Rathbone.

   To help you find a file quickly, click the Search button in the Windows Explorer window.

   Once Office loads your file and the program that created it, such as Excel or PowerPoint, you can start editing the information.

Opening an Office file within a program

If you are already running a particular Office program, such as Word or Excel, you can open an existing file by following these steps:

1. **Choose one of the following:**

   - Click File➪Open

   - Press Ctrl+O

   - Click the Open icon on the Standard toolbar

   Whichever method you chose, an Open dialog box appears.

2. **Click the file that you want to open.**

   If the file you want to open is buried in another folder or even on another drive, click in the Look In list box and choose a different drive or folder, such as Local Disk (C:) or the My Documents folder.

3. **Click Open.**

   Office loads your file into your currently running program.

Office allows you to open multiple files so that you can quickly switch back and forth between the files you need at the moment.

Taking a Shortcut

Rather than wade through multiple menus or the less than intuitive Windows Explorer, you can create shortcuts to your favorite Office programs or files. You can put these shortcuts directly on your Windows desktop or on the Start menu. That way, you can just double-click the shortcut and go to the program or file you want right away.

A *shortcut* is nothing more than an icon that represents a specific file. This file can be an actual program (such as Microsoft Word) or a file created by another program (such as your résumé written in Word).

Putting a shortcut on the desktop

To place a shortcut of a program or file on the Windows desktop, follow these steps:

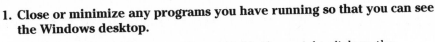

1. **Close or minimize any programs you have running so that you can see the Windows desktop.**

   You can see the Windows desktop quickly if you right-click on the Windows Start bar at the bottom of the screen and when a pop-up menu appears, click Show the Desktop.

2. **Right-click the mouse on the Windows desktop.**

   A pop-up menu appears, as shown in Figure 1-6.

3. **Choose New⇨Shortcut.**

4. **Click the Browse button.**

   A Browse For Folder dialog box appears.

5. **Locate the Microsoft Office program or file that you want to place on your Windows desktop.**

   For example, if you want to put a shortcut to Excel on the Windows desktop, look for the Excel icon. By default, Microsoft Office XP stores its program files in the `C:\Program Files\Microsoft Office\ Office11` folder.

   To help you decipher the cryptic names Microsoft gives its programs, here's a table you can refer to:

Program	*Icon Name Displayed in the Browse Dialog Box*
Access	Msaccess
Excel	Excel
Outlook	Outlook
PowerPoint	Powerpnt
Word	Winword

6. **Click a program icon, such as Mspub or Powerpnt, or a file and click Open.**

   The Create Shortcut dialog box appears again.

7. **Click Next.**

   The Create Shortcut dialog box asks you for a descriptive name for your desktop icon. If you don't type a name, Windows uses the program icon name by default, such as Msaccess or Winword.

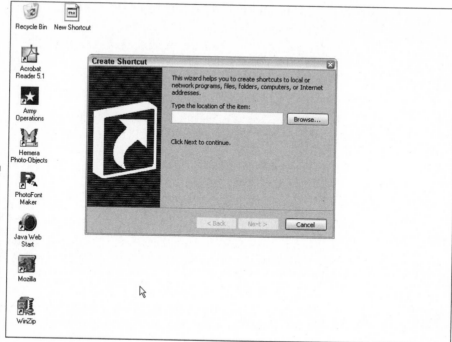

Figure 1-6:
The Create
Shortcut
dialog box
guides you
through the
process of
finding and
naming a
shortcut.

8. **Type a descriptive name for your program or file, such as Microsoft Word or Letter of Resignation, and click Finish.**

   The Windows desktop appears with your chosen shortcut on the desktop. Shortcuts are easy to spot because they have a little black-and-white arrow in the lower-left corner.

9. **Double-click your shortcut to run the program or load your file.**

If you want to delete a shortcut icon from your desktop, right-click it and choose Delete from the pop-up menu.

Putting a program shortcut on the Start menu

The Start menu lists your most recently used programs for easy access. However, you might want to store shortcuts to your favorite programs on the Start menu yourself. To do this, follow these steps:

1. **Click the Start button.**

   The Start menu appears.

2. **Click All Programs.**

   A pop-up menu appears.

3. **Click Microsoft Office.**

   A pop-up menu appears that lists all the Microsoft Office programs available.

4. **Right-click the program you want to store on the Start menu.**

   A pop-up menu appears, as shown in Figure 1-7.

5. **Click the Pin to Start menu command.**

   Your chosen program appears as a shortcut icon on the Start menu.

   If you ever want to delete a shortcut icon from the Start menu, right-click that icon and then click the Remove from This List command from the pop-up menu.

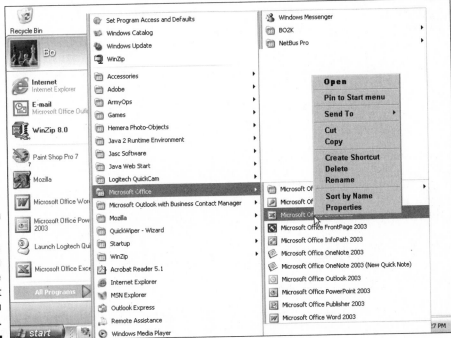

Figure 1-7:
The pop-up menu displays the Pin to Start menu command.

Saving a File

Unless you want to keep typing the same data into your computer over and over again, you should save your files. If you create a new file and then save it, you need to specify a name for your file and a location where you want to store it, such as on your hard drive or in a specific folder, such as the My Documents folder. When you edit an existing file, Office 2003 simply saves your data in the current file.

To save a file, just choose one of the following:

- Click File⇨Save.
- Click the Save icon on the Standard toolbar, as shown in Figure 1-8.
- Press Ctrl+S.

Save icon

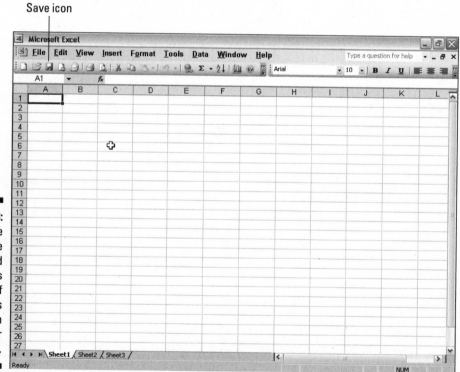

Figure 1-8:
The Save icon on the Standard toolbar is just one of the ways you can save your file.

You should save your data periodically while you're working, such as every ten minutes or whenever you take a break and walk away from your computer. That way, if the power suddenly goes out, your hard disk crashes, or something else goes horribly wrong with your computer, you lose only a little bit of the data you typed in since the last time you saved your file.

For extra security, save a copy of your file on removable media such as a floppy disk or a rewritable CD, then store that removable media in a separate location away from your computer. That way if a fire, flood, or other type of disaster wipes out your computer, you'll (hopefully) be able to recover your data on your removable media later.

Closing a File

After you open a file to edit or add new data, you eventually have to close that file again so that you can do something else with your life besides use Microsoft Office 2003. There are two ways to close a file:

- ✔ Click File⇨Close in case you want to stop editing a specific file but still want to keep using Office 2003.

If you have multiple files open in the same program, such as multiple Word documents, you can close them all at the same time if you hold down the Shift key and then click File⇨Close All. The Close All command only appears when you hold down the Shift key.

- ✔ Click File⇨Exit

For a fast way to close a file and the program that created it, click the Close box of the program window. (The *Close box* is a little box with an X in it, which appears in the upper-right corner of a program window.)

If you made any changes after you save your file and then choose the File⇨ Exit command, Microsoft Office 2003 asks whether you want to save the changes and offers you the following options: Yes, No, or Cancel.

- ✔ Click Yes to save your file.
- ✔ Click No if you don't want to save any recent changes.
- ✔ Click Cancel (or press the Esc key on your keyboard) if you suddenly don't want to exit after all.

Chapter 2

Common Office 2003 Commands

*I*n an effort to make Microsoft Office 2003 easier to use, nearly every Office 2003 programs shares similar mouse and keyboard commands so you can (theoretically) switch from one Office 2003 program to another without much hassle or mental anguish.

Of course, until you learn how to give commands to one Office 2003 program, you can't use any Office 2003 programs, so this chapter shows you the common ways to control every Office 2003 program with your mouse or keyboard.

Using Your Menus

The menu bar appears at the top of every Office 2003 program window and consists of several menu titles that organize different program commands by categories. Some of the commonly shared menu titles among Office 2003 programs include:

- ✔ **File:** Contains commands for opening, saving, and printing files.

- ✔ **Edit:** Contains commands copying, deleting, pasting, searching, and replacing data.

- ✔ **View:** Contains commands to change the way your data appears on the screen.

- **Insert:** Contains commands for putting different types of information in a file such as lines, graphs, or hyperlinks.

- **Format:** Contains commands for changing the way your data appears such as fonts or different ways to represent numbers such as dates or scientific notation.

- **Tools:** Contains commands for manipulating the data in your file, such as checking the spelling. Also contains commands for customizing the way your Office 2003 program looks and works.

- **Windows:** Contains commands for manipulating windows within a particular Office 2003 program.

- **Help:** Contains commands for getting help using that Office 2003 program.

To view the commands trapped under a particular menu title, just click that menu title, such as the File or Help menu title. If you look carefully, you'll notice that every menu title has a single letter underlined. This underlined letter represents a hot key that you can press to view that particular menu title as well.

For example, the File menu title has the letter *F* underlined. This means that you can press the Alt key and then the F key to view the File menu without using the mouse.

If you just press the Alt key, Office 2003 highlights the File menu. Now you can use the left/right arrow keys to highlight a different menu title and press the down arrow key or the Enter key to view the highlighted menu title.

Moving the menu bar

The menu bar normally appears near the top of every Office 2003 program window. In case you'd rather put the menu bar somewhere else, follow these steps:

1. **Move the mouse pointer over the menu bar handle.**

   When the mouse pointer appears directly over the menu bar handle, the mouse pointer turns into a four-way pointing arrow as shown in Figure 2-1. This figure shows what the menu bar looks like as a floating window and at the top of the program window.

2. **Drag the mouse (hold down the left mouse button and move the mouse).**

   As you drag the mouse, the menu bar appears as a floating window.

3. **Release the left mouse button when you're happy with the location of the menu bar.**

If you drag the title bar of the menus back to the top of the program window, the menu bar "snaps" back in place.

Customizing the menu bar

Because Office 2003 contains so many different commands, each menu title can display commands in one of three ways:

- ✔ Display every possible command at all times. This lets you see all the possible commands you can choose but can also overwhelm you with too many choices.

- ✔ Hide the commands you rarely use. If you want to see all the commands stored under a particular menu title, you have to click the Expand button at the bottom of the menu title.

- ✔ Hide the commands you rarely use but display them automatically after a few seconds.

Menu bar

Handle

Title bar

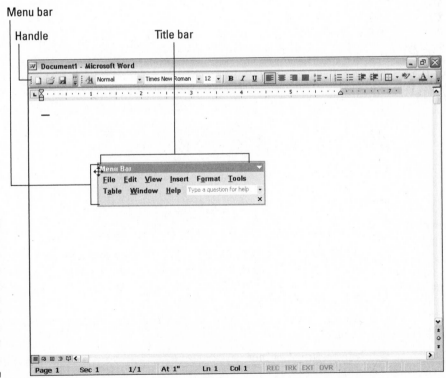

Figure 2-1:
You can move the menu bar by dragging the menu bar handle to a new location.

To change the way menus work, follow these steps for each Office 2003 program:

1. **Choose one of the following:**

   • Click Tools⇨Customize.

   • Click View⇨Toolbars⇨Customize.

A Customize dialog box appears, as shown in Figure 2-2.

2. **Click the Options tab.**

3. **Click or clear one of the following check boxes:**

   • **Always Show Full Menus:** If checked, this option makes the drop-down menus display every possible command as shown in Figure 2-3.

   • **Show Full Menus After A Short Delay:** If checked, this option waits a few seconds before showing the less-frequently used commands on a menu.

4. **Click Close.**

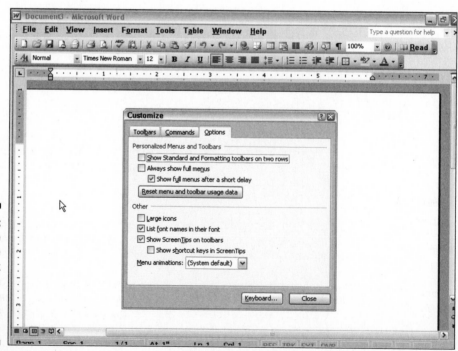

Figure 2-2: The Customize dialog box lets you modify the way menus work.

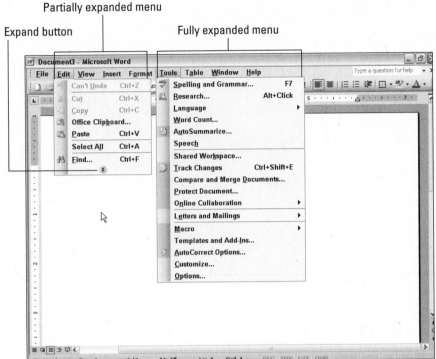

Figure 2-3:
Menus can
display all
commands
at all times.

Using Your Toolbars

Toolbars contain icons that represent the most commonly used commands. That way, you can just click an icon to choose a command rather than dig through a menu or press an obscure keystroke combination, such as Ctrl+P. The two common toolbars that every Office 2003 program shares are the Standard and the Formatting toolbars.

The Standard toolbar contains icons that represent common commands from the File, Edit, and Insert menus. The Formatting toolbar contains icons that represent commands from the Format menu.

To use a toolbar, just click the icon that represents the command you want. If you don't know what each icon represents, move the mouse pointer over the icon and wait a second or two. Office 2003 kindly displays a short description of the command that the icon represents, as shown in Figure 2-4.

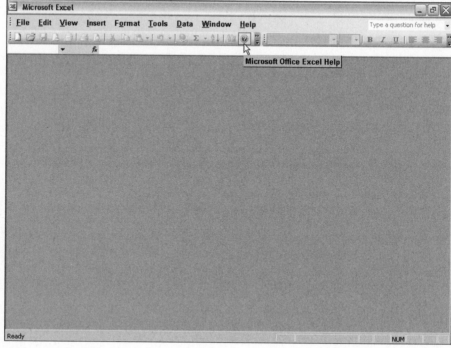

Figure 2-4:
When you
point to an
icon on a
toolbar, you
can see
what
command
that icon
represents.

Smashing (or stacking) the Standard and Formatting toolbars

To save space, Microsoft Office 2003 may smash the Standard and Formatting toolbars together on a single row. Unfortunately, this prevents both toolbars from displaying all the icons available.

When the Standard and Formatting toolbars share one row, you have to click the Toolbar Options button to display a drop-down menu that contains any toolbar icons that are not displayed on the toolbar, as shown in Figure 2-5.

If you want to stack the Standard and Formatting toolbars on top of each other so that you can see all the commands available in each toolbar, follow these steps:

1. **Choose one of the following:**

   • Click Tools⇨Customize.

   • Click View⇨Toolbars⇨Customize.

A Customize dialog box appears.

2. **Click the Options tab.**

3. **Click or clear the Show Standard and Formatting Toolbars on Two Rows check box.**

4. **Click Close.**

   Office 2003 displays the Standard and Formatting toolbars on separate rows as shown in Figure 2-6.

Hiding and displaying toolbars

Besides the Standard and Formatting toolbars, Office 2003 includes a handful of additional toolbars that contain additional commands that you might need. To save space, Office 2003 normally keeps these other toolbars tucked out of sight, but if you use specific commands often, you might want to use a toolbar that displays your commonly used commands.

Toolbar Options button

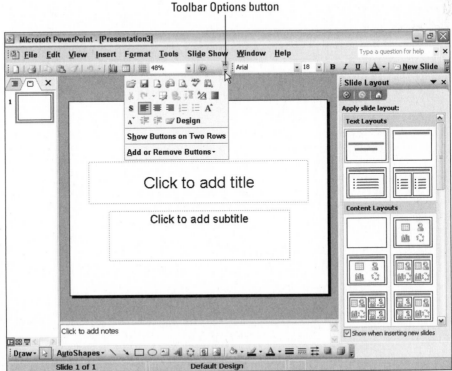

Figure 2-5:
Clicking the
Toolbar
Options
button to
see the rest
of the icons.

Figure 2-6: When the Standard and Formatting toolbars appear on separate rows, you can see all the icons available.

Of course, the more toolbars you display, the less screen space you have to actually see what you're doing, so Office 2003 can also hide your toolbars from view at any time. To hide or display a toolbar, follow these steps:

1. **Choose View⇨Toolbars.**

   The Toolbars drop-down menu appears, as shown in Figure 2-7. Check marks appear next to those toolbars currently displayed.

2. **Click the toolbar that you want to display (or hide).**

   Office 2003 obediently displays or hides your chosen toolbar.

Moving a toolbar

Like the menu bar, toolbars can either appear near the edges of the screen or as a floating window in the middle of the screen. To move a toolbar, follow these steps:

1. **Move the mouse pointer over the handle of the toolbar that you want to move. (If the toolbar appears in the middle of the screen, move the mouse pointer over the title bar of the toolbar.)**

When you move the mouse pointer over a toolbar handle, the mouse pointer turns into a four-way pointing arrow, as shown in Figure 2-8. If you move a toolbar that appears in the middle of the screen, you don't see the four-way pointing arrow mouse pointer until you hold down the left mouse button.

2. **Hold down the left mouse button and drag the mouse.**

   The toolbar appears as a separate window (see Figure 2-8).

3. **Release the left mouse button when the toolbar window appears where you want it.**

   If things floating in the middle of the screen make you nervous, you can smash the toolbar to one side or to the bottom of the screen and stick it there.

If you leave the toolbar in the middle of the screen as a floating window, you can resize the toolbar window. Just move the mouse pointer over one edge of the toolbar window, wait until the mouse pointer turns into a double-pointing arrow, and then hold down the left mouse button and drag the mouse to resize the toolbar window.

Resizing a toolbar

If you keep the Standard and Formatting toolbars smashed together on a single row, you may want to alter the size of one of the toolbars so you can see more icons on the other toolbar. To change the size of a toolbar, follow these steps:

1. **Move the mouse pointer over the toolbar handle that appears in the middle of the screen.**

   When you move the mouse pointer over a toolbar handle, the mouse pointer turns into a four-way pointing arrow (see Figure 2-8).

2. **Hold down the left mouse button and drag the mouse.**

   The toolbar either shrinks or expands, depending on which way you drag the mouse.

3. **Release the left mouse button when the toolbar appears at the size that you find acceptable.**

If the toolbar appears as a floating window in the middle of the screen, follow these steps:

1. **Move the mouse pointer over one edge of the floating toolbar.**

   When you move the mouse pointer over a toolbar handle, the mouse pointer turns into a two-way pointing arrow.

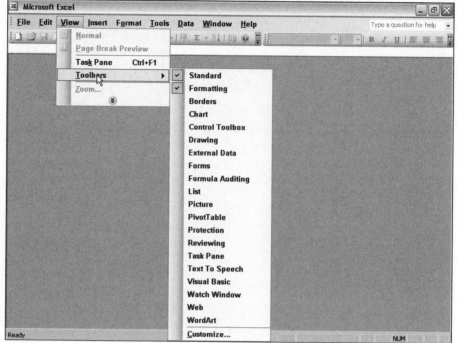

Figure 2-7:
To hide or display a toolbar, just click in the toolbar you want to display (or hide).

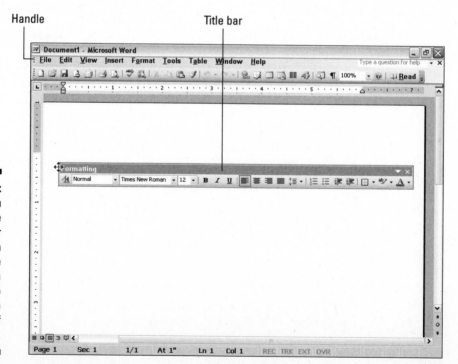

Figure 2-8:
You can drag the toolbar handle with the mouse to move a toolbar to the middle or side of the screen.

2. **Hold down the left mouse button and drag the mouse.**

   The toolbar either shrinks or expands, depending on which way you drag the mouse.

3. **Release the left mouse button when the toolbar appears at the size that you find acceptable.**

Showing or hiding icons from a toolbar

In case you find the Standard and formatting toolbars too cluttered, you can hide the icons that you rarely use. That way your toolbars only contain the icons of your most frequently used commands. To hide or display icons on a toolbar, follow these steps:

1. **Click on the Toolbar Options button on either the Standard or Formatting toolbar.**

   A pull-down menu appears that shows all the icons available for that particular toolbar, as shown in Figure 2-9.

2. **Click Add or Remove Buttons.**

   Another menu pops up as shown in Figure 2-10.

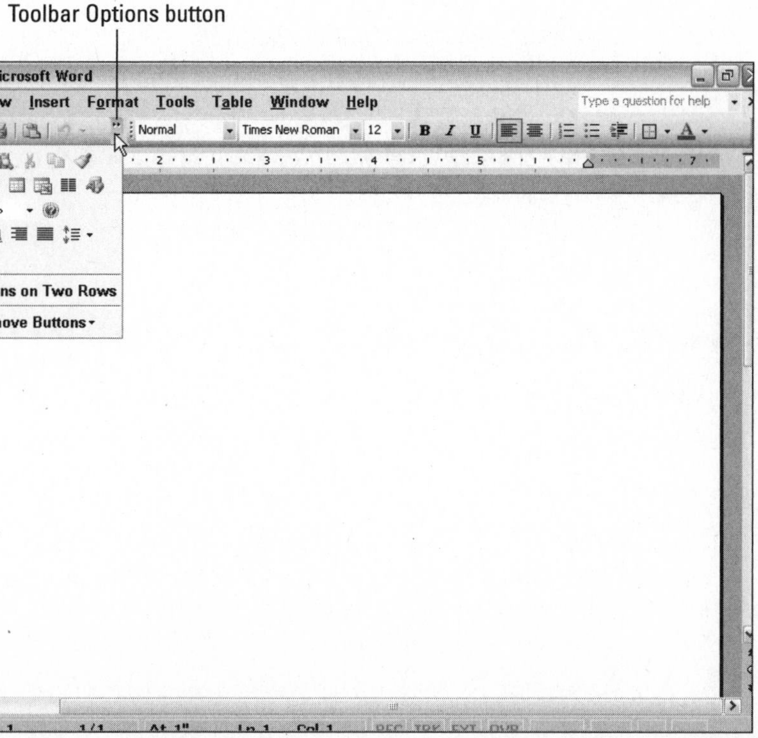

Toolbar Options button

Figure 2-9: To customize a toolbar, you need to click on the Toolbar Options button.

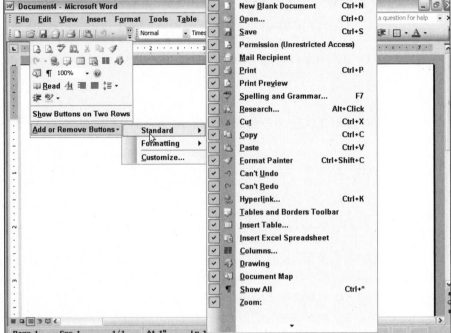

Figure 2-10:
A check mark appears next to every icon that currently appears on the toolbar.

3. **Click Standard and Formatting.**

4. **Click to the left of the icon that you want to display on the toolbar. (Clear a check mark from any icons that you want to hide on the toolbar.)**

   Office 2003 immediately displays or hides the icons you chose.

5. **Click anywhere on the screen to get rid of the pull-down menus.**

Working with the Task Pane

Sometimes when you choose a command, such as the New command in the File menu, Microsoft Office 2003 needs more information from you before it can do anything else. In the case of the New command, Office 2003 has no idea whether you want to create a new blank file or a new file based on a template.

So when Office 2003 needs to display additional options for you to choose from, Office 2003 shows those options as links in a window, called the task pane, which appears to the right side of the screen, as shown in Figure 2-11.

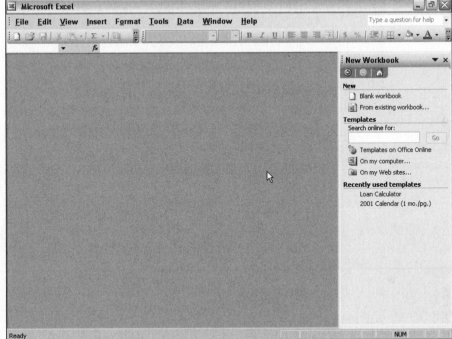

Figure 2-11:
The task
pane
displays
different
options
while still
letting you
see the
contents of
your file on
the screen.

Every Office 2003 program includes several different types of task panes. Each type provides options for performing one particular task, such as creating a new slide (in PowerPoint), creating a mail merge document (in Word), or displaying help for that particular program (in all Office 2003 programs).

Using the task pane

When you choose a command, the task pane may appear to show you all the options available. To choose an option, just click a link, which appears highlighted in blue.

You can also identify links in the task pane by moving the mouse pointer over text. If the text appears underlined and the mouse pointer turns into a pointing hand icon, that means the mouse pointer is over a link.

After you choose an option from the task pane, Office 2003 removes the task pane from view so you can get back to work again.

Hiding and displaying the task pane

In case you want to display the task pane without waiting to choose a command that will open the task pane for you, do one of the following:

- ✔ Click View⇨Task pane
- ✔ Press Ctrl+F1

If you want to hide the task pane from view, just click the Close box of the task pane.

Navigating through the task pane

The task pane can display different types of information at various times, which means there's a good chance that the task pane won't display the information you want to see at any given moment. Fortunately, you can change the type of information that appears in the task pane by using either the task pane list box or the Back, Forward, or Home buttons (shown in Figure 2-12).

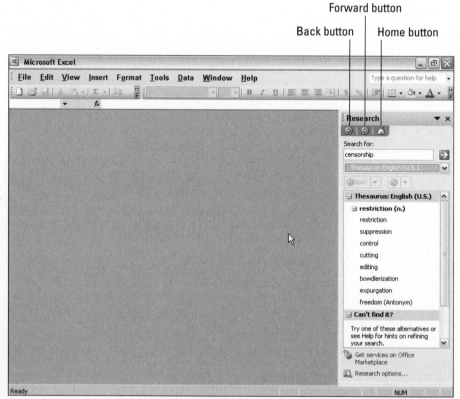

Forward button

Back button   Home button

Figure 2-12:
The task pane gives you additional options to choose while working in an Office 2003 program.

The Home button displays the home page of the task pane, which is where you can create a new file or open an existing one. If you click a link in the task pane, the task pane displays different information.

Clicking the Back button displays the previous information that appeared in the task pane. If you click the Back button and suddenly decide you want to return to that task pane, just click the Forward button.

If you click on the Task Pane list box, you can view all the other types of information that the task pane can display, such as the Help task pane or the Clipboard task pane as shown in Figure 2-13.

Task Pane list box

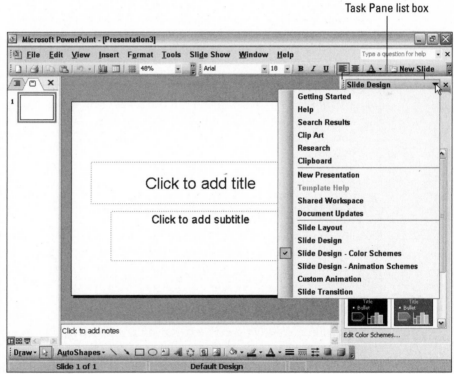

Figure 2-13: The Task Pane list box lets you quickly see all the types of information the task pane can display.

Opening Multiple Windows

With the exception of Outlook and Access, every Office 2003 program can open multiple files. For example, one window could display a résumé you're writing in Word while a second window could display your letter of resignation in Word. By opening multiple files in separate windows, you can work with several files at the same time and copy data from one file to another.

Switching between multiple windows

When you open multiple windows, only one window can be active at any given time. To switch to a different window, choose one of the following:

- Click anywhere inside the window that you want to switch to (provided you can see that window).
- Click the Window menu and then click the name of the window to switch to.
- Click the window name that appears on the Windows taskbar at the bottom of the screen (or wherever you may have moved the Windows taskbar).

Arranging multiple windows

If you open two or more windows, you may want to see the contents of all windows simultaneously. That way, you can view the contents of one window while you edit another. To display multiple windows on the screen, follow these steps:

1. **Choose Window⇨Arrange All.**

   All your currently open files arrange themselves on the screen as separate windows.

   If you have multiple windows open, you can choose Windows⇨Cascade to neatly stack your windows in layers, like index cards with their edges showing.

2. **Click in the window that you want to edit.**

   The active window (the one you're currently editing) highlights its title bar while the other windows dim their title bar.

You can resize windows or move them by dragging the title bar of a window anywhere on the screen. By doing this, you can arrange your windows in any way you choose.

Saving and closing multiple windows

After a while, you may not want multiple windows cluttering up your screen. To close a window, do one of the following:

- ✔ Click the Close box of all the windows you want to close. (The Close box is that little X in the upper-right corner.)
- ✔ Click the Minimize box of all the windows you want to keep open but hide out of view for the moment. (The Minimize box has a little horizontal line.)

If you click in the Close box at the top of the program window, you may exit out of the program altogether.

If you have two or more windows open, you can close and save windows more conveniently using the Close All command.

The Close All command is not available in Access or Outlook.

To close every open window, do the following:

1. **Hold down the Shift key.**

2. **Choose File⇨Close All.**

   When you hold down the Shift key, the File menu changes the Close command to Close All. If you haven't saved a file, Office XP displays a dialog box that asks whether you want to save your data before closing the file.

Copying and Pasting with the Office Clipboard

When you copy objects (such as text or graphics) in an Office 2003 program, your computer stores the copied object on the *Windows Clipboard,* which temporarily stores items that you can use again in the future. Unfortunately, the Windows Clipboard can hold only one item at a time. The moment you copy a second item, the Windows Clipboard erases anything currently stored on the Clipboard.

To avoid this problem, Microsoft Office 2003 comes with a special Office Clipboard, which works exactly like the Windows Clipboard except that the Office Clipboard can hold up to 24 (count them, 24) items at a time.

The major limitation of the Office Clipboard is that you can use this feature only while working within one or more Office 2003 programs. The (ahem) *polite* term for features that work like this is *proprietary technology* — it means the features work only with programs created by a particular maker (in this case, Microsoft) in a bid to make rival programs look obsolete. (Subtle, isn't it?)

Each time you cut or copy an item from within an Office 2003 program, that cut or copied item appears on both the Office Clipboard and the ordinary Windows Clipboard. That way if you switch to a non-Office 2003 program, you can paste that item into another program. If you cut or copy another item from an Office 2003 program, this second item gets stored in the Office Clipboard but erases anything in the Windows Clipboard.

Copying stuff to the Office Clipboard

To copy or cut an object (such as text or a graphic image) to the Office Clipboard, do the following:

1. **Highlight the text or graphic object that you want to copy or cut.**

2. **Choose one of the following:**

   - Click Edit⇨Copy (or Cut).

   - Press Ctrl+C to copy (or Ctrl+X to cut).

   - Click the Copy or Cut icon on the Standard toolbar.

Whenever you cut or copy an object, Office 2003 magically pastes that object onto the Office Clipboard. After you cut or copy 24 items, Office 2003 starts erasing the oldest item on the Clipboard to make room for each new item you cut or copy.

When you turn off your computer, the Office Clipboard "forgets" (erases) any items stored on it.

Pasting stuff from the Office Clipboard

After you have copied or cut an item from within an Office 2003 program, you can paste an object from the Office Clipboard by doing the following:

1. **Click where you want to paste an object from the Office Clipboard.**

2. **Choose Edit➪Office Clipboard.**

   The task pane appears and displays the Clipboard as shown in Figure 2-14.

3. **Move the mouse pointer over the object you want to paste from the Office Clipboard.**

   Your chosen object appears highlighted and displays a downward-pointing arrow to the right.

4. **Click the downward-pointing arrow.**

   A drop-down menu appears.

5. **Choose Paste. (To paste all the objects from the Office Clipboard, just click the Paste All button in Office Clipboard.)**

If you press Ctrl+V, choose Edit➪Paste, or click the Paste button on the Standard toolbar, you paste only the last object that you cut or copied from another program.

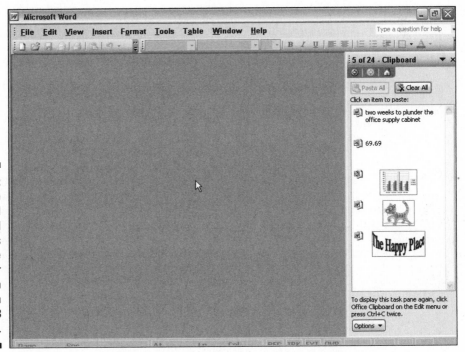

Figure 2-14:
The Office Clipboard displays all the items you have cut or copied from within an Office 2003 program.

Cleaning out your Office Clipboard

Because Office XP blindly stores everything you cut or copy to the Office Clipboard, you may want to delete some items to make room for items you really want to use again. (If you don't delete an item from the Office Clipboard, Office XP starts deleting the oldest stored items to make room for any new items you copy or cut to the Office Clipboard.) To delete an object from the Office Clipboard, do the following:

1. **Choose Edit⇨Office Clipboard.**

   The Office Clipboard appears, displaying all the items currently available (refer to Figure 2-11).

2. **Move the mouse pointer over the object you want to delete from the Office Clipboard.**

   Your chosen object appears highlighted and displays a downward-pointing arrow to the right.

3. **Click the downward-pointing arrow.**

   A drop-down menu appears.

4. **Choose Delete.**

   Office 2003 deletes your chosen item from the Office Clipboard.

To delete all the objects from the Office Clipboard, just click the Clear All button in Office Clipboard.

Chapter 3

Getting Help from Microsoft Office

Microsoft Office 2003 tries to offer every imaginable feature possible, although most people will barely use 10 percent of those features. The trouble is that each person uses a different 10 percent of Office 2003 features, which means nearly everyone winds up trying to wade their way through the other 90 percent of the Office 2003 features they don't want or need to use.

With so many features buried in the programs, Office 2003 can sometimes seem more complicated to use than necessary. To help you out, Microsoft Office 2003 comes with a built-in help system, which tries to answer any questions you might have in using Office 2003. Although it's no substitute for a knowledgeable person or a program that's intuitively easy to use in the first place, the Office 2003 help system can often answer your questions regarding most of the tasks you may want to perform in Office 2003.

Getting Help From Office 2003

The best way to learn how to use any program on your computer is to try something and then turn to an expert sitting nearby whenever you have a question. Because even Microsoft can't afford to hire a real-live expert to sit at everyone's desk, the next best (cheapest) solution is to provide every Office 2003 program with a feature (known as a help system) designed to help you find the answers you need.

Perhaps the best way to learn any new skill is the "trial and error" method. Feel free to experiment with any command just to see what it might do. Then if it screws up your data, choose Edit➪Undo or press Ctrl+Z to reverse the last command you just chose. By removing any possibility for permanent failure, the Undo command gives you the freedom to experiment with anything in Office 2003.

The Office 2003 help system lets you type one or more words (known as keywords) to ask Office 2003 what type of information you want help on. So if you type the word *printing* into the Office 2003 help system, the help system responds with a list of printing related topics, such as how to set the paper size while printing or how to change the order of the pages to print.

To give you the illusion of freedom and choice (except when it comes to choosing an operating system), Microsoft provides three ways to type a keyword into the help system (see Figure 3-1):

Office Assistant text box   Help text box

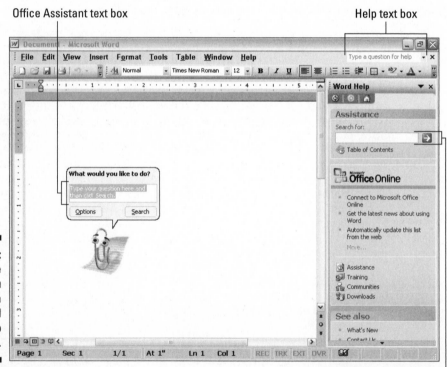

Figure 3-1:
The three places you can type a keyword into the help system.

Task Pane Search text box

✓ Through the Help text box in the upper right corner

✓ Through the Search text box in the Help task pane

✓ Through the Office Assistant text box (yes, the Office Assistants are still there in Office 2003)

Using the Help text box

The Help text box appears on the menu bar of every Office 2003 program. To use the Help text box, follow these steps:

1. **Click in the Help text box.**

2. **Type one or more keywords, such as *file* or *table margins* and press Enter.**

   The Help task pane appears with a list of topics related to the keywords you typed in Step 1, as shown in Figure 3-2.

   When you type a keyword, make sure you spell it correctly; otherwise, the help system won't know what type of help you need.

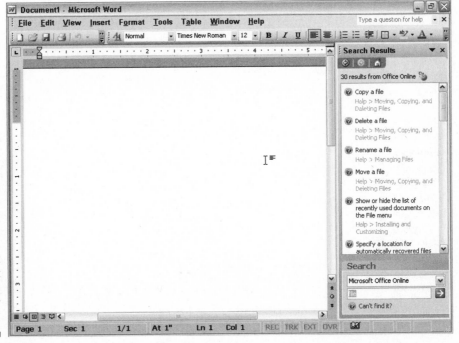

Figure 3-2:
The Help task pane displays a list of topics so you can choose the one that seems most likely to answer your question.

3. Click one of the displayed topics.

Another window appears that displays step-by-step instructions for the topic you chose in Step 2, as shown in Figure 3-3.

You may need to scroll up or down to see the entire list of topics that the help system displays.

4. Click one of the displayed topics.

A help window appears that displays step-by-step instructions for the topic you chose in Step 2, as shown in Figure 3-3.

If you click the Print icon in the Help window, you can print a hard copy of the step-by-step instructions. That way, you can save the instructions for future reference.

5. Click the Close box of the help window and the Help task pane to make them go away.

Print icon

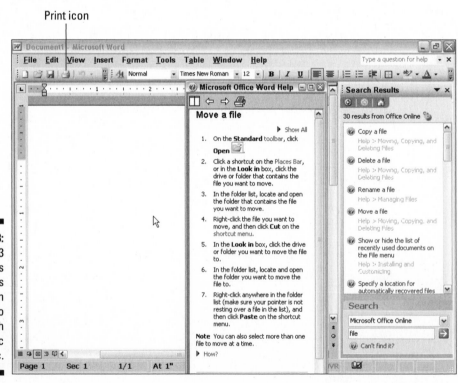

Figure 3-3:
Office 2003 displays instructions that explain how to accomplish a specific topic.

Using the Search text box in the Help task pane

The Search text box in the Help task pane works exactly like the Help text box that appears in the menu bar of every Office 2003 program. To use the Search text box, follow these steps:

1. **Choose one of the following:**

   • Press F1.

   • Choose Help⇨Microsoft Office _____ Help, where the blank is the name of the Office 2003 program you're using.

   • If the Task Pane is already visible, click in the Task Pane list box and choose Help.

   The Help task pane appears (refer to Figure 3-1).

2. **Click in the Search text box.**

3. **Follow Steps 2 through 5 in the previous section, "Using the Help text box."**

Using the Office Assistant

The Office Assistant is a cartoon character that performs the same function as the Help task pane. In previous versions of Microsoft Office, the Office Assistant was the only way to get help, but so many people found the Office Assistants annoying that now they're optional.

In case you're still one of the few people who still like using the Office Assistant, you can still use it by following these steps:

1. **Choose Help⇨Show the Office Assistant.**

   The Office Assistant pops up on the screen (refer to Figure 3-1).

2. **Click the Office Assistant.**

   The Office Assistant text box appears within a cartoon voice box.

3. **Click in the Office Assistant text box.**

4. **Follow Steps 2 through 5 in the previous section, "Using the Help text box."**

In case you're bored, you can make your Office Assistant amuse you if you right-click the Office Assistant and then click Animate from the pop-up menu.

Getting Help from the Table of Contents

In case you find that typing in a keyword or two is too clumsy, you can just use the table of contents of the help system instead. Basically, this table of contents lists various topics that you can browse, so you can (hopefully) find the answers you need to get something done.

The table of contents basically lists all the information that would normally appear in the instruction manual that comes with Office 2003. But because it's cheaper not to print an actual manual, the table of contents just acts like the electronic equivalent of a printed manual instead.

To browse the table of contents, follow these steps:

1. **Choose one of the following:**

   • Press F1.

   • Choose Help⇨Microsoft ____ Help, where the blank is the name of the Office 2003 program you're using.

   • If the Task Pane is already visible, click in the Task Pane list box and choose Help.

   The Help task pane appears (refer to Figure 3-1).

2. **Click the Table of Contents link that appears directly under the Search text box.**

   The Help task pane displays the table of contents where each heading appears next to a book icon as shown in Figure 3-4.

3. **Click the book icon next to the heading that you want to browse.**

   The book icon turns into an open book icon and displays a list of additional headings that may also display book icons. You may need to repeat this step several times until you find a specific topic that you want to read. Topics appear with a document icon with a question mark next to it.

4. **Click the topic that you want to read.**

   A help window appears and displays step-by-step instructions for your chosen topic.

5. **Click the Close box of the help window and Help task pane to make them go away.**

Headings

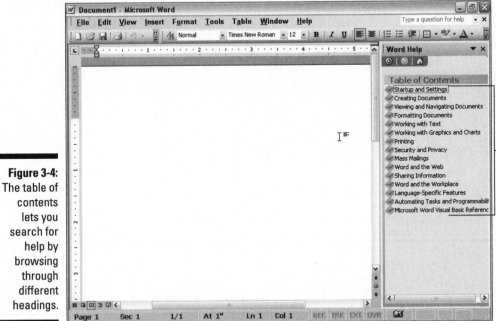

Figure 3-4:
The table of
contents
lets you
search for
help by
browsing
through
different
headings.

Getting Help on the World Wide Web

To provide you with the latest software updates, patches, bug fixes, program
news, tips, and software add-ons, Microsoft runs its own Web site (www.
microsoft.com). To help you reach Microsoft's Web site quickly and easily,
every Office 2003 program has a special *Microsoft Office Online* command.

Before you can use this Microsoft Office Online command, you must have an
existing Internet account or be willing to create (and pay for) an Internet
account.

To access the Microsoft Web site, which is full of useful Microsoft Office 2003
information, software, news, or bug updates, do the following:

1. Choose Help⇨Microsoft Office Online.

Office 2003 starts up the Internet Explorer browser and loads the
Microsoft Office Online Web page.

2. **Browse the pages until you find the information you need.**

3. **Choose File➪Exit or click the close box of your browser to make the browser go away.**

Exiting from your Web browser may not always disconnect you from the Internet. To make sure you disconnect from the Internet, click the Dial-Up Connection icon, which appears in the lower right-hand corner of the Windows taskbar. When a dialog box appears, click Disconnect.

Recovering from Crashes with Office 2003

If your computer ever freezes, crashes, or acts erratically for no apparent reason, it's probably nothing that you've done but most likely the fault of your computer because computers can be so unreliable. Since computers aren't likely to become more reliable in the future, Microsoft Office 2003 offers two ways to protect yourself:

✔ Repairing Microsoft Office 2003 programs

✔ Protecting documents corrupted during a computer crash

Repairing Microsoft Office 2003

Each program (such as Word, Excel, and PowerPoint) consists of several files with cryptic file extensions, such as .exe, .dll, and .olb. If even one of these cryptic files gets deleted or corrupted through your own mistakes or a virus, Microsoft Office 2003 program may no longer work.

To protect you from this problem, Microsoft Office 2003 contains a special Detect and Repair command which — what else? — checks to make sure that all those important files still exist on your hard disk and are in working order.

(Of course, the big problem is that if a file is missing or corrupted, you may not be able to run any Microsoft Office 2003 programs in the first place in order to use the Detect and Repair command. In that case, you may have to reinstall the entire program . Be sure to make backups of your important data just in case the installation procedure goes awry and messes up your hard disk completely.)

So, the next time any Office 2003 program starts acting flaky, try to fix it by using the Detect and Repair command:

1. **Run a Microsoft Office 2003 program, such as Word or PowerPoint.**

2. **Insert your Microsoft Office 2003 CD in your computer.**

3. **Choose Help⇨Detect and Repair. (You may have to click the expand button, which appears as a double rightward-pointing arrow at the bottom of the Help menu, before you can see the Detect and Repair command.)**

   The Detect and Repair dialog box appears, as shown in Figure 3-5.

4. **Click the check boxes to choose any options you want.**

   The two options for repairing Microsoft Office include the following:

   • **Restore my shortcuts while repairing:** Makes sure any desktop shortcuts you may create continue pointing to the right programs and documents.

   • **Discard my customized settings and restore default settings:** Returns your copy of Office 2003 back to its original settings, wiping out any custom changes you may make to menus or toolbars.

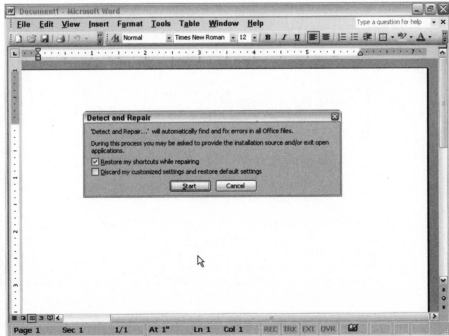

Figure 3-5:
The Detect and Repair dialog box can help fix most problems you may have with Office 2003.

5. **Click Start.**

   Follow the on-screen instructions as Microsoft Office 2003 valiantly tries to fix itself if it detects any problems.

Protecting files from a computer crash

If your computer crashes or fails for any reason, it often decides to take out as many files with it as possible, usually the most important ones you need at the time. Because you can never predict when a computer crash will happen (except knowing that it *will* happen one day), Microsoft Office 2003 provides several options for minimizing the chance of losing data during a computer crash:

- ✔ **Timed saving of files:** Automatically saves information about your document at specific time intervals. By saving document information, you can increase the chances that Office 2003 can recover your data in the event of a crash. Available only in Word, Excel, PowerPoint, and Outlook.

- ✔ **Hang manager:** Allows you to attempt to restart Word, Excel, or PowerPoint if they crash.

- ✔ **Corrupt document recovery:** Attempts to recover a file that may have been corrupted when the program crashed. Available only in Word and Excel.

The best way to protect your data is to save your files often and store backup copies of your data in separate locations, such as on a rewritable CD or external hard disk.

Saving files automatically

For your first line of defense in protecting your data, you can make Word, Excel, and PowerPoint save your files automatically at specific intervals, such as every ten minutes, by following these steps:

1. **Choose Tools⇨Options.**

   The Options dialog box appears.

2. **Click the Save tab.**

   The Save tab displays the Save AutoRecover Info check box, as shown in Figure 3-6.

3. **Make sure a check mark appears in the Save AutoRecover Info check box.**

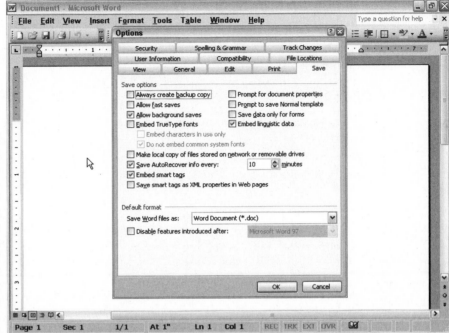

4. **Click the minutes text box and type the number of minutes you want to wait before saving your document information automatically, such as every ten minutes.**

5. **Click the Always create backup copy check box. (Optional.)**

   If you click this option, Office 2003 creates a duplicate copy of your file so in case your original file gets corrupted, you might be able to recover your data by opening the duplicate copy of that same file. The big disadvantage of this option is that it gobbles up more disk space since it makes two copies of every file you create and edit.

6. **Click OK.**

Restarting a frozen application

Instead of crashing, Office 2003 may *hang* or *freeze*, which means the program still appears on the screen although nothing seems to work (such as the keyboard or the mouse). When this happens (notice the emphasis on *when* and not *if*), you can attempt to restart your frozen Office 2003 program by running the Microsoft Office Application Recovery Tool, as follows:

1. **Click the Start button on the Windows taskbar.**

   A pop-up menu appears.

2. **Choose All Programs⇨Microsoft Office Tools⇨Microsoft Office Application Recovery.**

   The Microsoft Office Application Recovery dialog box appears, as shown in Figure 3-7.

3. **Click the crashed program that you want to restart and click Recover Application.**

   If you're lucky, Microsoft Office 2003 restarts your chosen application. If nothing happens, click End Application and try to restart the application again.

After a program crashes, there's a greater chance that it'll crash again. So, after you restart a crashed application, you should immediately save any opened documents and exit the previously crashed application before you start up the application again. For extra safety, consider also restarting your entire computer.

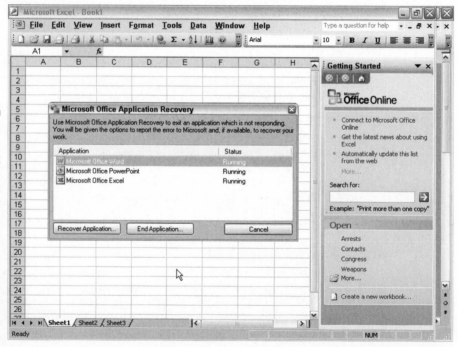

Figure 3-7:
The Microsoft Office Application Recovery dialog box shows you which Office programs are running and which ones have crashed.

Recovering corrupted files

No matter how careful you may be, if Microsoft Office 2003 crashes, it could mangle any documents that you were working on at the time of the crash. If this happens, Word, Excel, and PowerPoint can attempt to recover your files the next time you start the program. To attempt to recover your files, do the following:

1. **Load Word, Excel, or PowerPoint immediately after your Office 2003 program crashed.**

   A Document Recovery pane appears, as shown in Figure 3-8.

2. **Click the document you want to recover.**

   Office 2003 loads your chosen document.

 If you right-click a document in the Document Recovery pane, a pop-up menu appears. You can click Save As to save your recovered document under a different name, just to make sure that it doesn't overwrite the original file that got corrupted.

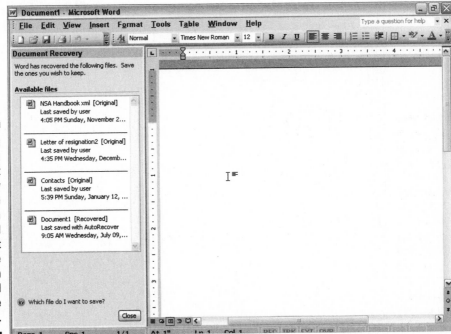

Figure 3-8:
The Document Recovery pane displays a list of all files that may have been corrupted during the last crash.

Both Word and Excel offer another way to recover files corrupted during a computer crash. To use this option, follow these steps:

1. **Load either Word or Excel.**

2. **Choose File⇨Open (or press Ctrl+O).**

   The Open dialog box appears.

3. **Click the file you want to recover.**

4. **Click the downward-pointing arrow that appears to the right of the Open button in the lower right-hand corner.**

   A pop-up menu appears, as shown in Figure 3-9.

5. **Click Open and Repair.**

   Word or Excel attempts to load your chosen file and repair any problems that may have occurred during a crash.

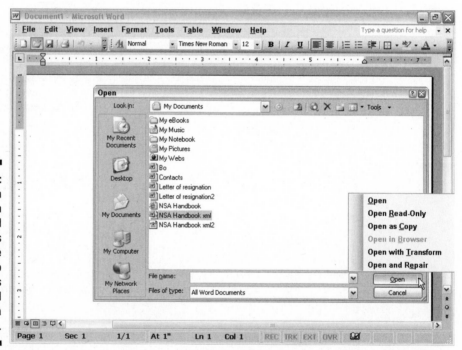

Figure 3-9: The Open dialog box in Word and Excel offers an alternate way to recover files corrupted during a crash.

Chapter 4

Sharing Data

In This Chapter

▶ Playing with file formats

▶ Using smart tags

▶ Linking and embedding data

After you've stored data in an Office 2003 program, the next problem is finding a way to share that data with another Office 2003 program or even with another person using an entirely different program altogether (such as someone using a Macintosh). Although Microsoft would just love for everyone to shell out a few hundred dollars to buy a copy of Microsoft Office so they can share data back and forth, not everyone in the world is likely to own a copy of Microsoft Office 2003. So when you want to share data, you may need to get a bit creative by using one or more of the techniques described in this chapter.

Saving Data in Different File Formats

When you save data in any program, such as Word or PowerPoint, that program saves your data in a specific way, known as a file format. File formats just define how a particular program stores data in a file. Unfortunately, every program in the world stores data in a different file format, which would be like one person in an office speaking Japanese, another French, and a third Spanish, and then wondering why nobody can communicate effectively with each other.

So to partially solve this problem, many programs including Office 2003, allow you to convert data into a different file format so another program can understand it. Essentially, when you save a file in a different format, you're translating your data into a format that another program can understand, much like translating a Spanish textbook into English so an English speaker can read it.

The Wonderful World of XML

One of the biggest problems with computers, besides the fact that they're too hard to use and understand, is that they don't have a universally accepted format for storing data. The earliest attempt to create a universal file format, called ASCII, simply stored text but without any type of formatting, such as fonts or underlining.

Rather than agree on a universal file format, every computer and software company simply created their own proprietary file format in hopes that their format would become the de facto standard for storing data. Unfortunately, even computer and software companies constantly change their own file format standards to add additional features, which explains why new versions of a program often save data in a newer file format that's incompatible with file formats used by older versions of that same program. So if you save a word processor file in Word 11, you can't open the file using an ancient copy of Word 95.

To solve this problem, computer companies finally decided to agree on a universal file format standard dubbed XML (which stands for eXtensible Markup Language). The basic idea behind XML files is that they define data in a way that other programs can understand and use without any messy file conversion headaches. Theoretically, this means you can store your word processor report as an XML document and load that data into a database or spreadsheet.

Although XML still isn't perfect or widely accepted, it will become a growing universal standard. So rather than save your files in a proprietary file format, such as dBase IV or WordPerfect 5.2, save your files as an XML document instead. Now you just have to hope that when you share your XML files with someone else, they actually have a program that can understand XML files as well.

Any time you convert data to another file format, there's a good chance you'll lose some type of formatting along the way. If your file consists of nothing but plain text, you probably won't lose anything but if your file consists of tables filled with numbers neatly aligned, converting this file may scramble your data all over the place. The data will still be there, it just won't be neatly organized the way you originally formatted it.

Converting a file to another format

Every Office 2003 program can convert your data to another file format to share with someone using another program, such as WordPerfect. Because Office 2003 offers so many different ways to save your data in another file format, you may be wondering which file format you should use, so here are some general guidelines.

If you need to convert your file for a specific version of a program, such as WordPerfect 5.0, try to save your file in that specific file format, in this case WordPerfect 5.0. When you save a file in the exact file format that another program uses, you can save most of your formatting when you convert your file.

If you can't find the exact version number of a program, use the closest version number you can find. For example, if you need to save an Excel file to give to someone who uses Lotus 1-2-3 Millennium Edition, save your Excel file as a WK4 (1-2-3) file format, which is a file format used by Lotus 1-2-3 version 4.0. Nearly every program can recognize data stored in a file format used by an earlier version of that same program.

A bigger problem arises when Office 2003 can't convert a file into the exact file format used by another program. For example, you may need to share an Office 2003 file with someone who uses AppleWorks on a Macintosh. In these cases, you may have to save your file into an intermediate format that most programs can also understand, although there's a good chance that you may lose some or all of the formatting of your original file.

To give you some general guidelines on converting file formats, take a look at the following:

- When you're converting a *word processor* document, you have two options:

  - Save your file in a *Rich Text File* format. This format preserves most of your formatting, and most word processors can understand it.

  - As a last resort, you can save your file as *Plain Text* format, but this format strips away all formatting.

- When you're saving an *Excel* file, save your file as a *Lotus 1-2-3* file format (which the Excel Save As dialog box abbreviates as WK4, WK3, WK!, or WKS).

  As a last resort, save your file as a *DIF, CSV,* or *Text (tab delimited)* format, which strips away all formatting but preserves your data.

- When you're saving an *Access* file, you have three options:

  - Save your file as a *dBase 5, dBase IV,* or *dBase III* format, which most database programs can understand.

  - Try saving your file in a *Lotus 1-2-3* file format (WK4, WK3, etc.).

  - As a last resort, save your data as Text Files format, which preserves your data but may not load properly in another program.

To convert your data, follow these steps:

1. **Choose File⇨Save.**

   Saving your file first ensures that, when you convert your file to another format, that file contains the latest data.

2. **Choose File⇨Save As. (In Access, choose File ⇨Export.)**

   A Save As dialog box appears.

3. **Click the Save As Type list box.**

   A list of available file formats appears, as shown in Figure 4-1.

   Every Office 2003 program can save files as an XML document, which is the new universal file format that nearly every program will soon be able to understand. So to be part of the future, you may want to save a copy of your file as an XML document.

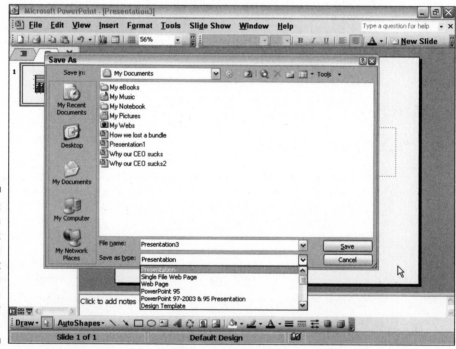

Figure 4-1:
The Save as type list box shows you the most popular file formats to save your data in.

4. **Click a file format to use.**

5. **If you want to name the file, click in the File name text box and type a name.**

6. **Click Save.**

Opening a file stored in another file format

In case someone using another program hands you a file, there's a good chance that Office 2003 will be able to open it. (For best results, that other person should try to save the file in a Microsoft Office file format, such as Word or Excel.)

To open a foreign file format, follow these steps:

1. **Choose File⇨Open.**

   An Open dialog box appears.

2. **Click in the Files of Type list box and choose All Files.**

   If you know the specific file format of the file that you're trying to open, click that file format in the Files of Type list box.

3. **Click the file that you want to open and click Open.**

   Whenever you open a file stored in another file format, there's a chance that the data may be disorganized. For example, numbers may no longer appear neatly aligned in rows and cells inside Excel, or paragraphs may have weird indenting in Word.

Sharing Data within Office 2003 with Smart Tags

When you type data into Word, Excel, or PowerPoint, Office 2003 can often recognize what type of data that might be such as a date, telephone number, or a name. When Office 2003 recognizes specific data types, it can identify it within your file with a smart tag. A smart tag gives you an option to do something else, such as create a new e-mail message or check your calendar.

Word, Excel, and PowerPoint are the only Office 2003 programs that offer smart tags.

Turning smart tags on or off

If you want to use smart tags, you have to turn them on. Word provides smart tags by default, but you can turn them off. Neither Excel nor PowerPoint allows smart tags by default, so you must turn them on.

To turn smart tags on or off, follow these steps:

1. **Choose Tools➪AutoCorrect Options.**

   The AutoCorrect dialog box appears.

2. **Click the Smart Tags tab.**

   The Smart Tags dialog box appears, as shown in Figure 4-2.

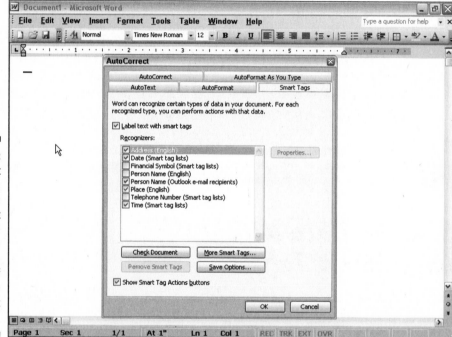

Figure 4-2:
The Smart Tags dialog box lets you turn smart tags on and off and define the type of smart tags you want to use.

3. **Click in the Label text with smart tags check box to turn smart tags on or off.**

   If a check mark appears in the Label text with smart tags check box, smart tags are turned on. If no check mark appears, smart tags are turned off.

4. **Click in any additional check boxes to define other types of smart tags, such as the Address or Financial Symbol Smart Tag check box.**

5. **Click OK.**

Using smart tags

When you have turned on smart tags within Word, Excel, or PowerPoint, Office 2003 automatically underlines in purple any text that it recognizes as a smart tag, such as a date or name. To use a smart tag, follow these steps:

1. **Move the mouse pointer or cursor over the smart tag text.**

   The smart tag icon appears.

2. **Right-click the smart tag icon.**

   A drop-down menu appears, showing you the different options available, as shown in Figure 4-3.

3. **Click an option in the smart tag drop-down menu.**

   Depending on the action you take, Office 2003 may open another Office 2003 program, such as Outlook, and allow you to do something else with your smart tag data, such as create a new e-mail message.

Smart tag

Smart tag icon

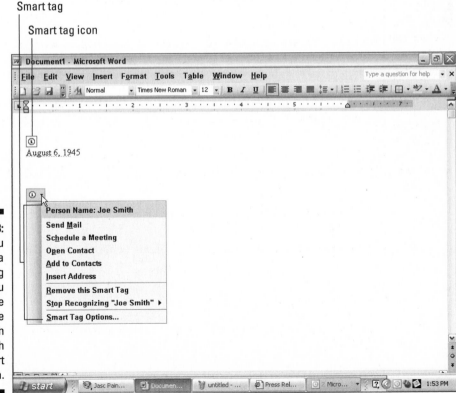

Figure 4-3: When you right-click a smart tag icon, you can see what else you can do with your smart tag data.

Linking and Embedding Data

Office 2003 allows you to copy, cut, and paste data from one Office 2003 program to another, such as copying a list of numbers from Excel and pasting it into a PowerPoint presentation. Unfortunately, if you paste data from one Office 2003 program to another and that data later changes, you'll have to copy and paste that new data into your other Office 2003 program all over again to keep it updated.

Rather than do this yourself, let Office 2003 do it for you automatically. The two ways that Office 2003 can do this are called linking and embedding.

Linking data

Many times you may create data in a specific Office 2003 program, such as Excel, but may want to display that information in a different Office 2003 program, such as PowerPoint or Word. To avoid making separate copies of data (and risk creating nearly identical data with different information in them), Office 2003 allows you to link data from one program to another.

Essentially, linking lets an Office 2003 file point to data stored in another file. So if you create a PowerPoint presentation, you can create a link to an Excel spreadsheet. Now any changes you make to your Excel spreadsheet automatically appear within your PowerPoint presentation. It's actually the same data, but linking just gives you the illusion that this same data appears in two different places.

To link data between two Office 2003 programs, follow these steps:

1. **Create and save data in an Office 2003 program, such as Word or Excel.**

   The data you create in this step will be the data that appears in another Office 2003 program through a link.

2. **Highlight the data you want to link and choose Edit➪Copy.**

3. **Open another Office 2003 program.**

   This Office 2003 program will display the data created by the program in Step 1.

4. **Move the cursor or click the mouse pointer where you want to insert the linked data.**

5. **Choose Edit⇨Paste Special. (You may need to click the Expand button at the bottom of the Edit menu to find the Paste Special command.)**

    A Paste Special dialog box appears, as shown in Figure 4-4.

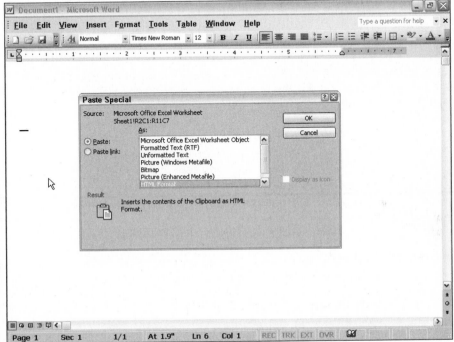

Figure 4-4:
The Paste
Special
dialog box
lets you link
to data
created and
stored in
another file.

6. **Click in the Paste link radio button.**

7. **Click the data listed in the As: list box that you want to link to your current Office 2003 program.**

    In Figure 4-4, you would click Microsoft Excel Worksheet Object.

8. **Click OK.**

    Office 2003 displays your copied data from Step 1 in your current Office program. Any changes you make to the original data now automatically appears in the other Office 2003 file, as shown in Figure 4-5.

If you want to edit linked data, you have to open the original Office 2003 program that created that data.

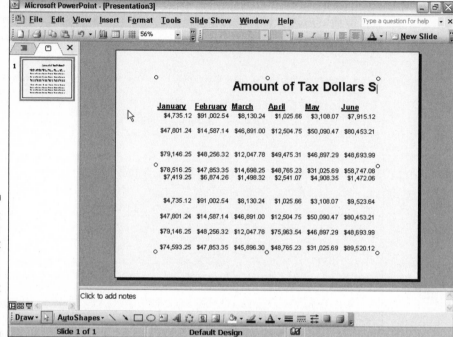

Figure 4-5:
An Excel
worksheet
appears
inside a
PowerPoint
presen-
tation.

Embedding data

When you link data between two different Office 2003 programs, you can only edit that data from the original Office 2003 program that created it. An alternative to linking is embedding, which allows you to edit data in both the program that created it and in the program that displays it.

For example, you can copy a worksheet from Excel and embed that worksheet inside a Word document. Now you can update that data by either loading Excel and editing the worksheet, or by double-clicking on the Excel worksheet within your Word document. When you double-click on embedded data, Office 2003 automatically loads the program that created that data (Word, Excel, etc.) so you can edit it.

To embed data in another Office 2003 program, follow these steps:

1. **Create and save data in an Office 2003 program, such as Word or Excel.**

   The data you create in this step will be the data that appears in another Office 2003 program through a link.

2. **Highlight the data you want to link and choose Edit⇨Copy.**

3. **Open another Office 2003 program.**

This Office 2003 program will display the data created by the program in Step 1.

4. **Move the cursor or click the mouse pointer where you want to embed the data.**

5. **Choose Edit⇨Paste Special. (You may need to click the Expand button at the bottom of the Edit menu to find the Paste Special command.)**

   A Paste Special dialog box appears (see Figure 4-4).

6. **Click in the Paste radio button.**

7. **Click the data listed in the As: list box that includes the word Object in it, such as Microsoft Excel Worksheet Object.**

8. **Click OK.**

   Office 2003 embeds your data in the current Office 2003 program.

Embedded data looks exactly the same as linked data. The main difference is that if you double-click embedded data, you can edit the embedded data, as shown in Figure 4-6. Although you may not notice it in Figure 4-6, the Power Point menu bar and toolbars have been replaced by the Excel menu bar and toolbars, so that you have full access to Excel's commands while you edit the embedded Excel data.

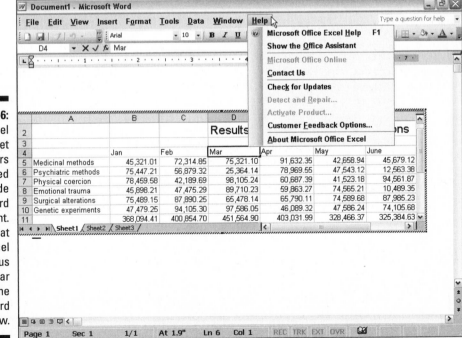

Figure 4-6: An Excel worksheet appears embedded inside a Word document. Note that the Excel menus appear within the Word window.

Part II
Working with Word

The 5th Wave   By Rich Tennant

"I don't know what program you been usin' Frank, but it ain't the right one. Look—your menu bar should read, File, Edit, Reap, Gather..."

In this part . . .

*W*ord processing remains the most popular use for a
personal computer (right after playing games and
wasting hours exploring the Internet), so this part of the
book gently guides you into using the powerhouse word
processor known as Microsoft Word. By using the 2003
version of Word, you can create anything from a simple
letter to a resume or business report.

Along the way to discovering how to use Word's powerful
features, this part of the book also teaches you how to
write, edit, spell-check, and grammar-check your writing,
and how to format text to make it look really pretty. If you
need to share your documents with others, this part of
the book also shows you how to collaborate and merge
the ideas of different people into a single document for
everyone to see.

Word may seem like an ordinary word processor at first
glance, but this part of the book unlocks the techniques
that summon Word to help you write, create, and print
your ideas as fast as you care to type them. (Just as long
as your computer doesn't crash on you.)

Chapter 5

Manipulating Your Words

As its name implies, Word lets you write words so that you can create letters, reports, proposals, brochures, newsletters, pink slips, ransom notes, and practically anything else that requires a rudimentary command of the written language. This chapter guides you through the process of turning your ideas into words and storing them inside a Microsoft Word document.

Editing a Document

Writing well means rewriting. Even the best writers in the world rarely churn out a paragraph, or even a complete sentence, that says exactly what they want to say the first time. Most writers follow a two-step process: Get your ideas into words as quickly as possible and then go back and edit your text so that it reads better than before.

When you edit a document, you'll spend most of your time adding new text, deleting old text, and rearranging existing text.

Deleting text

Word provides three ways to delete text. If you want to delete text one character at a time, you can do one of the following:

✔ Press the Backspace key (erases one character to the left)

✔ Press the Delete key (erases one character to the right)

The Backspace key deletes the character that appears immediately to the left of the cursor (not the mouse pointer). The Delete key deletes one character to the right of the cursor. If you hold down the Backspace or Delete key, Word keeps deleting characters until you release the Backspace or Delete key.

You can move the cursor by either

✔ Pressing the ←, →, ↓, or ↑ arrow keys

✔ Clicking the mouse pointer anywhere in your text

The Backspace and Delete keys are handy for erasing short amounts of text. To quickly erase larger chunks of text, follow these steps:

1. **Highlight the text that you want to delete.**

   You can highlight text in one of two ways:

   • Drag the mouse to highlight the text

   • Hold down the Shift key and press one of the arrow keys

2. **Press Backspace or Delete.**

   Word deletes your chosen text.

If you think you might need the text you highlighted in Step 1 at a later time, choose Edit⇨Cut, press Ctrl+X, or click the Cut icon on the Standard toolbar. Then, you can choose the Paste command (Ctrl+V) to paste your cut text somewhere else.

Adding text

Adding text can be as simple as moving the cursor where you want to add the text and start typing. If you want to add text within an existing chunk of text, Word gives you two choices:

✔ **Insert mode:** When you move the cursor in between existing text and start typing, your new text pushes the old text to the side.

✔ **Overwrite mode:** If you move the cursor between existing text and start typing, the new text erases anything to the right of the cursor as you type. If you type a four-letter word in Overwrite mode, Word replaces the first four characters to the right of the cursor with your new text.

To switch between Insert and Overwrite mode, press the Insert key. When Word is in Overwrite mode, you'll see the letters OVR in the bottom of the status bar.

For a quick way to delete text and add new text, highlight the text you want to delete and then start typing the new text you want to add.

Rearranging text

After writing, you may find that some paragraphs or sentences should be someplace else in your document. The traditional way to move text from one place to another is to use the Cut and Paste commands as follows:

1. **Highlight the text that you want to move.**

   You can highlight the text by dragging the mouse over the text or holding down the Shift key and highlighting the text by pressing the arrow keys.

   If you hold down the Ctrl key and use the mouse to highlight text, you can select multiple chunks of text that aren't next to each other, such as the first word in a sentence and the last word in that same sentence.

2. **Choose Edit⇨Cut, press Ctrl+X, or click the Cut icon on the Standard toolbar, as shown in Figure 5-1.**

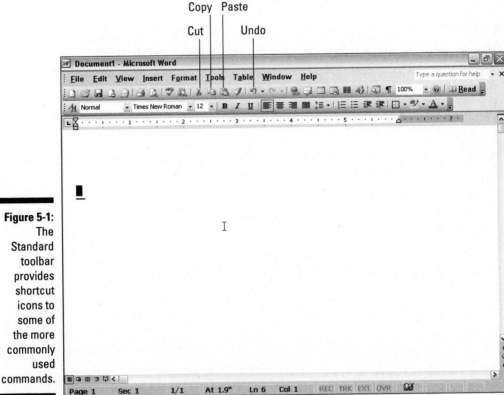

Figure 5-1: The Standard toolbar provides shortcut icons to some of the more commonly used commands.

Word temporarily deletes your highlighted text.

Copying text keeps your highlighted text in its original location but lets you paste a second copy of that text somewhere else. If you want to copy text, choose Edit⇨Copy, press Ctrl+C, or click the Copy icon instead.

3. **Move the cursor where you want to move the text.**

   You can move the cursor by either pressing the arrow keys or clicking the mouse.

4. **Choose Edit⇨Paste, press Ctrl+V, or click the Paste icon on the Standard toolbar.**

   The text you highlighted in Step 1 appears in its new location in your document.

While the standard Cut and Paste commands can move text from one place to another, you can use the mouse to do this faster by following these steps:

1. **Highlight the text that you want to move.**

   You can highlight the text by dragging the mouse over the text or holding down the Shift key and highlighting the text by pressing the arrow keys.

2. **Move the mouse pointer anywhere inside your highlighted text, hold down the left mouse button, and drag the mouse.**

   The mouse pointer turns into an arrow icon with a box at the end, and Word displays a dotted line cursor to show you where your text will move to when you release the mouse button.

   If you hold down the Ctrl key while dragging the mouse in Step 2, you can copy your highlighted text.

3. **Drag the mouse to move the dotted line cursor where you want to move your highlighted text.**

4. **Release the left mouse button.**

   Word moves your highlighted text.

Cut and pasting text with the Spike

If you need to cut multiple chunks of text and paste them somewhere else (even in another document), you can use Word's Spike feature.

The Spike acts like a super version of the ordinary cut and paste commands. To use the Spike, follow these steps:

1. **Highlight the text that you want to cut.**

2. **Press Ctrl+F3.**

   Word cuts your highlighted text and puts it on the Spike (which you can't see).

   When you store text on the Spike, you can't access that text using the ordinary Paste command.

3. **Repeat steps 1 and 2 for each chunk of text that you want to cut.**

4. **Move the cursor where you want to paste the text stored on the Spike.**

5. **Press Ctrl+Shift+F3.**

   Word pastes your text in the reverse order that you cut it in steps 1 and 2.

   When you press Ctrl+Shift+F3, Word empties out all text stored on the Spike. If you want to paste text off the Spike while keeping it on the Spike for future pasting, follow these steps:

1. **Repeat steps 1- 4 above.**

2. **Choose Insert➪AutoText➪AutoText.**

   The AutoCorrect dialog box appears.

3. **Move the cursor where you want to paste the text stored on the Spike.**

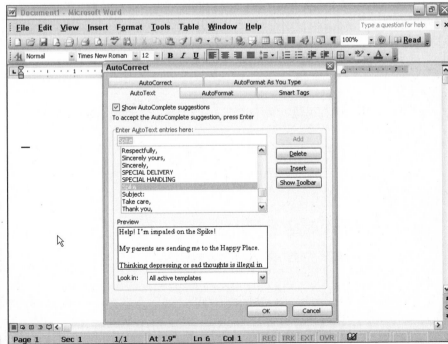

Figure 5-2:
The AutoCorrect dialog box lets you view the contents of the Spike.

4. **Scroll through the Enter AutoText entries here: list box and click on the word Spike.**

   The AutoCorrect dialog box displays the text currently impaled on the Spike as shown in Figure 5-2.

5. **Click the Insert button.**

   Word pastes all the text from the Spike and leaves a copy of the text still on the Spike.

Reversing your mistakes

Deleted something you wish you hadn't deleted? Pasted text in the wrong place? You can reverse your last command by doing one of the following:

- Choose Edit⇨Undo
- Press Ctrl+Z
- Click the Undo icon on the Standard toolbar

 Each time you choose the Undo command, you reverse the previous command you chose. In case you choose the Undo command too many times, you can choose the Redo command by doing one of the following:

- Choose Edit⇨Redo
- Press Ctrl+Y
- Click the Redo icon on the Standard toolbar

Moving Through a Word Document

If you create a large document, Word can show you only a small part of your text at any given time. To look at different parts of your document, use the mouse or the keyboard to scroll or jump to different parts of your document.

Using the mouse to jump around in a document

The mouse is often the quickest way to move around a document. When you use the mouse, you can use the vertical scroll bar, as shown in Figure 5-3.

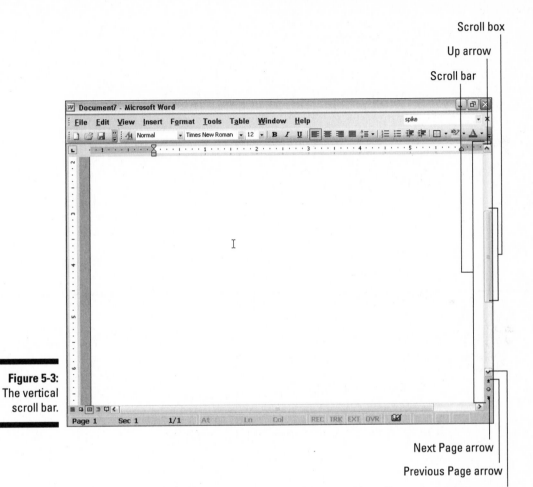

Scroll box

Up arrow

Scroll bar

Figure 5-3:
The vertical
scroll bar.

Next Page arrow

Previous Page arrow

Down arrow

You can use the scroll bar to do the following:

- Click the up or down arrow to scroll up or down, one line at a time.
- Drag the scroll box in the desired direction to jump to an approximate location in your document.
- Click the scroll bar above or below the scroll box to page up or down one window at a time.
- Click the Previous Page or Next Page arrows at the bottom of the scroll bar to jump to the top of the previous or next page.

If your mouse has a wheel in the middle, you have two choices:

✔ Roll the middle wheel on your mouse to scroll a line at a time up or down.

✔ Press the middle wheel and drag the mouse up or down to scroll up or down.

Using the keyboard to jump around in a document

For those who hate the mouse (or just like using the keyboard), here are the different ways to jump around in your document by pressing keys:

✔ Press the ↓ key to move down one line in your document.

✔ Press the ↑ key to move up one line in your document.

✔ Hold down the Ctrl key and press ↑ or ↓ to jump up or down a paragraph at a time.

✔ Press the PgDn key (or Page Down, on some keyboards) to jump down the document one window at a time.

✔ Press the PgUp key (or Page Up, on some keyboards) to jump up the document one window at a time.

✔ Press Ctrl+Home to jump to the beginning of your document.

✔ Press Ctrl+End to jump to the end of your document.

Using the Go To command

When you want to jump to a specific part of your document, the Go To command is much easier and faster than either the mouse or the keyboard. Besides jumping to a specific page number, the Go To command can also jump to the following:

✔ A specific line number

✔ A comment written by a specific person

✔ A bookmark that you or someone else placed in the document

To use the Go To command, do the following:

1. **Choose Edit⇨Go To or press Ctrl+G.**

   The Go To tab of the Find and Replace dialog box appears, as shown in Figure 5-4.

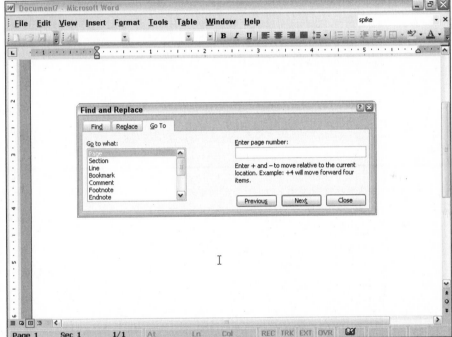

Figure 5-4:
The Go To tab allows you to jump to a specific part of your document, such as a page number.

2. **Type a page number (or click the item you want to go to, such as a specific line number, and then type what you want to find) and press Enter.**

   Word jumps to your chosen item, such as a page number or line number.

3. **Click Close or press Esc to make the Go To dialog box go away.**

Finding and Replacing Words

One common editing task involves finding a word or phrase to read the information around it or to replace that word or phrase with new text.

Finding text

If you just want to find text in a document, follow these steps:

1. **Choose Edit➪Find, or press Ctrl+F.**

   A Find dialog box appears, as shown in Figure 5-5.

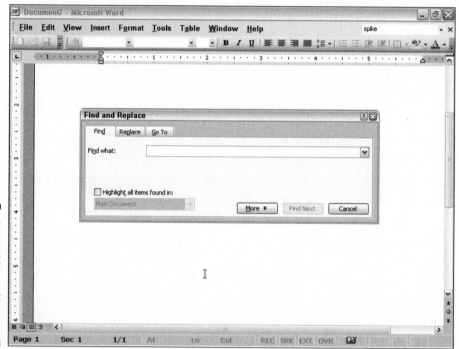

Figure 5-5:
The Find
dialog box
lets you
search a
document
for a word
or phrase.

2. **Click in the Find what text box and type the word or phrase you want to find.**

   If you misspell a word in the Find what text box, Word may not find the word or phrase you want.

3. **Click Find Next.**

   Word highlights the text if it can find it in the document. If you click the Find Next button again, Word will look for additional occurrences of the text.

4. **Click the Close box of the Find dialog box to make it go away.**

If you click the More button in the Find dialog box, you can choose additional options for searching for text, as shown in Figure 5-6. For example, you may want to search for whole words (to prevent Word from finding words buried in another word such as the *rat* inside *rather*), or text that exactly matches the case of the text you typed in the Find What text box.

Figure 5-6: The More button lets you define additional options for searching a document for text.

Finding and replacing text

Many times, you may want to find certain text and replace it automatically with different text. For example, if you typed a letter of resignation using four-letter words, you might want to find and replace all four-letter words and replace them with milder adjectives.

To find and replace text, follow these steps:

1. **Choose Edit⇨Replace, or press Ctrl+H.**

   The Find and Replace dialog box appears, as shown in Figure 5-7.

2. **Click in the Find What text box and type the word or phrase you want to find.**

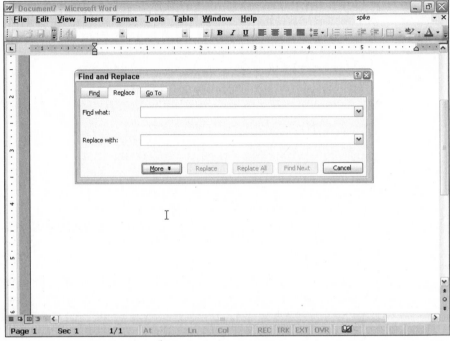

Figure 5-7:
The Find and Replace dialog box lets you specify the text you want to find and the text that you want to use to replace it.

If you misspell a word in the Find what text box, Word may not find the word or phrase you want.

3. **Click in the Replace With text box and type the word or phrase you want to appear instead.**

4. **Choose one of the following:**

   • **Click Replace:** This action highlights the text you want to find and gives you the option to skip or replace this text.

   • **Click Replace All:** Automatically replaces all occurrences of the text you want to find.

5. **Click the Close box of the Find and Replace dialog box to make it go away.**

Checking Your Spelling and Grammar

The final step to polishing your text involves checking your spelling and grammar so mistakes don't detract from the message you want to deliver.

Checking your spelling and grammar

Word provides several ways to check the spelling and grammar in your document. The simplest way is to follow these steps:

1. **Highlight the text that you want to spell check. (Skip this step if you want to check the spelling or grammar of your entire document.)**

2. **Choose one of the following:**

   • Press F7

   • Click the Spell Check icon on the Standard toolbar

   • Choose Tools⇨Spelling and Grammar

   Each time Word finds a word that may be misspelled or a grammatical error, the Spelling and Grammar dialog box appears and highlights the misspelled word or grammatical error, as shown in Figure 5-8.

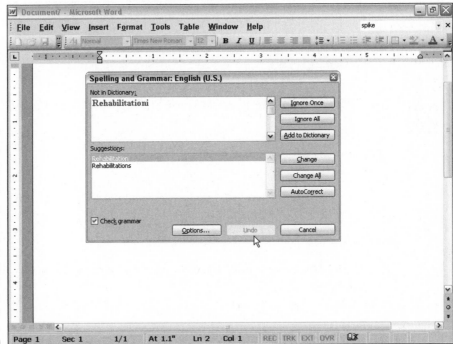

Figure 5-8:
The Spelling and Grammar dialog box shows you what words may be misspelled and lets you choose an alternate spelling.

3. **Choose one of the following:**

   • Click a suggested change and click Change to correct the problem.

   • Click Ignore Once to skip over this problem once.

   • Choose Ignore All or Ignore Rule to ignore all problems of this type.

When Word can no longer find any misspelled words, a dialog box appears to let you know that the spelling check is done.

4. Click OK.

Spell and grammar checking as you type

Word gives you the option of spell and grammar checking as you type. The moment you type a misspelled word, Word underlines that word with a red wavy line. If you type a grammatically incorrect sentence, Word underlines that sentence with a green wavy line.

To correct the spelling or grammar of a word highlighted by a red or green wavy line, follow these steps:

1. Right-click the word that appears highlighted by a red or green wavy line.

A pop-up menu appears that lists several alternate spellings for the highlighted word, as shown in Figure 5-9.

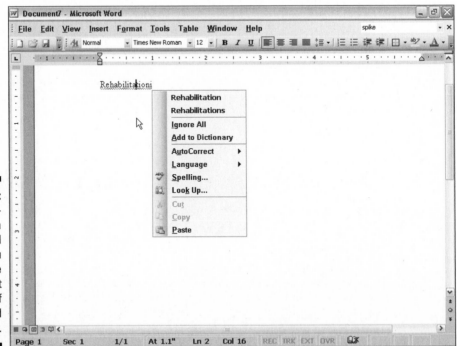

Figure 5-9:
By right-clicking a misspelled word, you can choose the correct spelling of a word right away.

A red wavy line means the word may be misspelled. A green wavy line means that the word may be grammatically incorrect.

2. Choose one of the following:

- Click the correct spelling or grammatical use of the highlighted word.

- Click Add to Dictionary if the word is actually spelled correctly and you don't want Word to keep flagging it as misspelled.

- Click Ignore Once to ignore the problem.

- Click Ignore All in case the word is spelled correctly but you don't want to add it to Word's dictionary.

Word removes the red or green wavy line from under the misspelled word.

Although it can be handy to let Word check your spelling and grammar as you type, you may want to turn this feature off (or on again in case you already turned it off). To turn this feature on or off, follow these steps:

1. Choose Tools⇨Options.

An Options dialog box appears.

2. Click the Spelling & Grammar tab.

The Spelling and Grammar options appear, as shown in Figure 5-10.

3. Click in the Check Spelling As You Type check box or the Check Grammar As You Type check box.

If a check mark appears, Word automatically checks your spelling or grammar as you type. If a check mark does not appear, Word won't check your spelling or grammar as you type.

4. Click OK.

Correcting your spelling automatically

Rather than worry about spell checking your document, let Word automatically correct any spelling mistakes. The moment you misspell a word, Word corrects it automatically so you don't have to worry about it.

This handy feature, called AutoCorrect, lets you define a common misspelling of a word and then define the correct way the word should be spelled. That way the next time you misspell a word wrong, such as typing *thje,* Word will automatically change this to the correct spelling of *the.*

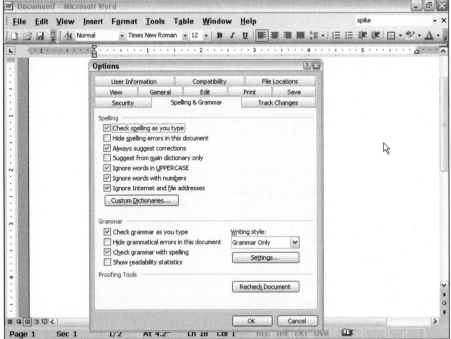

Figure 5-10:
You can turn
Word's spell
checking
feature on
or off in
case you
don't want
to check
your
spelling as
you type.

To modify Word's AutoCorrect feature, follow these steps:

1. **Choose Tools⇨AutoCorrect Options.**

   The AutoCorrect options appear, as shown in Figure 5-11.

2. **Click in the Replace text box and type a word that you commonly misspell.**

   If you scroll down the list, you can see all the misspelled Words that Word already recognizes.

3. **Click in the With text box and type the correct spelling of the word.**

4. **Click OK.**

You can use the AutoCorrect Options feature to create acronyms that represent phrases you may use frequently. For example, if you type NATO into the Replace text box and then type North Atlantic Treaty Organization into the With text box, every time you type NATO, Word will automatically replace NATO with North Atlantic Treaty Organization.

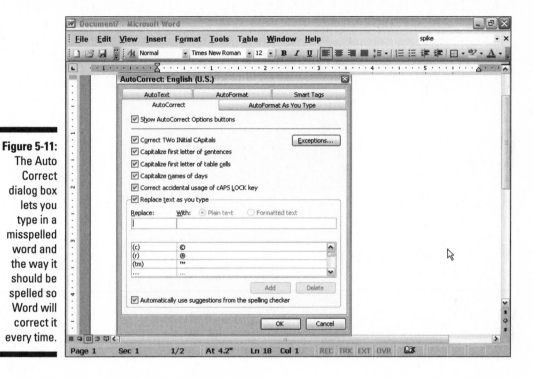

Counting Your Words

Sometimes you may need to keep your writing within a certain number of words for publication in a magazine or for an essay paper you need to turn in for class. To show you how many words you've already typed, you can use Word's handy word counting feature by following these steps:

1. **Highlight the text that you want to count. (Skip this step if you want to count the words in your entire document.)**

2. **Choose Tools⇨Word Count.**

   A Word Count dialog box appears that shows you how many words, pages, paragraphs, and lines are in your highlighted text or document, as shown in Figure 5-12.

3. **Click Close.**

Figure 5-12:
The Word
Count dialog
box lets you
see how
many words
you've typed
in your
document.

Saving Your Stuff

Normally, if you take the time and trouble to write something in Word, you probably want to save your work so that you can use it again in the future. Word provides several ways to save your words.

Saving your document

To save your document, choose one of the following methods:

- ✔ Press Ctrl+S.
- ✔ Click the Save icon on the Standard toolbar (the button that looks like a floppy disk).
- ✔ Choose File⇨Save.

If you're saving a document for the first time, Word asks you to name your file. Ideally, you should make your filename as descriptive as possible, such as Letter To Dad or Subpoena To Ex-Spouse, so it jars your memory about the document's contents when you haven't looked at the file for a while.

If you have multiple documents open and want to save them all in one keystroke, hold down the Shift key and choose File➪Save All.

The longest filename that Word can handle is 255 characters. Filenames must not include the forward slash (/), backslash (\), greater-than sign (>), less-than sign (<), asterisk (*), question mark (?), quotation mark ("), pipe symbol (|), colon (:), or semicolon (;).

Making backups of your file automatically

In case you're terrified of losing data (a completely justified fear, given the penchant for computers to crash at any time for no apparent reason whatsoever), you may want to use Word's backup feature.

The *backup feature* creates a second copy (a backup) of your document every time you save your document. This backup file is called Backup of (Name of Original Document). So if you save a document called Plan for World Domination, the backup file is called Backup of Plan for World Domination and is stored in the same folder as your original document. (This also means that if you accidentally wipe out the folder containing the original document, you also wipe out the backup copy as well.)

To turn on Word's backup feature, follow these steps:

1. **Choose Tools➪Options.**

   The Options dialog box appears.

2. **Click the Save tab.**

   The Save options appear, as shown in Figure 5-13.

3. **Make sure a check mark appears in the Always Create Backup Copy check box.**

4. **Click OK.**

Word also provides an Allow Fast Saves check box that you can click after Step 3. The Fast Saves option saves your files quickly (hence the name Fast Save) because it only stores any changes you make in a smaller, separate, temporary file on the disk. If you choose the Fast Saves option, you should clear the Allow Fast Saves check box periodically so that Word consolidates all changes into a single file.

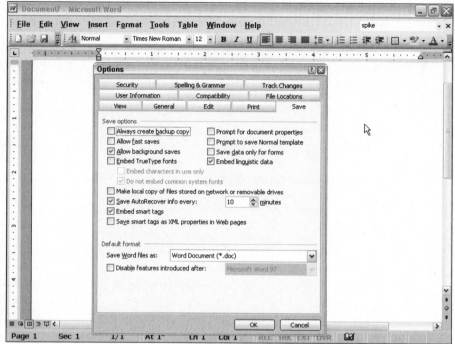

Figure 5-13:
The Save
options in
the Options
dialog box
give you all
sorts of
ways to
save your
text from
ever getting
lost again.

Chapter 6

Making Your Words Look Pretty

*W*ords alone will never sway an audience. Besides writing clearly (something you rarely see in most computer manuals), you should also make your text look nice by formatting it. The better looking your document is, the more likely that someone will take the time to read it.

Microsoft Word gives you two ways to format text: by hand or by using something called a *style template* (explained later in this chapter, so don't worry about the exact meaning for now). Formatting text by hand takes longer but gives you more control. Formatting text using a style template is faster but may not format the text exactly the way you want, which means you may have to go back and format the text by hand anyway.

So which method should you use? Both. If you're in a hurry, use a style template. If you just need to do a little formatting or you want to format text a specific way, do it yourself.

Formatting Text Manually

To modify the appearance of your text, you can change one or more of the following:

✔ Font and font sizes

✔ Type *styles* (such as bold, italics, and underline)

✔ Text color

Picking a font and font size

Your computer comes with a variety of fonts that you probably don't even know exist. A *font* defines the appearance of individual letters. Depending on which fonts your computer has, you can make your text look like it was printed in a newspaper or written with a feather quill. Some examples of different fonts are

- ✔ Times New Roman
- ✔ Courier
- ✔ Arial

When you click the Font list box on the Formatting toolbar, Word conveniently displays a list of all available fonts and shows you what they look like, as shown in Figure 6-1.

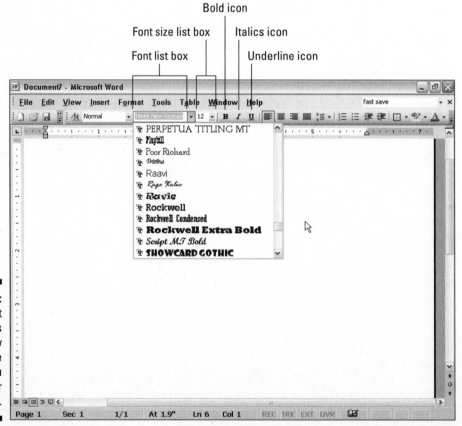

Figure 6-1:
The Font list box allows you to view and pick the font you want for your text.

The font size makes your text bigger or smaller, regardless of the type of font you choose. Some fonts look better large, some fonts look good small, and some fonts look horrible no matter what font size you choose.

If you're not sure whether to change the font or font size of your text, experiment with a few font and font size combinations to see whether they improve the readability of your text.

If you plan to share documents with others, stick to common fonts, such as Times New Roman or MS Sans Serif. Not all computers have some of the more bizarre fonts installed, so if you use those fonts, your text may look really weird on someone else's computer.

To change the font and font size of text, do this:

1. **Highlight the text that you want to modify.**

2. **Click the Font list box on the Formatting toolbar and choose a font.**

   Word displays your highlighted text in your chosen font.

3. **Click the Font Size list box on the Formatting toolbar and choose a font size.**

   Word displays your highlighted text in your chosen font size.

If you choose a font and font size with the cursor at the end of your document, Word automatically uses your chosen font and font size on whatever text you type next.

Choosing a type style

Just to give you a little extra control over your text, Word also lets you display text as bold, italicized, or underlined, regardless of the font or font size you choose.

- ✔ **This sentence appears in bold.**
- ✔ *This sentence appears in italics.*
- ✔ <u>This sentence is underlined.</u>
- ✔ **<u>This sentence shows that you can combine styles — bold and underlined *with italics*, for example.</u>**

To change the type style of text, follow these steps:

1. **Highlight the text that you want to modify.**

2. **Choose one or more of the following, depending on how you want your text to look:**

   • Click the Bold icon (which looks like a B) on the Formatting toolbar or press Ctrl+B.

   • Click the Italic icon (which looks like an I) on the Formatting toolbar or press Ctrl+I.

   • Click the Underline icon (which looks like a U) on the Formatting toolbar or press Ctrl+U.

   Word displays the selected text in your chosen style.

If you choose a type style with the cursor at the end of your document, Word automatically uses your chosen style, such as italic or underline, on whatever text you type next.

Making a splash with color

Because the cost of color printers is falling as rapidly as the net worth of the United States government, you may want to experiment with using different colors to display text. (By the way, adding color doesn't have to be just an aesthetic choice. Color is very useful when you want to highlight portions of text or strain the eyes of the people forced to read your document.)

To change the background color of your text (which makes your text look like someone colored it with a highlighting marker), do the following:

1. **Highlight the text that you want to modify.**

2. **Click the Highlight icon. (If you want to choose a different color, click the downward-pointing arrow to the right of the Highlight icon on the Formatting toolbar.)**

   A palette of different colors appears as shown in Figure 6-2.

3. **Click the color that you want to use on the background.**

   Word magically changes the background color of your text.

To change the color of the actual letters that make up your text, do the following:

1. **Highlight the text that you want to modify.**

2. **Click the Font Color icon. (If you want to choose a different color, click the downward-pointing arrow to the right of the Font Color icon on the Formatting toolbar.)**

   A palette of different colors appears.

Font Color icon

Highlight icon

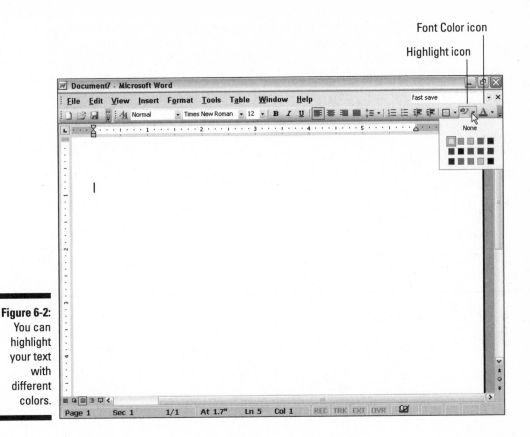

Figure 6-2:
You can
highlight
your text
with
different
colors.

3. Click the color that you want to use on the text.

Word changes the color of your text.

Painting text with the Format Painter

Suppose you have a chunk of text formatted perfectly — font, font size, type style, and so on. Do you have to go through the whole laborious process again to make another chunk of text look exactly the same? Of course not! Use the Format Painter.

The Format Painter tells Word, "See the way you formatted that block of text I just highlighted? I want you to use that same formatting on this other chunk of text."

By using the Format Painter, you don't have to format the individual characteristics of text yourself, which saves time so you can do something that's more important (like make plans for lunch or print your résumé on company time).

To use the Format Painter, follow these steps:

1. **Highlight the text that contains the formatting that you want to use on another chunk of text.**

2. **Click the Format Painter button (it looks like a paintbrush and appears to the right of the Paste icon) on the Formatting toolbar.**

   The mouse cursor turns into an I-beam cursor with a paintbrush to the left. The paintbrush lets you know that Word automatically formats the next chunk of text that you select.

   You may need to click the Toolbar Options button on the Standard toolbar to access the Format Painter icon, as shown in Figure 6-3.

3. **Drag the mouse over the text that you want to format.**

   As soon as you release the left mouse button, Word formats the text with all the formatting characteristics of the text you selected in Step 1.

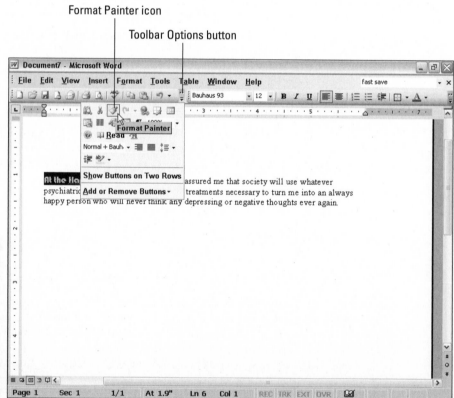

Format Painter icon

Toolbar Options button

Figure 6-3:
The Format
Painter icon
appears
when you
click the
Toolbar
Options
button.

If the text that you select in Step 1 contains a variety of formatting character-istics, Word copies only the formatting characteristics that the entire chunk of selected text has in common. For example, if you select text that's in Times New Roman font with one sentence underlined, a second sentence in bold, and a third sentence with a yellow background, Word formats your new text with the only shared formatting characteristic — the Times New Roman font.

Formatting Your Document the Easy Way

If you really love using Word, you can format your text manually. However, Word provides three shortcuts for changing the overall appearance of your documents:

- ✔ **Themes:** Define the color and graphical appearance of bullets, text, hori-zontal lines, and the background of a document
- ✔ **Style templates:** Provide one or more styles for creating common types of documents, such as résumés, business letters, or fax cover pages
- ✔ **Styles:** Define the format for a paragraph using specific margins, font sizes, or underlining

Choosing a theme

A *theme* lets you choose the decorative appearance of your document. If you don't choose a theme, your text appears in boring black and white. Themes mostly make your document look pretty. If you don't care about appearances, you probably don't need to use themes.

To choose a theme, follow these steps:

1. **Choose Format⇨Theme.**

   The Theme dialog box appears, as shown in Figure 6-4.

2. **Click the theme you want to use in the Choose a Theme list.**

   Each time you click a theme, Word politely shows you a sample of how that theme can change the appearance of your document. You may need to insert your Office 2003 CD in your computer to install your chosen theme.

3. **Choose or clear one or more of the following check boxes:**

   - **Vivid Colors:** Adds (or removes) additional colors to text
   - **Active Graphics:** Adds (or removes) additional graphics to make bullets and horizontal lines look more interesting
   - **Background Image:** Adds (or removes) the background graphic

Figure 6-4:
The Theme
dialog box
can create a
formatted
document
for you
quickly and
easily.

4. **Click OK after you find and define a theme to use.**

    Word displays your chosen theme on the currently displayed document.
    Don't worry. You can still format text individually after you have defined
    a theme for a document.

Choosing a style template

A *style template* provides formatting for common types of documents (faxes,
reports, proposals, memos, and so on). So, if you need to write a fax cover
sheet or a business letter, you could write the whole thing from scratch and
waste a lot of time in the process. Or, you could use a special fax or business
letter template that provides the formatting (styles) for creating a fax or business letter. Then all you have to do is type the text and let Word worry about
the formatting.

To choose a style template, follow these steps:

1. **Choose Format➪Theme.**

    The Theme dialog box appears (see Figure 6-4), showing you the theme
    used in your current document.

2. **Click the Style Gallery button.**

   The Style Gallery dialog box appears, as shown in Figure 6-5.

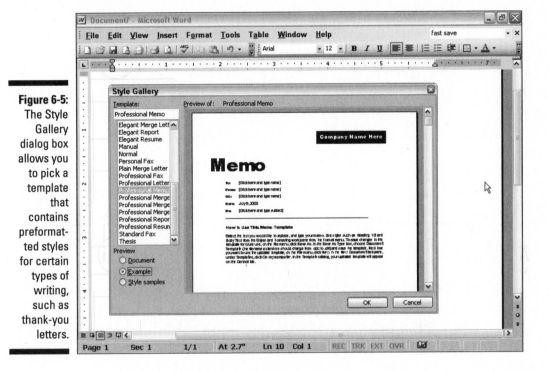

Figure 6-5:
The Style
Gallery
dialog box
allows you
to pick a
template
that
contains
preformat-
ted styles
for certain
types of
writing,
such as
thank-you
letters.

3. **Click one of the style templates listed in the Template box, such as Elegant Fax or Contemporary Report.**

   You can scroll up or down the list under the Template box to see more style templates.

4. **Click one of the following option buttons in the Preview group:**

   • **Document:** Shows what your current document looks like with the selected style template

   • **Example:** Shows how a typical document can look with the selected style template

   • **Style samples:** Shows the different styles that make up the style template

5. **Click OK after you find a style template that you want to use.**

Formatting paragraphs with different styles

Styles define the overall appearance of the text, such as the fonts used to display text or the size of text. By using different styles in a document, you can keep your document from looking like a boring typewritten page (provided, of course, that you still remember what a typewriter is).

To choose a style, use the Style list box on the Formatting toolbar as described in the following steps:

1. **Click in the paragraph that you want to format with a particular style.**

   If you haven't typed any text yet, Word applies the style to whatever text you type in Step 4.

2. **Click the Style list box on the Formatting toolbar to choose a style.**

   A list of different styles appears, as shown in Figure 6-6.

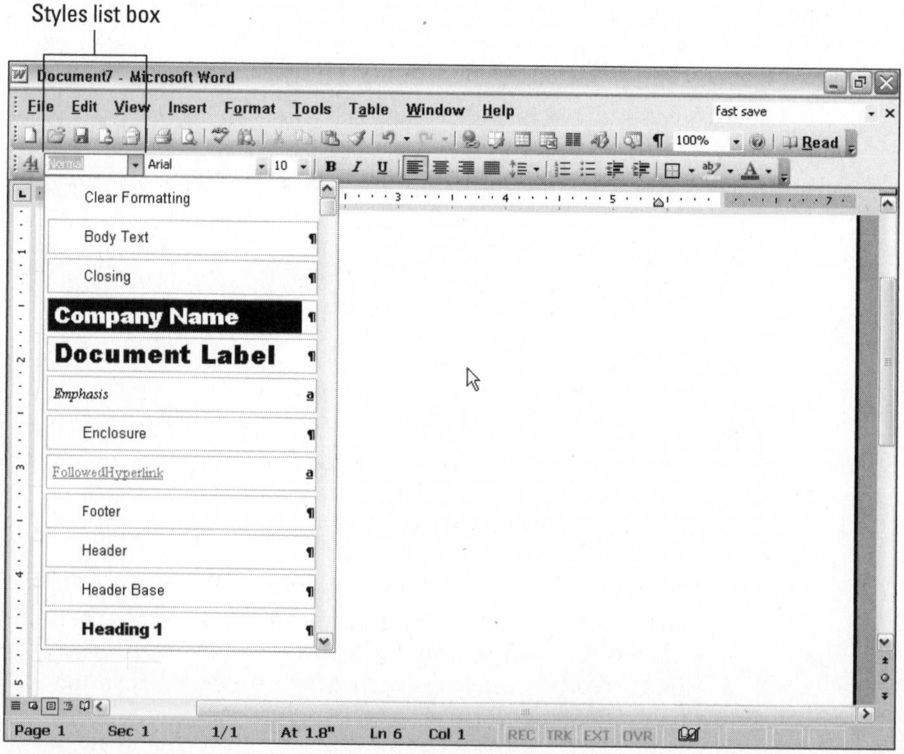

Styles list box

Figure 6-6: Depending on the style template your document uses, you can choose from a variety of preformatted styles for your text.

3. **Click the style that you want to use.**

4. **Type your text and watch Word format it before your eyes. (Or Word formats your text right away, if you moved the cursor to an existing block of text in Step 1.)**

Aligning Text

Another way you can change the appearance of your text is by aligning it within the left and right margins of your page. Word provides several easy ways to align text, but if you want exact control over your text alignment, you can define those margins using the ruler.

Aligning text to the right and the left

Word lets you choose an alignment for your text, which can be left, center, right, or justified, as shown in Figure 6-7. Most of the time, you probably want to left-align text, but occasionally, you may want to center a heading in the middle of the page or justify an entire paragraph. Don't worry too much about right-aligning text unless you like displaying your text in strange ways.

In a nutshell, here's what the four alignment possibilities do to your text:

- ✔ **Left-align text:** The left margin is a straight line, and the right margin is uneven.

- ✔ **Center text:** Each line is centered in the middle of the page. Consequently, both the left and right margins look ragged when you have several lines of unequal length centered.

- ✔ **Right-align text:** The right margin is a straight line, and the left margin is uneven.

- ✔ **Justify text:** Both the left and right margins are straight, and the letters in between look somewhat spaced apart.

To align text, do the following:

1. **Click anywhere inside the paragraph that you want to align.**

2. **Click the Align Left, Center, Align Right, or Justify icon on the Formatting toolbar, depending on how you want the text to look.**

   As soon as you click a button, Word aligns your text.

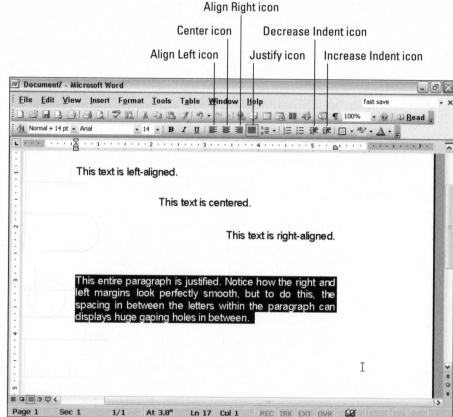

Align Right icon

Center icon   Decrease Indent icon

Align Left icon   Justify icon   Increase Indent icon

Figure 6-7:
Four
different
ways to
align text.

If you choose an alignment where the cursor doesn't appear inside any text, Word applies your chosen alignment to whatever text you type next.

Indenting text

Rather than align text, you may just want to indent it instead. Indenting text can make a block of text stand out so it's easy to find and read. To indent text, do the following:

1. **Highlight the paragraph that you want to indent.**

   You can just highlight part of a paragraph, and when you choose the Indent command, Word is smart enough to indent the entire paragraph.

2. **Click the Increase Indent or Decrease Indent icons on the Formatting toolbar.**

   Clicking the Increase Indent button moves the text to the right. Clicking the Decrease Indent icon moves the text to the left.

Defining margins with the ruler

In case you want to specify exactly how your text aligns on the left and right margins, you can use the ruler. The *ruler* defines the margins and tabs of your document, and if you create a multicolumn document, the ruler also shows the column margins and the distance between the columns. By using the ruler, you can make margins wider (or smaller) and change the indentation of paragraphs.

Word provides five different types of tabs (shown in Figure 6-8) that you can set on the ruler where each tab type performs a specific function:

- ✔ **Left tab (looks like an L):** Moves text toward the right edge of the page as you type

- ✔ **Center tab (looks like an upside-down T):** Centers text around the tab

- ✔ **Right tab (looks like a backward L):** Moves text toward the left edge of the page as you type

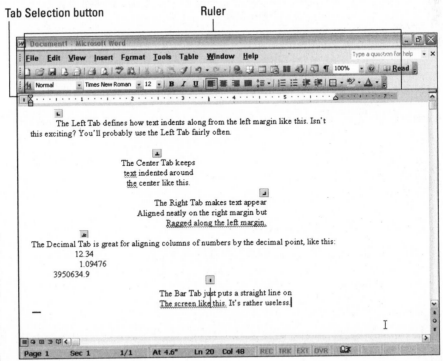

Figure 6-8:
The five different types of tabs you can place on a ruler.

- ✔ **Decimal tab (looks like an upside-down T with a dot next to it):** Aligns decimal numbers in a column on the decimal point, as in this example:

  24.90

    1.9084

  58093.89

- ✔ **Bar tab (looks like a straight line, like |):** Draws a vertical line on the document

To place a tab on the ruler, follow these steps:

1. **Click the Tab Selection button (which appears to the left of the ruler) until it displays the tab that you want to use.**

2. **Click the ruler where you want to place the tab.**

To move an existing tab on the ruler, do the following:

1. **Move the mouse pointer over the tab you want to move.**

2. **Hold down the left mouse button until you see a dotted line appear directly below the tab.**

3. **Move the mouse to where you want to move the tab.**

4. **Release the left mouse button.**

To remove a tab from the ruler, do the following:

1. **Move the mouse pointer on the tab you want to remove.**

2. **Hold down the left mouse button until you see a dotted line appear directly beneath the tab.**

3. **Move the mouse off the ruler.**

4. **Release the left mouse button.**

Indents on your ruler

To help you indent paragraphs, the Tab Selection button also displays two types of indentation icons, as shown in Figure 6-9:

- ✔ **First Line Indent icon:** This icon looks like an upside-down house and defines the left margin of the first line in a paragraph.

- ✔ **Hanging Indent icon:** This icon looks like a big U on the Tab Selection button and has a right-side-up house above the Left Indent icon on the ruler. The icon defines the left margin of every line but the first line in a paragraph.

Left indent

Hanging indent

Right indent

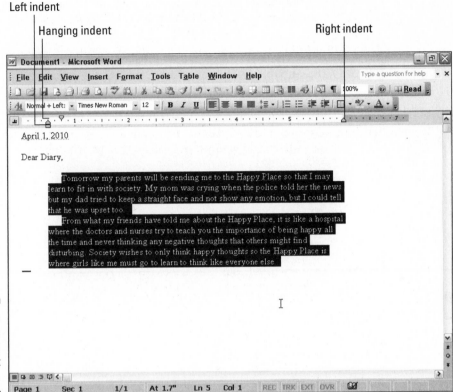

Figure 6-9:
Using the
ruler, you
can indent
text.

To provide more indentation options, the ruler displays two indent icons that
can indent your text left and right:

- ✔ **Left Indent icon:** This icon does not appear in the Tab Selection button.
  It cannot be separated from the Hanging Indent icon where it also
  defines the left margin of every line except the first line of a paragraph.

- ✔ **Right Indent icon:** This icon does not appear in the Tab Selection
  button. It defines the right margin of every line of a paragraph.

The ruler can display only one indent (whether First Line, Hanging, Left, or
Right) per paragraph.

To indent paragraphs with the First Line Indent, Hanging Indent, Left Indent,
and Right Indent markers, follow these steps:

1. Highlight the paragraphs that you want to indent.

Skip this step if you haven't written any paragraphs to indent yet. Any
indentation that you apply to a blank document affects the entire future
document.

2. **Move the mouse pointer on a marker (First Line Indent, Hanging Indent, Left Indent, or Right Indent) and hold down the left mouse button.**

   Word displays a dotted vertical line directly under the marker.

3. **Move the mouse where you want to indent the paragraph and then release the mouse button.**

Instead of moving the indent markers on the ruler, you can click the Tab Selection button until the First Line or Hanging Indent icon appears, and then click the ruler where you want to put the First Line or Hanging Indent marker.

Making Lists

Some people like making lists so that they know what they're supposed to do, what they're supposed to buy, and what they really don't feel like doing but feel guilty enough about that they try to do it anyway. To help accommodate list makers all over the world, Word creates lists quickly and easily.

Word lets you make two types of lists, as shown in Figure 6-10:

✔ **Numbered list:** Displays each item with a number in front

✔ **Bulleted list:** Displays a bullet in front of each item

You can left-align, right-align, center, or justify any of your bulleted or numbered lists. Aren't computers an exciting example of how technology can empower the average user?

Making lists the fast way

To create a numbered or bulleted list quickly, follow these steps:

1. **Click the Numbering or Bullets icon on the Formatting toolbar.**

   Word displays a number or bullet.

2. **Type your text and press Enter.**

   Each time you press Enter, Word displays another number or bullet.

3. **Click the Numbering or Bullets icon again to turn off the numbering or bullets feature.**

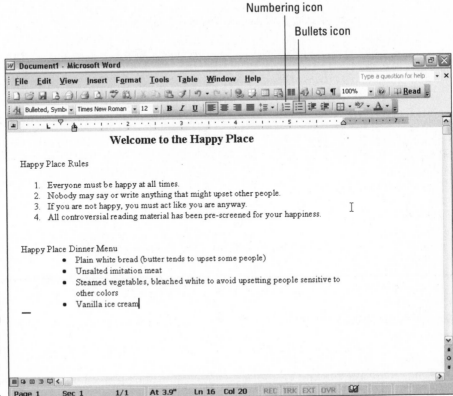

Figure 6-10:
A numbered
list and a
bulleted list.

Customizing the way your lists look

In case you want to have more control over the type of numbering or bullets Word uses, follow these steps:

1. **Highlight the text that you want to turn into a list.**

   If you highlight an existing list, you can change the numbering or bullet style that appears.

2. **Choose Format➪Bullets and Numbering.**

   The Bullets and Numbering dialog box appears, as shown in Figure 6-11.

3. **Click the Bulleted tab to define the appearance of a bulleted list or the Numbered tab to define the appearance of a numbered list.**

   The dialog box displays two rows of boxes that show the various numbering or bullet styles.

4. **Click inside the box that shows the type of bullets or numbering that you want to use; then click OK.**

   Word automatically converts your selected text into a list.

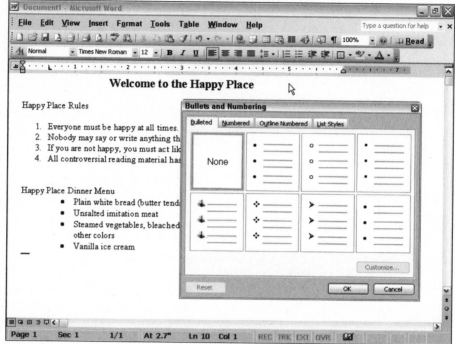

Figure 6-11:
The Bullets
and
Numbering
dialog box
shows you
different
bullet and
numbering
styles you
can choose.

In case you find Word's automatic list-making feature more annoying than useful, you can turn it off by following these steps:

1. **Choose Tools⇨AutoCorrect Options.**

2. **Click the AutoFormat As You Type tab and click the Automatic Bulleted List or Automatic Numbered Lists check boxes to clear them.**

3. **Click OK.**

Aligning Text with Tables

Tables organize information in rows and columns, which can be useful for displaying information in an easy-to-read format. With a table, you can organize essential text so that people can find and read it easily, rather than trying to find important information buried inside a paragraph.

Before you start working with tables, you need to know some things about rows and columns, including the following:

> ✔ A *row* displays information horizontally.
>
> ✔ A *column* displays information vertically.
>
> ✔ A *cell* is a single box formed by the intersection of a row and a column.

Making a table

You may be happy to know that Word provides three different ways to make a table in your documents:

> ✔ Draw the table in your document with the mouse
>
> ✔ Define the size of a table by typing in the exact number of rows and columns
>
> ✔ Convert a chunk of text into a table

Drawing a table with the mouse

If you want to create tables right away, you can draw the table's approximate size by using the mouse. You can modify its height and width later. To create a table using the mouse, do the following:

1. **Choose Table⇨Draw Table.**

   The Tables and Borders toolbar appears, and the mouse pointer turns into a pencil icon.

2. **Move the mouse where you want the table to appear.**

3. Hold down the left mouse button and drag the mouse to draw the table, as shown in Figure 6-12.

4. **Release the left mouse button.**

   Word displays your table as a solid line.

5. **Drag the mouse inside the table where you want to draw a row or column. You can draw a line vertically, horizontally, or diagonally to define your cells.**

   Repeat this step as many times as necessary.

   In case you make a mistake, just click the Eraser icon on the Tables and Borders toolbar and click the line that you want to erase. Then click the Draw Table icon again to start drawing your table once more.

6. **Press Esc when you finish drawing your rows and columns.**

   The mouse cursor changes from a pencil icon back to an I-shaped icon. At this point, you can click inside a cell and type text in your newly created table.

7. **Click the Close box of the Tables and Borders toolbar to make it go away.**

Defining a table from the Table menu

Drawing a table with the mouse can be especially useful when you want to create tables where one row or column is a different size than another. If you want to create a table with uniform rows and columns, or a table with large numbers of rows or columns, it's easier to create a table from the menus. To do this, follow these steps:

1. **Choose Table⇨Insert⇨Table.**

   The Insert Table dialog box appears, as shown in Figure 6-13.

2. **Click in the Number of Columns box and type the number of columns you want.**

3. **Click in the Number of Rows box and type the number of rows you want.**

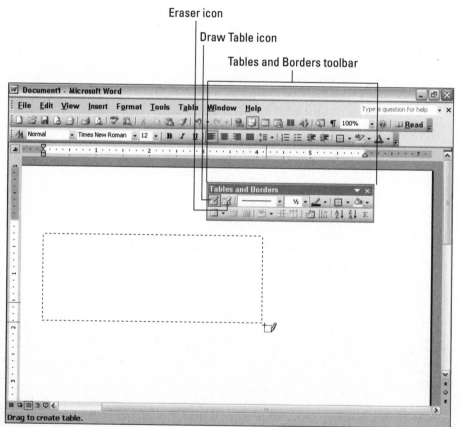

Figure 6-12: You can draw a table with the mouse.

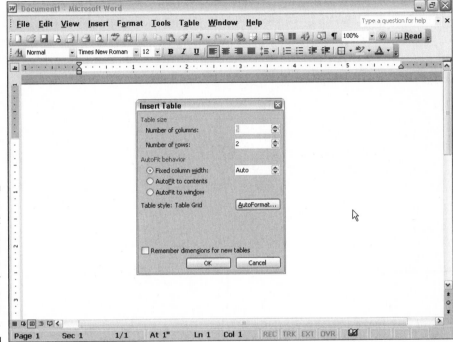

4. **In the AutoFit Behavior area, click one of the following option buttons:**

   • **Fixed Column Width:** You can choose Auto to force Word to make column widths the size of the longest item stored in the entire table, or you can define a specific value, such as 0.5 inches.

   • **AutoFit to Contents:** Adjusts column widths depending on the longest item in each column.

   • **AutoFit to Window:** Adjusts the table based on the size of the window used to display the table.

5. **Click the AutoFormat button.**

   The Table AutoFormat dialog box appears, as shown in Figure 6-14.

6. **Click one of the table formats (such as Classic 3 or Simple 1) in the Table Styles list and try out the various formatting options available in the dialog box.**

   The Preview window shows a sample of the selected table format. When you click any check boxes in the Apply Special Formats To group in the Table AutoFormat dialog box, the Preview window shows how these options affect the selected table format's appearance.

7. **After you select your table format preference and any optional formatting options, click OK.**

   The Insert Table dialog box appears again (refer to Figure 6-13).

8. **Click OK.**

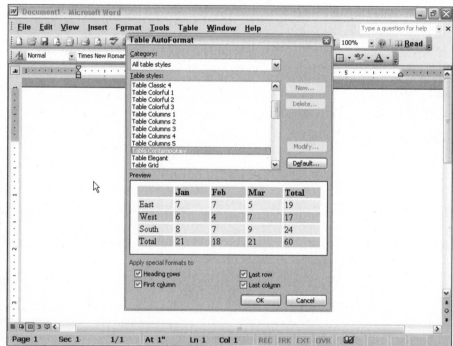

Figure 6-14:
The Table
AutoFormat
dialog box
can quickly
format your
table with
a minimal
amount of
effort.

Converting text into a table

If you have text separated by commas, paragraphs, or tabs, you can convert that blob of text into a neatly organized table. To convert text into a table, follow these steps:

1. **Highlight the text you want to convert into a table.**

2. **Choose Table➪Convert➪Text to Table.**

   The Convert Text to Table dialog box appears as shown in Figure 6-15. The options displayed in this dialog box show you the default table Word will create based on the text you highlighted in Step 1. If you want to modify the table's appearance, you can define the number of rows and columns along with the formatting by clicking the AutoFormat button. When you're done making any changes, go to Step 3.

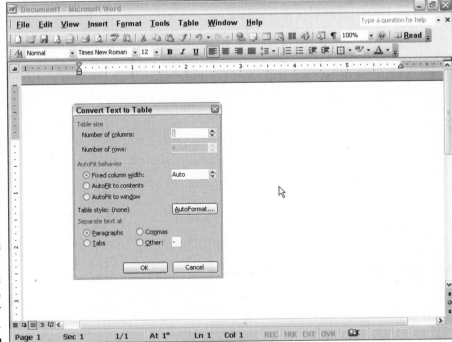

Figure 6-15:
The Convert
Text to Table
dialog box
lets you
define the
number of
rows and
columns
you want to
create for
your table.

3. Click OK.

Word converts your highlighted text into a table. Depending on the text
you highlighted, the table may look perfect or may contain text scattered in separate cells, so you may need to cut and paste some of the
data to make everything look nice and neat.

Entering and editing table data

A blank table is pretty useless, so you may want to add data inside the tables
you create. To enter and edit data, just click the desired cell and use the keyboard to type or edit. You can also use the following methods to move
around within the table:

- Press the Tab key to move the cursor to the next cell to the right in the
same row.
- Press Shift+Tab to move backward (to the left) in the row.
- Use the ↑ and ↓ keys to move from row to row.

Deleting tables

Word gives you two ways to delete a table:

- ✔ Delete just the contents of the table (leave the blank cells and formatting intact).
- ✔ Delete the entire table, including the contents of the table.

To delete only the data inside the table but not the table itself, follow these steps:

1. **Click the mouse anywhere inside the table containing the data you want to delete.**

2. **Choose Table➪Select➪Table.**

   Word highlights your chosen table.

3. **Press Delete.**

   Word deletes the data inside your chosen table.

To delete the data and the table, follow these steps:

1. **Click the mouse anywhere inside the table.**

2. **Choose Table➪Delete➪Table.**

   Word deletes your chosen table and any data inside it.

If you delete your table or data by mistake, press Ctrl+Z right away to return your data and table back to your document again.

Adding or deleting rows, columns, and cells, oh my!

After you create a table, you may want to make it bigger or smaller by adding or deleting rows and columns. To delete a row or column, do the following:

1. **Put the cursor in the row or column that you want to delete.**

   You can either use the keyboard arrow keys or click the table using the mouse.

2. **Choose Table➪Delete➪Columns (or Rows).**

To delete a single cell, which may make your table look funny, do the following:

1. **Put the cursor in the cell that you want to delete.**

   You can either use the keyboard cursor keys or click in the cell.

2. **Choose Table⇨Delete⇨Cells.**

   The Delete Cells dialog box appears.

3. **Click a radio button (such as Shift Cells Left) and click OK.**

To add a row or column to your table, do this:

1. **Put the cursor in any row or column.**

2. **Choose Table⇨Insert⇨Columns to the Left (or Columns to the Right or Rows Above or Rows Below).**

To add a single cell, do the following:

1. **Put the cursor in the table where you want to add a cell.**

2. **Choose Table⇨Insert⇨Cells.**

   The Insert Cells dialog box appears.

3. **Click a radio button (such as Shift Cells Right) and click OK.**

Changing the dimensions of a table's columns and rows

Normally, Word displays all columns with the same width and all rows with the same height. However, if you want some rows or columns to be a different size, Word gives you two options for changing them:

- ✔ Use the mouse to change the height or width of rows and columns visually.
- ✔ Define exact dimensions for the height or width of rows and columns.

Changing the height of a row or the width of a column visually

To change the row height or column width of a table visually, follow these steps:

1. **Choose View⇨Print Layout or click the Print Layout View icon in the bottom left-hand corner of the screen.**

   Word displays a vertical ruler on the left side of the screen and a horizontal ruler at the top of the screen.

2. Click inside the table that you want to modify.

The Adjust Table Row and Adjust Column markers appear, as shown in Figure 6-16.

3. Place the mouse cursor over one of the Adjust Table Row or Move Table Column markers on the vertical or horizontal ruler.

4. Hold down the left mouse button and drag the mouse up or down (or right and left).

Word displays a dotted line to show how your chosen row or column will look when you release the mouse button.

5. Release the left mouse button when you're happy with the height of your row or width of your column.

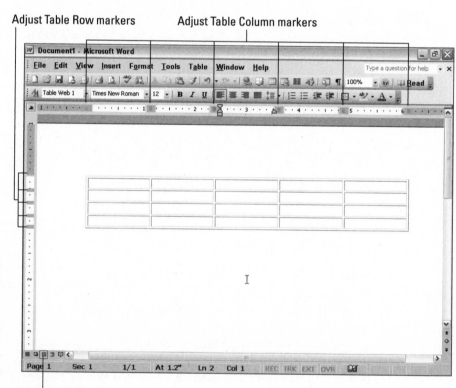

Figure 6-16:
You can use the markers to adjust the rows and columns.

Defining exact dimensions for the height of a row or the width of a column

To tell Word to use exact dimensions for the height of a row or width of a column, follow these steps:

1. **Click in the row or column that you want to adjust.**

2. **Choose Table⇨Table Properties.**

   The Table Properties dialog box appears, as shown in Figure 6-17.

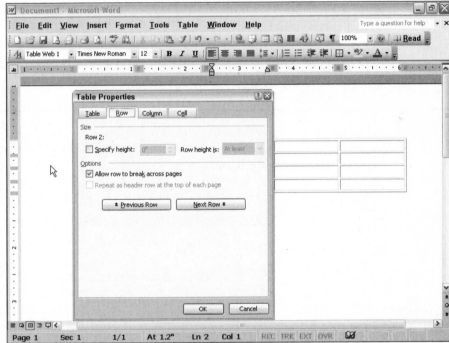

Figure 6-17: The Table Properties dialog box can help you precisely define the widths and heights of your table's columns and rows.

3. **Click the Row or Column tab.**

   The Row or Column tab appears in the Table Properties dialog box.

4. **Click in the Specify Height (or Preferred Width) box and click the up or down arrows to choose a height or width, such as 0.74 inches.**

5. **Click in the Row Height Is box and choose At Least or Exactly. (If you're adjusting the width of a column, click in the Measure In box and choose Inches or Percent.)**

If you choose the At Least option for the row height, your rows will never be smaller than the dimensions you specify, but rows may be larger, depending on the amount of text you type in it. If you want rows to remain a fixed height, choose the Exactly option instead.

6. **Click OK.**

Converting a table into text

A table may organize your text nicely, but one day you may decide that you don't need a table in your document but you still want to keep the text inside that table. To save your text, you can use Word's magic command that converts a table into a chunk of text by following these steps:

1. **Click anywhere inside the table that you want to convert into text.**

2. **Choose Table⇨Convert⇨Table to Text.**

   The Convert Table to Text dialog box appears, as shown in Figure 6-18.

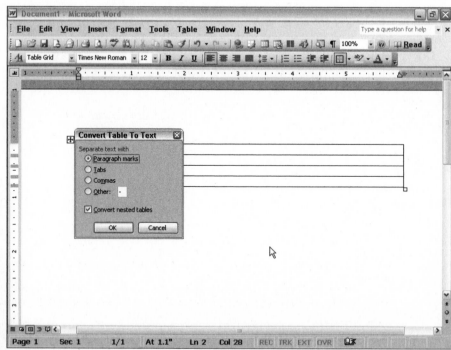

Figure 6-18:
The Convert Table to Text dialog box asks you how you want to separate your text on the page.

3. **Click an option button to define how to separate your text.**

   - **Paragraph marks:** Displays the contents of every cell on a separate line. If you have a table with multiple columns, this arranges your text as one huge stack.

   - **Tabs:** Leaves the text exactly on the screen as it appears, but without the table borders around it.

   - **Commas:** Displays each row as one line of text where the contents of each cell appear separated by a comma.

   - **Other:** Allows you to type a character to use to separate the text in each cell, such as typing a dash (-) or a / character.

4. **Click OK.**

   Word converts your table into text.

In case you don't like the way Word converted your table into text, press Ctrl+Z to restore your table back to its original condition.

Chapter 7

Creating Fancy Pages

●●

●●

ou can use Word to write letters, reports, or threatening notes to people you don't like. With a little bit of creativity and a lot of patience, you can also use Word's limited desktop publishing features to make simple newsletters, brochures, and flyers without having to wrestle with a separate desktop publishing program (such as Microsoft Publisher). The prettier the presentation of your text, the more credibility people will give it, in most cases without even bothering to read it.

Playing with Footers and Headers

Headers and footers are chunks of text that appear at the top and bottom of your pages. *Headers* appear at the top of the page (think of where your head appears in relation to your body), while *footers* appear at the bottom (think of where your feet appear).

Both headers and footers can appear on each page of a document and contain information, such as the publication title, the section or chapter title, the page number, and/or the author's name. If you look at the odd-numbered pages in this book, you can see that the chapter number, chapter title, and page number appear at the top of the page as a header. Headers and footers are useful for displaying identical (or nearly identical) text on two or more pages — for example, document titles or page references (such as *Page 4 of 89*). Although you can type this same text over and over again on each page (but why?), letting Word do the work for you is much easier.

You have two ways to view a document's headers and footers:

- ✔ Choose View➪Header and Footer.
- ✔ Choose View➪Print Layout (or click the Print Layout View icon in the bottom-left corner of the screen).

If you switch to Print Layout view, you can see how your headers and footers will look on each page, but you won't be able to edit them in that view.

Adding headers and footers

To add a header or footer, follow these steps:

1. **Choose View➪Header and Footer.**

   Word displays the Header and Footer toolbar along with a Header (or Footer) text box where you can type a header (or footer), as shown in Figure 7-1.

2. **Type your header (or footer) text in the Header (or Footer) text box and/or click a toolbar button to have Word insert the page number, number of pages, date, or time.**

   - If you press Tab once, Word moves the cursor to the center of the header text box. If you press Tab again, Word moves the cursor to the right of the head text box.

   - If you click the Insert Page Number, Insert Number of Pages, Insert Date, or Insert Time buttons to insert the page number, date, or time in your header, Word automatically updates this information from page to page (for the page number information) or each time you open the document (for the date and time information).

   - You can also click Insert AutoText on the toolbar to have Word insert commonly used text for headers and footers (for example, Page X of Y).

3. **Click the Switch between Header and Footer button.**

   Word displays the Footer text box (or the Header text box if you created a header in Step 2).

4. **Type your text in the Footer (or Header) text box and/or click a toolbar button.**

   Refer to Step 2 for directions.

5. **Click Close on the Header and Footer toolbar to make the toolbar disappear.**

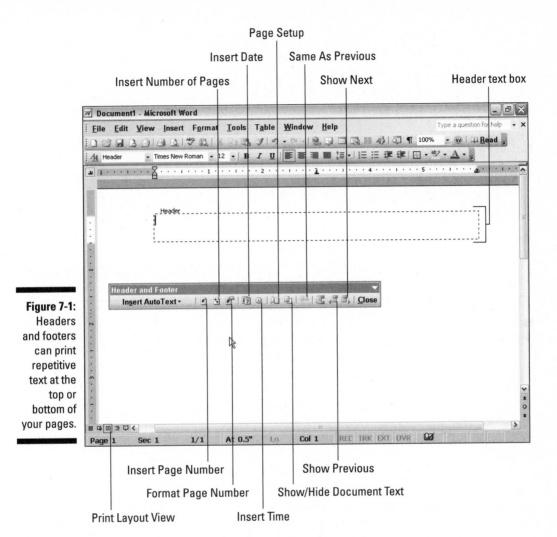

Page Setup

Insert Date   Same As Previous

Insert Number of Pages   Show Next   Header text box

Figure 7-1:
Headers
and footers
can print
repetitive
text at the
top or
bottom of
your pages.

Insert Page Number   Show Previous

Format Page Number   Show/Hide Document Text

Print Layout View   Insert Time

Modifying page numbering

When you tell Word to include page numbers in your headers or footers, Word starts numbering from page one and displays Arabic numerals such as 1, 3, and 49. If you want to number your pages differently (for example, numbering them as i, ii, iii, or a, b, c), or if you want Word to make 97 the first page number in your document, you have to use the Page Number Format button on the Header and Footer toolbar. To use the Page Number Format button, follow these steps:

1. **Choose View⇨Header and Footer.**

   The Header and Footer toolbar appears (refer to Figure 7-1).

2. **Highlight the page numbers that appear in your Header (or Footer) text box.**

   The page number appears shaded gray. If page numbers do not appear in your Header (or Footer) text box, click the Insert Page Number button on the Header and Footer toolbar and then highlight the number that appears.

3. **Click the Format Page Number icon on the Header and Footer toolbar.**

   The Page Number Format dialog box appears (as shown in Figure 7-2) offering ways to change the way Word displays numbers or starts numbering in your header or footer.

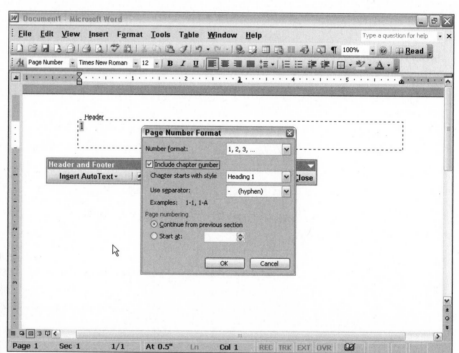

Figure 7-2:
The Page
Number
Format
dialog box.

4. **Click in the Number Format list box and choose a page numbering style (such as 1, 2, 3 or i, ii, iii).**

5. **In the Page Numbering group, click one of the following radio buttons:**

   - **Continue from Previous Section:** Numbers pages sequentially

   - **Start At:** Lets you define the starting page number as a number other than 1

6. **Click OK.**

Creating Multicolumn Documents

To create a newsletter or brochure, you may want to display text in two or more columns to give it a professional look. Word can divide your documents into multiple columns — but remember that if you use more than four columns on a single page, none of the columns can display much text.

Making columns the fast way

To create multiple columns quickly, follow these steps:

1. **Highlight the text that you want to turn into columns.**

   If you want to divide your entire document into columns, skip this step.

2. **Click the Toolbar Options icon on the Standard toolbar.**

   A list of additional icons appears as shown in Figure 7-3.

3. **Click the Columns icon on the Standard toolbar.**

   The Column menu appears, giving you the choice of dividing a page into two, three, or four columns.

4. **Highlight the number of columns you want by dragging the mouse to the right.**

   Word immediately converts your document into a multicolumn document.

Making custom columns

To create customized columns, follow these steps:

1. **Highlight the text that you want to turn into columns.**

   If you want to divide your entire document into columns, skip this step.

2. **Choose Format➪Columns.**

The Columns dialog box appears (as shown in Figure 7-4), offering ways to define column widths and space between columns.

3. Click one of the column types shown in the Presets group or type the number of columns you want in the Number of columns box.

4. Click (or clear) the Equal column width check box.

If the Equal Column Width check box is clear, you can define the width of each column individually.

5. Click the Width box in the Width and spacing group and click the up or down arrow to specify the exact dimension of each column width.

You can also type a specific column width if you want.

6. Click the Spacing box in the Width and spacing group and click the up or down arrow to specify the exact dimension of the spacing between each column.

You can also type a specific spacing width if you want.

7. Click OK.

Word displays your document in multiple columns, customized to your specifications.

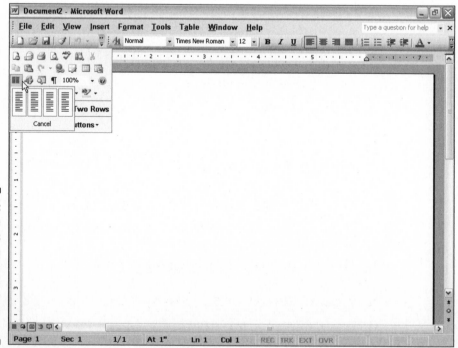

Figure 7-3:
The Columns icon appeared buried on the Standard toolbar.

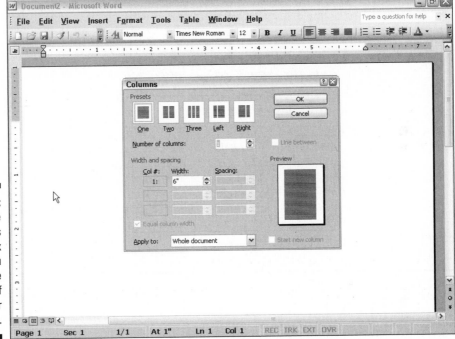

Figure 7-4:
The Columns dialog box lets you customize the size of your columns.

Adding Pictures to a Document

Because long stretches of text can often intimidate people from reading what you have to say, you may want to spice up your document with pictures. Word gives you several choices for inserting graphics into a document as shown in Figure 7-5:

- ✔ **Clip Art:** Gives you the option of inserting any picture from the Microsoft Office Clip Art gallery.

- ✔ **From File:** Adds a picture stored in a graphic file created by another program (for example, PaintShop Pro or Adobe Photoshop).

- ✔ **From Scanner or Camera:** Adds digital images or photographs captured by a scanner or digital camera.

- ✔ **AutoShapes:** Draws a common geometric shape (such as an oval, rectangle, or star) on your screen.

- ✔ **WordArt:** Creates text that appears in different colors and shapes.

- ✔ **Organizational Chart:** Creates a typical business chart that shows who's on top and who really does all the work.

- ✔ **New Drawing:** Creates drawings from geometric shapes, lines, or WordArt.

- ✔ **Chart:** Lets you add a business graph, such as a pie, line, or bar chart.

Organizational chart

WordArt

Clip art

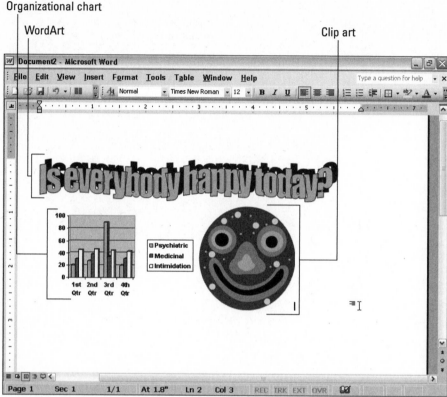

Figure 7-5:
Some
examples of
the different
types of
pictures that
Word can
display in a
document.

Putting clip art into your document

To add clip art to a document, follow these steps:

1. **Move the cursor where you want to insert the image.**

2. **Choose Insert⇨Picture⇨Clip Art.**

   The Clip Art task pane appears.

3. **Click in the Search For text box and type a word or two describing the type of clip art you want to use.**

   You may want to keep the description simple at first — *sailboat,* for example, instead of *catamaran,* or *hot dog* instead of *bratwurst.*

4. **Click Go or press Enter.**

   The Clip Art task pane displays all the clip-art images that match your search, as shown in Figure 7-6.

Figure 7-6:
The Clip Art task pane lets you search for clip art images by subject.

5. **Right-click the image you want to insert and when a pop-up menu appears, click Insert.**

   Word inserts your chosen clip art in your document.

6. **Click the Close box in the Insert Clip Art pane to make it go away.**

Putting existing graphic files into a document

If you've already drawn, copied, bought, or created a graphic file, you can shove it into a Word document. To add an existing graphic file to a document, follow these steps:

1. **Move the cursor where you want to insert the image.**

2. **Choose Insert➪Picture➪From File.**

   An Insert Picture dialog box appears.

3. **Click the folder containing the graphic file you want to add.**

4. **Click the file you want to use.**

   Word displays your chosen image.

5. Click Insert.

Word inserts your chosen image into your document. If you need to wrap words around your picture, follow the instructions in the "Wrapping words around a picture" section later in this chapter.

Using WordArt in a document

WordArt is a fancy way to make your text look pretty by combining colors, shapes, and fonts in a unique appearance. To add WordArt to a document, follow these steps:

1. Move the cursor where you want to insert the WordArt.

2. Choose Insert⇨Picture⇨WordArt.

A WordArt Gallery dialog box appears as shown in Figure 7-7.

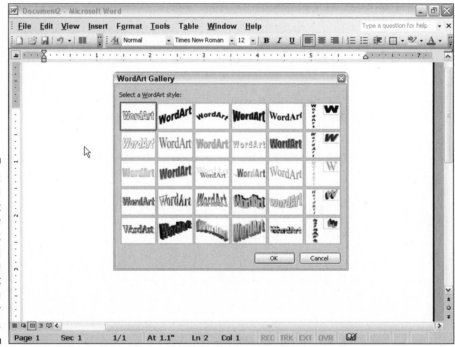

Figure 7-7:
The WordArt Gallery dialog box shows you all the different styles you can use for your text.

3. Click the type of WordArt that you want to add and click OK.

An Edit WordArt Text dialog box appears, as shown in Figure 7-8.

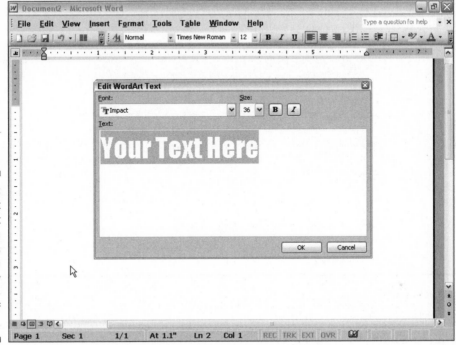

Figure 7-8:
The Edit
WordArt
Text dialog
box is
where you
can modify
the appear-
ance of
your text.

4. Type the text you want to display.

At this time you can change the font, adjust the size, or add bold or italics to your text.

5. Click OK.

Editing a Picture

After you've inserted a picture into a document, you may want to modify the
way that picture affects the text that surrounds it, move the picture to a new
location, or just delete the picture altogether.

Wrapping words around a picture

To wrap text around a picture, follow these steps:

1. Right-click the picture that you want words to wrap around.

A pop-up menu appears.

2. **Click Format Picture.**

   The Format Picture dialog box appears.

3. **Click the Layout tab.**

   Word displays several different ways to wrap text around your chosen picture, such as Square or Tight as shown in Figure 7-9.

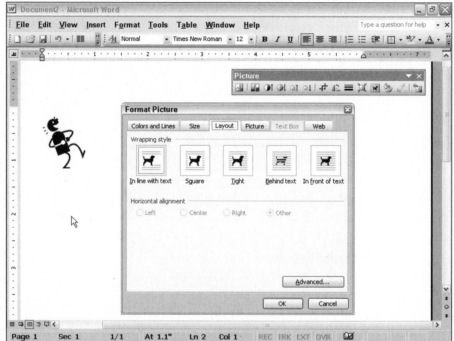

Figure 7-9:
The Format Picture dialog box gives you different ways to wrap text around a picture.

4. **Click an icon in the Wrapping Style group, such as Square or Tight.**

   The different icons in the Format dialog box show you how your text will wrap around your chosen object. For example, the Tight option makes text appear very close to the edges of your picture.

5. **Click OK.**

   If you click the Advanced button after Step 4, you can define the exact distance that separates text from the border of your picture.

Moving a picture in a document

After you place a picture in a document, you can always move it to a new location later. To move a picture, follow these steps:

1. **Click the picture that you want to move.**

   Handles appear around your chosen picture.

2. **Hold down the left mouse button and drag the mouse.**

   As you move the mouse, a gray vertical line appears in your text to show you where Word will move your picture the moment you release the left mouse button.

3. **Release the left mouse button when the picture appears where you want it.**

If you need to move a picture a large distance, such as from page 1 to page 230, you may find it easier to click on a picture, press Ctrl+X, move the cursor where you want the picture to move to, and then press Ctrl+V.

Resizing a picture in a document

You may find that a picture is too small or too large. You can resize it by following these steps:

1. **Click the picture that you want to resize.**

   Handles appear around your chosen picture.

2. **Move the mouse pointer over a handle, hold down the left mouse button, and drag the mouse.**

   As you move the mouse, Word displays a dotted line that shows you the approximate size of your picture.

3. **Release the left mouse button when the picture is the size you want it.**

Deleting a picture from a document

In case you suddenly decide that you don't want a picture in your document anymore, you can delete it by following these steps:

1. **Click the picture that you want to delete.**

   Handles appear around your chosen picture.

2. **Press the Delete key.**

   Word deletes your chosen picture.

Putting Borders on Your Pages

Another way to make your document look visually appealing is to put borders around the edges, top, or bottom of your page. Borders can consist of solid or dotted lines of varying width and color.

To add a border to your document, follow these steps:

1. **Choose Format⇨Borders and Shading.**

   The Borders and Shading dialog box appears, as shown in Figure 7-10.

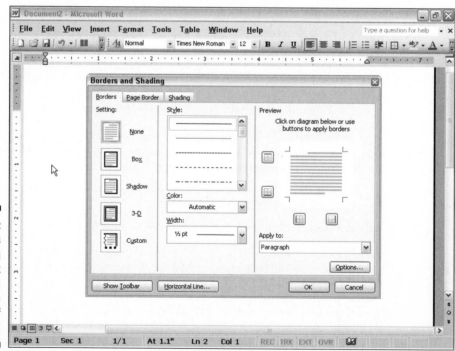

Figure 7-10: The Borders and Shading dialog box can place a border on any edge of your page.

2. **Click the Borders or Page Border tab.**

   Use the Borders tab to put a border around a paragraph. Use the Page Border tab to place a border around one or more pages of your document.

3. **In the Setting area, click an option, such as Box or Shadow.**

   The Preview box shows you what the border will look like.

4. **Click a line style in the Style list box, such as a solid or dotted line.**

5. **Click the Color list box and choose a color, such as Red or Black.**

6. **Click in the Width list box and choose a width, such as 1 pt or 3 pt.**

7. **Click the top-, bottom-, right-, and/or left-edge button in the Preview section to define where you want the border to appear.**

8. **Click in the Apply To list box and choose an option, such as Whole Document or This Section.**

9. **Click OK.**

   Word displays your border around your page. If you cannot see your borders, you may have to switch to Print Layout view by choosing View⇨Print Layout.

Previewing and Printing Your Documents

If you don't mind contributing to global deforestation, you're free to print every chance you get, just to see whether your documents are properly aligned. But if you're one of the growing crowd who cringe at the thought of wasting precious resources on unnecessary printing, use the Word Print Preview feature before you actually print out your work.

Putting Print Preview to work

Print Preview enables you to see how your document looks before you print it. That way, you can check to see whether your margins are aligned properly and your page numbers appear in the right place.

To use the Print Preview feature, follow these steps:

1. **Choose File⇨Print Preview.**

   Word displays your document in minuscule print, as shown in Figure 7-11, and displays the cursor as a magnifying glass.

2. **Move the mouse cursor (the magnifying glass) over the document and click to view your document in its full size.**

3. **Click Close to close Print Preview.**

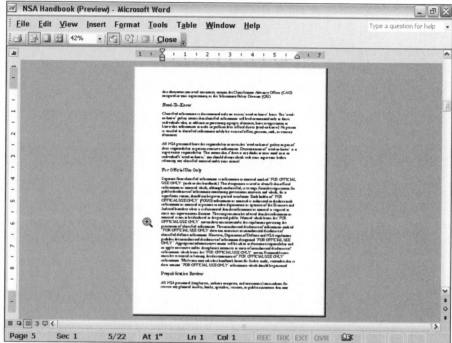

Figure 7-11:
Print
Preview
shows you
what your
document
will look like
when you
eventually
print it.

Defining your pages

Before you print your Word documents, you may want to define your page margins and paper size. To define your pages, follow these steps:

1. **Choose File⇨Page Setup.**

   The Page Setup dialog box appears.

2. **Click the Margins tab and click the Top, Bottom, Left, or Right boxes to define the margins you want to set.**

The Margins tab appears in Page Setup dialog box, shown in Figure 7-12.

3. **Click the Paper tab and then click in the Paper Size list box to define the paper size (such as Legal or A4).**

   You may also want to define the specific width and height of your pages.

4. **Click in the First Page and Other Pages list boxes under the Paper Source group to define the location of the paper you want to use for your printer.**

5. **Click the Layout tab.**

   The Layout tab lets you define whether you want your headers and footers to appear differently on odd or even pages, or whether they should appear on the first page or not.

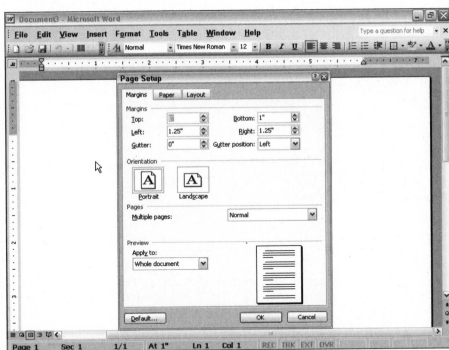

Figure 7-12:
Using the Page Setup dialog box, you can define the margins, layout, and type of paper for printing your document.

6. **Click OK.**

   After this exhaustive and tedious process of defining the paper you're going to use, you're ready to actually print your Word documents.

Printing your work

Sooner or later, you must succumb to the need to print something that you created in Word. To print a Word document, follow these steps:

1. **Choose File⇨Print or press Ctrl+P.**

   The Printer dialog box appears, as shown in Figure 7-13.

2. **Click the Name list box and choose the printer to use.**

3. **In the Page range group, click a radio button to choose the pages you want to print, such as All or Current page.**

   If you click the Pages radio button, you can selectively choose the pages you want to print, such as page 1, 3, or 5 – 12.

4. **Click the Number of copies box and type the number of copies you want.**

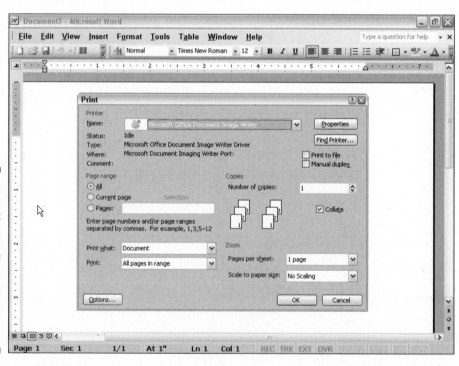

Figure 7-13: You can use the Print dialog box to define the number of copies and the page range you want to print.

5. **Click the Print list box and choose what you want to print, such as Odd or Even pages.**

6. **Click OK.**

When you click the Print icon on the Standard toolbar, Word immediately starts printing your entire document, bypassing the Print dialog box. If you want to print specific pages or a certain number of copies, go through the menu instead (or press Ctrl+P).

Part III

Playing the Numbers Game with Excel

In this part . . .

If adding, subtracting, multiplying, or dividing long lists of numbers sounds scary, relax. Microsoft endowed Office 2003 with the world's most popular spreadsheet program, dubbed Microsoft Excel. By using Excel, you can create budgets, track inventories, calculate future profits (or losses), and design bar, line, and pie charts so you can see what your numbers are really trying to tell you.

Think of Excel as your personal calculating machine that plows through your numbers for you, whether you need to manage something as simple as a home budget or something as wonderfully complex as an annual profit-and-loss statement for a Fortune 500 corporation.

By tracking numbers, amounts, lengths, measurements, or money with Excel, you can quickly predict future trends and likely results. Type in your annual salary along with any business expenses you have, and you can calculate how much income tax your government plans to steal from you in the future. Or play "What if?" games with your numbers and ask questions, such as "Which sales region sells the most useless products," "How much can I avoid paying in taxes if my income increases by 50 percent," and "If my company increases sales, how much of an annual bonus can I give myself while letting my employees starve on minimum wages?"

So if you want to get started crunching numbers, this is the part of the book that shows you how to use Excel to calculate results.

Chapter 8

The Basics of Spreadsheets: Numbers, Labels, and Formatting

*W*hile a program like Microsoft Word lets you manipulate text, Microsoft Excel lets you manipulate numbers. Although both Word and Excel can store and display numbers in neat rows and columns, Excel also lets you perform mathematical calculations on your numbers.

So if you're embezzling funds from your company, you might create a list of how much money you've stolen each month, such as:

January	$12 million
February	$8 million
March	$11 million

Adding the total for a short list like this can be fairly trivial using a calculator, but as you add more numbers, the odds that you'll type in the wrong number on a calculator start to increase.

Excel solves that problem by letting you type and store numbers (like Word) but also add them up automatically (like a calculator). Just as long as you type in the correct numbers the first time, you can be assured that Excel will always correctly add the total no matter how many numbers you type in.

Introducing the Parts of a Spreadsheet

In the old days, accountants wrote long columns of numbers on sheets of green ledger paper divided by lines to ease the task of entering and organizing information in neat rows. Excel mimics green ledger paper by displaying a worksheet on the screen, divided into rows and columns.

Many people use the terms *spreadsheet* and *worksheet* interchangeably. When you create a file in Excel, that file is called a *workbook;* it consists of one or more *worksheets*.

A worksheet consists of rows and columns where you can type in text, numbers, and formulas. A typical Excel file consists of the following, as shown in Figure 8-1:

- ✔ **A worksheet divided into rows and columns:** A *worksheet* acts like a page on which you can type numbers and labels. Each worksheet contains up to 256 vertical columns and 65,535 horizontal rows. Columns are identified by letters (such as A, B, and C). Rows are numbered (such as 1, 2, and 3).

- ✔ **Cells:** A *cell* is the intersection of a row and a column. When you type data into a worksheet, you have to type it in a cell. Cells are identified by their column letters followed by their row numbers. For example, the cell at the intersection of column G and row 12 is called cell G12.

- ✔ **Numbers:** *Numbers* can represent amounts, lengths, or quantities, such as $50.54, 309, or 0.094.

- ✔ **Labels:** *Labels* identify what your spreadsheet numbers mean, in case you forget. Typical labels are "May," "Western Sales Region," and "Total Amount We Lost Through Fred's Stupidity."

- ✔ **Formulas:** *Formulas* let you calculate new results based on the numbers you type in. Formulas are as simple as adding two numbers together or as complicated as calculating third-order differential equations that nobody really cares about. (Chapter 9 provides more information about creating formulas.)

Worksheets may look like a boring list of numbers, but their real power comes from the ability to let you change numbers and have Excel automatically calculate the new results. This forecasting and budgeting capability lets you ask what-if questions such as, "What would happen if the cost of oil changed from $42 dollars a barrel to $38 dollars a barrel?" "What would happen if our sales plummeted 90 percent?" "What would happen if I gave myself a million-dollar raise despite the fact that sales have plummeted 90 percent?"

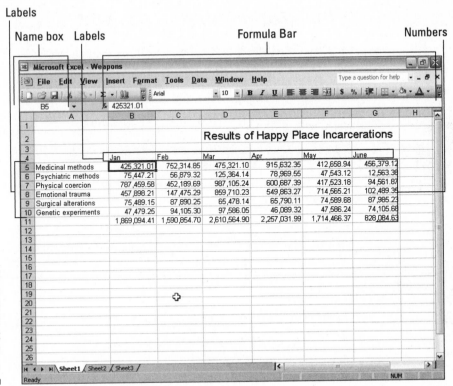

Figure 8-1:
The parts of
a typical
spreadsheet
as seen
in Excel.

Every Excel file is called a *workbook* where each workbook can hold several thousand individual worksheets (the limit depends on your computer's memory and your willingness to keep creating more worksheets).

Putting Stuff in a Worksheet

After you start Excel, an empty worksheet appears on the screen. Because an empty worksheet is useless by itself, you need to type data into the worksheet's cells. The three types of data that you can type into a cell are numbers, labels, and formulas.

Numbers represent your actual data, labels help you identify what your numbers represent, and formulas tell Excel how to calculate results based on the numbers stored in your worksheet.

Entering information in a cell

To type data into a cell, follow these steps:

1. **Click a cell with the mouse where you want to type data.**

   Excel highlights your cell with a dark border around the edges. The highlighted cell is called the *active cell* and is the Excel way of telling you, "If you start typing something now, this is the cell where I'm going to put it."

   You can also use the arrow keys to highlight a cell, although the mouse is usually easier and faster to use.

2. **Type a number (such as** 8.3**), label (such as** My Loot**), or formula (such as** =A1+F4-G3**).**

   As you type, Excel displays what you're typing in your chosen cell and in the Formula bar (refer to Figure 8-1).

3. **Do any one of the following actions to make your typed data appear in your chosen cell:**

   • Press Enter.

   • Click the Enter (green check mark) button, next to the Formula bar.

   • Press an arrow key to select a different cell.

   • Click a different cell to select it.

Putting numbers in a cell

When you type a number into a cell, you can either use the numbers located at the top of the keyboard or the numbers on the numeric keypad to the right of the keyboard. After you type a number into a cell, you may want to control the way that number appears. The way your numbers appear in a cell depends on the formatting of that cell.

Formatting is purely cosmetic and just changes the way your numbers look. Unless you specifically change the formatting, Excel uses a format called General.

In Excel, numbers can appear in a variety of formats, such as Currency, Fractions, or Dates. To change the formatting of a cell, follow these steps:

1. **Highlight the cells that contain the numbers you want to format.**

   You can also highlight empty cells so that, when you later type numbers into them, Excel will know how you want those numbers to appear automatically.

2. Choose Format⇨Cells, or press Ctrl+1.

The Format Cells dialog box appears, as shown in Figure 8-2.

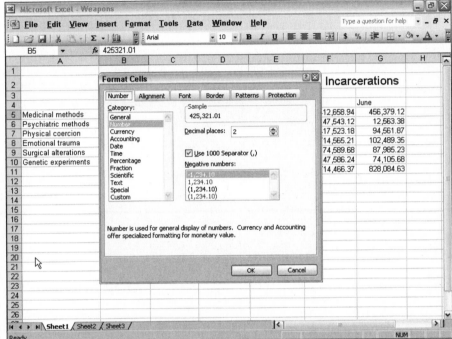

Figure 8-2:
The Format
Cells dialog
box gives
you a
variety of
ways to
display your
numbers.

3. Click a format you want to use.

Depending on the format you choose, you may need to select additional options, such as the number of decimal places to display or whether to display negative numbers in red or in parentheses.

4. Click OK.

Excel displays your numbers in your new format. If the cell you chose was empty, you'll see your number formatted as soon as you type a number in that cell.

If the formatting for a cell is General, you can type a time based on a 12-hour time clock, such as **7:45** followed by a space and **a** or **p** for AM or PM, respectively and Excel will automatically display this number in a time format. To put the current time in a cell, press Ctrl+Shift+: (colon). You can also type a date into a cell with the General format if you type either slashes or dashes, such as **4/7/2004** or **4-Mar-2005**. To put the current date in a cell, press Ctrl+; (semicolon). If you have already changed the formatting of a cell from General to something else, such as Time or Accounting, you won't be able to display dates in that cell until you change the formatting of that cell to Date or Time.

Typing a label in a cell

When you type a letter into a cell, Excel automatically treats everything you type as a label. Labels don't affect the way Excel calculates your numbers. Basically, labels help you identify what each particular row or column of number represents such as "Total Amount," "Height (inches)," or "Number of drunk drivers who crashed into my mailbox."

Sometimes, you may want to type a number as a label. Normally when you type a number into a cell, Excel assumes you want to perform some sort of calculation on that number, and depending on the formatting of that cell, may change the way that number looks from 12 to $12.00.

To make a number appear as a label, follow these steps:

1. **Highlight the cell that contains the numbers you want to appear as a label.**

   You can also highlight empty cells so that you can type numbers in them later and have those numbers appear as a label.

2. **Choose Format⇨Cells, or press Ctrl+1.**

   The Format Cells dialog box appears (see Figure 8-2).

3. **Click Text in the Category list and click OK.**

   Excel displays your number.

When you format a number as Text to make it a label, you cannot use that number in any formulas or calculations.

Typing long labels in a cell

Normally when you type text, Excel displays your text as a single line. If you want to display your text in a cell as multiple lines, press Alt+Enter to start a new line in the cell. So if you type **My income**, press Alt+Enter, and type **for 2005**, then Excel displays two lines in the cell. *My income* appears as the first line and *for 2005* appears as the second line in that same cell.

If you suddenly decide that you don't want your data to appear in the cell before you perform Step 3, press Esc or click the Cancel (red X) button, next to the Formula bar. If you already typed data in a cell and want to reverse your action, press Ctrl+Z or click the Undo icon.

For another way to display multiple lines of text within a cell, you can turn on word wrapping, which automatically wraps text to fit within the width of a cell. To turn on word wrapping, follow these steps:

1. **Highlight the cell (or cells) that you want to use word wrapping.**

2. **Choose Format⇨Cells, or press Ctrl+1.**

   The Format Cells dialog box appears (see Figure 8-2).

3. **Click the Alignment tab.**

   The Format Cells dialog box displays the Alignment tab as shown in Figure 8-3.

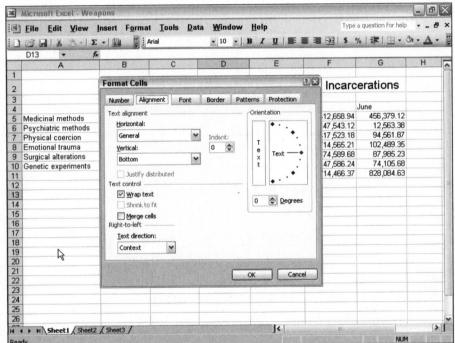

Figure 8-3: The Alignment tab lets you define how text appears in a cell.

4. **Click in the Wrap Text check box in the Text control category.**

   You can also change the alignment of text by clicking in the Horizontal or Vertical list boxes in the Text alignment category. In case you want to display text at an angle, you can even click in the Degrees box and click the up or down arrow.

5. **Click OK.**

   Excel changes the way your text appears in the highlighted cell.

Typing months or days in a cell

If you need to type the names of successive months or days in adjacent cells (such as January, February, March, and so on), Excel has a handy shortcut that can save you a lot of typing. To use this shortcut, follow these steps:

1. **Click a cell and type a month or day, such as** March **(or** Mar.**) or** Tuesday **(or** Tue.**).**

   The Fill handle — a black box — appears at the bottom-right corner of the cell that you just typed in.

2. **Place the mouse cursor directly over the Fill handle so that the cursor turns into a black crosshair.**

3. **Hold down the left mouse button and drag the mouse to the right or down.**

   As you move the mouse, Excel displays the successive months or days in each cell that you highlight, as shown in Figure 8-4.

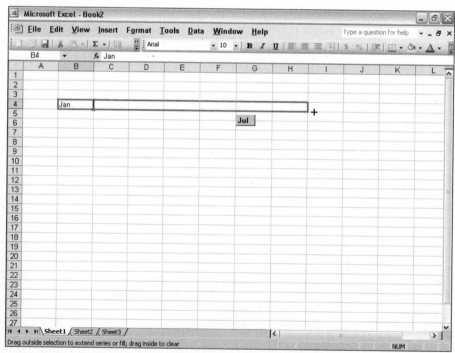

Figure 8-4:
Filling a row or column with labels the easy way.

4. **Release the left mouse button.**

   Excel automatically types the name of the months or days in the range of cells that you selected.

Deleting and Editing the Contents of a Cell

Sometimes you may need to edit what you typed in a cell, because you made a mistake, you just want to express your creative urges by typing something else in the cell, or you want to get that data out of there altogether.

To edit data in a cell, follow these steps:

1. **Click or use the arrow keys to select the cell containing the data that you want to edit.**

2. **Press F2, click in the Formula bar, or double-click the cell containing the data that you want to edit.**

3. **Press Backspace to delete characters to the left of the insertion point or press Delete to erase characters to the right of the insertion point.**

4. **Type any new data.**

5. **To make your typed data appear in your chosen cell, press Enter, click the Enter button (the green check mark next to the Formula bar), or select a different cell.**

To delete data in a cell or cells, follow these steps:

1. **Highlight the cell or cells containing the data that you want to delete.**

2. **Press Delete, or choose Edit⇨Clear⇨Contents.**

When you delete data from a cell or cells, you don't change the formatting you have defined for that cell, such as displaying the number as Currency or Fractions.

Navigating a Worksheet

A single worksheet can contain up to 256 columns and 65,536 rows. Unfortunately, your computer screen can't display such a large worksheet all at once, so you can see only part of a worksheet at any given time, much like viewing the ocean through a porthole in the side of a ship.

Because you can only see a limited portion of your worksheet at any given time, Excel provides different ways to view a different part of your worksheet using your mouse or keyboard.

Using the mouse to jump around a worksheet

To navigate a worksheet with the mouse, you have two choices:

✔ Click the vertical and horizontal scroll bars.

✔ Use the wheel on your mouse (provided, of course, your mouse has a wheel; not all mice have discovered it).

To jump around a document by using the vertical or horizontal scroll bar, you have these choices:

✔ Click the up/down, right/left scroll buttons at the ends of the scroll bars to scroll up and down one row or right and left one column at a time.

✔ Drag the scroll box along the scroll bar in the desired direction to jump to an approximate location in your document.

✔ Click the vertical scroll bar above or below the scroll box to page up or down one screen-length at a time.

✔ Click the horizontal scroll bar to the right or left of the scroll box to page right or left one screen-width at a time.

Using the keyboard to jump around a document

For those who hate the mouse or just prefer using the keyboard, here are the different ways to jump around your document by pressing keys:

✔ Press the ↓ key to move one row down in your worksheet.

✔ Press the ↑ to move one row up in your worksheet.

✔ Press the → to move one column to the right in your worksheet.

✔ Press the ← to move one column to the left in your worksheet.

✔ Hold down the Ctrl key and press ↓, ↑, →, or ← to jump up/down or right/left one adjacent row or column of data at a time.

✔ Press the PgDn key (or Page Down on some keyboards) to jump down the worksheet one screen-length at a time.

✔ Press the PgUp key (or Page Up on some keyboards) to jump up the worksheet one screen-length at a time.

✔ Press Home to jump to the A column in your worksheet.

✔ Press Ctrl+Home to jump to the A1 cell in your worksheet, which appears in the upper-left corner of every worksheet.

✔ Press Ctrl+End to jump to the last cell in your worksheet.

✔ Press the End key and then press ↓, ↑, →, or ← to jump to the end/beginning or top/bottom of data in the current row or column.

You can open any Excel worksheet (even a blank one will do) and practice using all the different methods of navigating around a worksheet. Then you can memorize the commands you find most useful and forget about the rest.

Using the Go To command

When you want to jump to a specific cell in your worksheet, the Go To command is a lot faster than the mouse or the keyboard.

To use the Go To command, follow these steps:

1. **Choose Edit⇨Go To or press Ctrl+G.**

   The Go To dialog box appears.

2. **Type a cell reference (such as** A4 **or** C21**) or click a cell reference or cell name displayed in the Go To list box.**

   Each time you use the Go To command, Excel remembers the last cell reference(s) you typed in. If you have any named cells or cell ranges (see the next section, "Naming cells and ranges"), Excel automatically displays these cell names in the Go To dialog box.

3. **Click OK.**

   Excel jumps to your chosen cell.

Naming cells and ranges

If you don't like referring to cells as E4 or H31, you can assign more meaning-ful names to a single cell or range of cells. Assigning names can make finding portions of a worksheet much easier. For example, finding your budget's 2004 income cell is a lot easier if it's called "income2004" instead of F22.

To assign a name to a cell or range of cells, follow these steps:

1. **Click the cell that you want to name, or select the range of cells that you want to name by dragging (holding down the left mouse button while moving the mouse) over the cells.**

    Excel highlights the cell as the active cell. (Or if you highlighted a range of cells, the first cell in the range becomes the active cell.) The active cell's address appears in the Name Box.

2. **Click in the Name Box.**

    Excel highlights the cell address.

3. **Type the name that you want to assign to the cell or cell range.**

4. **Press Enter.**

    The name that you assigned appears in the Name Box.

Names must start with a letter, must be one word, and cannot contain more than 255 characters. "MyIncome" is a valid cell name, but "My Income for 2004" is not, because of the spaces between the words. Rather than use a space, use underscores — for example, "My_Income_for_2004."

Jumping to a named cell or cell range

After you name a cell or cell range, you can jump to it from any other cell by following these steps:

1. **Click the downward-pointing arrow to the right of the Name Box.**

    Excel displays a list of all named cells or cell ranges in the current workbook.

2. **Click the cell name that you want to jump to.**

    Excel highlights the cell or range of cells represented by the name you chose.

Deleting a named cell or cell range

You may later decide that you don't need a name to represent a particular cell or cell range. To delete a cell name, follow these steps:

1. **Choose Insert➪Name➪Define.**

    The Define Name dialog box appears.

2. **Click the cell name that you want to delete and click Delete.**

    Repeat this step for each cell name that you want to delete.

3. **Click OK.**

Deleting a cell name doesn't delete the contents of any cells in the worksheet.

Making Your Worksheet Pretty with Formatting

Rows and columns of endless numbers and labels can look pretty dull. Because a plain, boring worksheet can be as hard to understand as a tax form, Excel gives you the option of formatting your cells.

By formatting different parts of your worksheet, you can turn a lifeless document into a powerful persuasion tool that can convince your boss to approve your budget proposals — and give the impression that you gave it more thought than you really did.

Excel offers an almost unlimited variety of formatting options. You can change fonts, borders, number styles, and alignment to make your worksheets look pretty.

Formatting just defines the way data looks but doesn't affect the way Excel manipulates that data in formulas.

Using AutoFormat

If you aren't a designer but want fancy formatting without having to do much work, use the Excel AutoFormat feature. AutoFormat can automatically format a range of cells for you, according to one of many formatting styles.

To use AutoFormat, follow these steps:

1. **Highlight two or more adjacent cells that you want to format.**

2. **Choose Format⇨AutoFormat.**

   The AutoFormat dialog box appears, as shown in Figure 8-5.

3. **Click a format that you want to use.**

4. **Click OK.**

   Excel automatically formats the range of cells that you selected in Step 1.

If you want to restrict the types of formatting that AutoFormat can apply, click the Options button in the AutoFormat dialog box and clear the check mark from any options you don't want to use. For example, if you don't want Excel to change fonts, remove the check from the Font check box by clicking it.

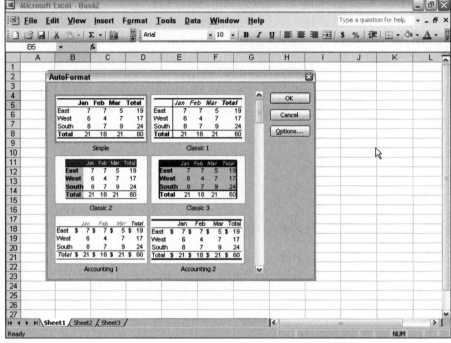

Figure 8-5:
The
AutoFormat
dialog box
offers you a
variety of
choices for
formatting
your cells
quickly and
easily.

Manually formatting your cells

For more control over the appearance of your cells, you may prefer to format them yourself. To format one or more cells, follow these steps:

1. **Highlight the cell or range of cells that you want to format.**

2. **Choose Format⇨Cells, or press Ctrl+1.**

   The Format Cells dialog box appears (see Figure 8-2).

3. **Click one of the following tabs to view different options available:**

   • **Number:** Defines the way numbers appear in cells, such as with a currency sign or in scientific notation.

   For a faster way to format numbers, click in a cell and then click the Currency Style, Percent Style, Comma Style, Increase Decimal, or Decrease Decimal button on the Formatting toolbar.

   • **Alignment:** Defines the way labels appear in a cell, using (for example) word wrapping within a cell or displayed at an angle.

   • **Font:** Defines the font, size, and colors of your text or numbers.

   • **Border:** Defines borders around the cells.

For a faster way to create borders around a cell, click in a cell and then click the Borders button on the Formatting toolbar. When a menu of different border styles appears, click the border style you want to use.

- **Patterns:** Defines background colors and patterns of cells.

- **Protection:** Protects cells from change if the entire worksheet is also protected by choosing the Tools⇨Protection⇨Protect Sheet or Protect Workbook.

4. **Make any changes, such as choosing a different color or font, and then click OK.**

   Excel displays your cells with your chosen formatting.

If you don't like the way your cells look, you can undo any formatting changes you made by pressing Ctrl+Z or clicking the Undo button right away.

Removing formatting

If you decide you want to remove formatting from one or more cells, you can do so at any time:

1. **Highlight one or more cells that you want to clear from any formatting.**

2. **Choose Edit⇨Clear⇨Formats.**

   Excel clears all formatting from your chosen cells.

Adjusting column widths

Unless you specify otherwise, Excel displays all columns in equal widths. However, you may soon find that some of your data appears truncated, scrunched, weird, or otherwise not displayed the way you intended. This problem occurs when your columns are too narrow.

To fix this problem, you can adjust columns to make them wider or narrower. To adjust the column widths quickly, follow these steps:

1. **Place the mouse cursor directly over one of the vertical borders of the column heading that you want to modify.**

   For example, if you want to adjust the width of column B, move the mouse cursor over the border between columns B and C.

2. **Hold down the left mouse button and drag the mouse to the left or right.**

   The mouse cursor appears as a double-headed arrow. Excel also displays a dotted vertical line to show you the approximate width of your column.

3. **Release the left mouse button when the column is the width you want.**

If you double-click the border between column headings, Excel automatically modifies the column on the left to make it just wide enough to display the longest entry in that column.

If you want to get real precise about defining your column widths, follow these steps:

1. **Click somewhere in the column you want to modify.**

   (Well, okay, this step doesn't have to be *all* that precise.)

2. **Choose Format➪Column➪Width.**

   A Column Width dialog box appears.

3. **Type a number to specify the column width (such as 14.5) and click OK.**

   Excel modifies your columns.

If you want to adjust the width of a column to match the width of data in a single cell, click that cell and choose Format➪Column➪AutoFit Selection.

Adjusting row heights

Excel normally displays all rows in equal heights. However, you may want to make some rows taller or shorter. To change the height of a row quickly, follow these steps:

1. **Place the mouse cursor directly over one of the horizontal borders of the row that you want to modify.**

   The mouse cursor turns into a double-pointing arrow.

2. **Hold down the left mouse button and drag the mouse up or down.**

   Excel displays a dotted vertical line along with a small box that tells you the exact height of the row.

3. **Release the left mouse button when the row is the height you want.**

For people who want to define the row height exactly, these steps are precisely the ones to follow:

1. **Click in the row you want to modify.**

2. **Choose Format⇨Row⇨Height.**

   A Row Height dialog box appears.

3. **Type a number to specify the column width (such as 12.95) and click OK.**

   Excel modifies your rows.

If you want to adjust the height of a row based on the height of data in a single cell, click that cell and choose Format⇨Row⇨AutoFit.

Printing a Worksheet

After you type numbers, labels, and formulas into a worksheet, you eventually want to print it out so that you don't have to drag everyone else over to look at your worksheet on your tiny computer screen. Before printing out a worksheet (and possibly wasting precious natural resources such as paper and ink), use the Print Preview feature first.

Using Print Preview to see your worksheet

Excel's Print Preview lets you see how your worksheet looks before you actually print it. That way, you can see things like whether your margins are aligned properly and whether columns or rows fit on a single page.

To use Print Preview, follow these steps:

1. **Choose File⇨Print Preview.**

   Excel displays your worksheet in minuscule print and displays the cursor as a magnifying glass, as shown in Figure 8-6.

2. **Move the mouse cursor (the magnifying glass) over the document and click to view your document in its full size.**

3. **Click Close to exit Print Preview or Print to start printing right away.**

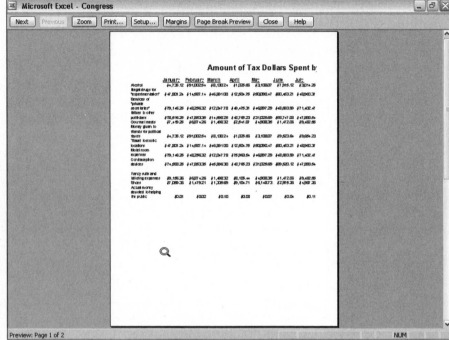

Printing worksheets

When you decide to print your worksheet, Excel gives you a variety of ways to do so:

1. **Make sure your printer is turned on, properly connected to your computer, loaded with paper, hasn't been drop-kicked through the third-story window out of frustration, and so on.**

2. **Choose one of the following ways to open the Print dialog box:**

   • Press Ctrl+P.

   • Choose File⇨Print.

3. **Click in the Name list box and choose the printer you want to use.**

4. **In the Print Range group, click an option button to choose the pages you want to print.**

   You can choose All, or type a page number or range to print in the From and To boxes.

5. **Click in the Number of Copies box and type the number of copies you want.**

6. **Click a radio button in the Print What area to choose what you want to print, such as Selection (which prints any cells you've already highlighted), Entire Workbook, or Active Sheet(s).**

7. **Click OK.**

If you want to print your entire worksheet right away, click the Print icon on the Standard toolbar. If you want to specify which pages you want to print and how many copies, choose one of the other methods (Ctrl+P or File⇨ Print).

Printing part of a worksheet

You may not always want to print your entire worksheet. Instead, you may want to selectively choose which parts of the worksheet to print. To do this, you first need to define something mysterious that Excel calls a *print area*. Here's the drill:

1. **Highlight one or more cells that you want to print.**

2. **Choose File⇨Print Area⇨Set Print Area.**

   Excel displays dotted lines around your chosen print area. You can define only one print area at a time.

With your print area established, you can now print out the selected portion of your worksheet as if it were just a regular worksheet. See the "Printing worksheets" section earlier in this chapter for the details.

To clear any print areas you have defined, choose File⇨Print Area⇨ Clear Print Area.

Chapter 9

Having Fun with Formulas and Functions

*T*he whole purpose of Excel lies in its ability to perform calculations on any numbers stored in different cells. When you create a formula in a cell, that formula tells Excel, "Grab some numbers stored in other cells, calculate a result, and store the result in this cell."

Besides doing your chores of addition, subtraction, division, and multiplication, Excel can also create more complicated calculations — statistical results, scientific calculations, or financial formulas to compare how much money you're losing in the stock market every month with how much cash you're spending on collectible baseball cards. For even more excitement, formulas can even rely on other formulas for the numbers they need to perform a calculation.

Creating Formulas

Excel works like a fancy calculator; it can whip up any type of result — as long as you know what you're doing in the first place. To tell Excel what to do, you can create a formula by using the following steps:

1. **Click the cell where you want to display the results of a calculation.**

2. **Type = (the equal sign) followed by your formula.**

   For example, if you want a formula that multiplies the contents of cell B3 by the contents of cell C3, type **=B3*C3**.

Instead of typing a cell reference, such as C3, you can just click the cell containing the data you want to use.

3. Press Enter.

Excel displays the results of your calculation. If your formula has an error in it, such as trying to add a number to a label, Excel displays an error message so that you can fix your mistake.

If your formula relies on numbers stored in other cells, those other cells must be in a row above or in a column to the left of the cell that contains your formula. So if you want to store a formula in cell D4, your formula can only use numbers stored in the following cells: A1, B1, C1, D1, A2, B2, C2, D2, A3, B3, C3, D3, A4, B4, and C4, as shown in the shaded area in Figure 9-1.

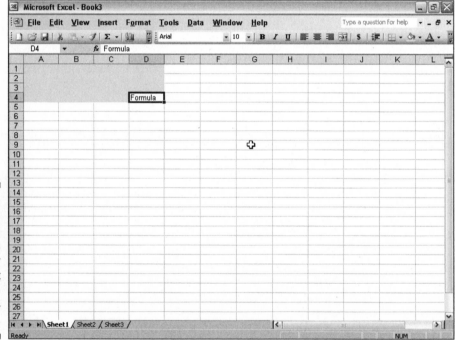

Figure 9-1:
The shaded area highlights the only cells that a formula in cell D4 can access.

To give you an idea of all the different types of formulas that you can create, Table 9-1 shows the most common mathematical operators you can use to create a formula. The numbers shown in the Example column represent data stored in other cells. For example, in the Addition row, you may actually type **=B3+G12**, where B3 contains the number 5 and G12 contains the number 3.4.

Table 9-1	Common Mathematical Operators		
Operator	*What It Does*	*Example*	*Result*
+	Addition	=5+3.4	8.4
-	Subtraction	=54.2-2.1	52.1
*	Multiplication	=1.2*4	4.8
/	Division	=25/5	5
%	Percentage	=42%	0.42
^	Exponentiation	=4^3	64
=	Equal	=6=7	False
>	Greater than	=7>2	True
<	Less than	=9<8	False
>=	Greater than or equal to	=45>=3	True
<=	Less than or equal to	=40<=2	False
<>	Not equal to	=5<>7	True
&	Text concatenation	="Bo the " & "Cat"	Bo the Cat

When you create a formula, you can either type numbers in the formula (such as 56.43+89/02) or use mysterious things called *cell references* (such as B5+N12). Although you may need to type numbers in a formula occasionally, the real power of Excel comes from using cell references.

Cell references let you take the contents of a specific cell and use those contents as part of your calculation. Now if the content of a specific cell changes, Excel automatically recalculates any formulas that use data from that specific cell.

What the heck are references?

Rather than forcing you to type exact numbers in all your formulas, references lets you tell Excel, "Just use whatever number is stored in this cell." Basically, references identify cells containing numbers that you want to use in a formula to calculate a result.

Referencing a single cell

In Excel, you can reference a cell in one of two ways:

- ✔ Use the column and row labels, such as A4 or C7.
- ✔ Use your own column and row labels, such as Feb or Sales.

For example, suppose you have numbers stored in cells B5 and B6, as shown in Figure 9-2. In this example, cell B7 contains the formula

```
=B5+B6
```

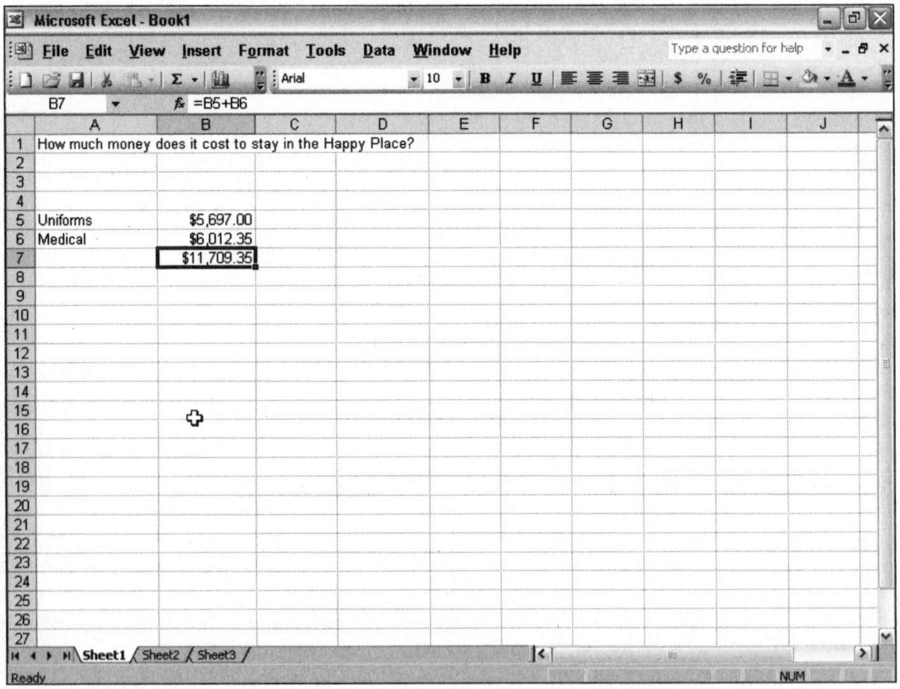

Figure 9-2:
Using cell
references
to calculate
a result.

(Screenshot of Microsoft Excel - Book1 showing:)

	A	B
1	How much money does it cost to stay in the Happy Place?	
5	Uniforms	$5,697.00
6	Medical	$6,012.35
7		$11,709.35

When you reference another cell, that cell can contain either data (such as numbers) or a formula (that calculates a result based on data obtained from other cell references).

The cell references in the preceding formula are B5 and B6, so the formula tells Excel, "Find the number stored in cell B5, add it to the number stored in B6, and display the result in cell B7."

Using cell references in a formula

To create a formula using a cell reference

1. **Click the cell where you want the results of the formula to appear.**

2. **Type = (the equal sign).**

3. **Choose one of the following methods:**

   • Type the cell reference, such as B4.

   • Click the cell containing the number that you want to use in your formula, such as B4.

4. **Type an operator, such as + (the plus sign).**

5. **Repeat Steps 3 and 4 as often as necessary to build your formula.**

6. **Press Enter.**

Now if you change the number in a cell that's referenced in another cell's formula, such as B5 in this example, Excel automatically calculates a new result.

To help you create the most common formulas, Excel has a special AutoSum feature. By clicking the AutoSum icon on the Standard toolbar, you can quickly add or find the average of a row or column full of numbers.

The AutoSum feature only calculates numbers stored in cells that appear in the same row or column. The moment the AutoSum feature finds an empty cell, it assumes there are no more numbers to include in its calculation.

One of the most convenient functions is the SUM function, which adds a row or column of numbers. To use the SUM function, follow these steps:

1. **Click in a cell below the column of numbers you want to add or to the right of a row of numbers you want to add.**

2. **Click the AutoSum icon on the Standard toolbar, as shown in Figure 9-3.**

   Excel highlights the cells that contain the numbers it will add up and automatically types in the equal sign and the SUM function name in the cell such as:

   ```
   =SUM(B3:B6)
   ```

   The preceding formula tells Excel to add all the numbers stored in cells B3 through B6.

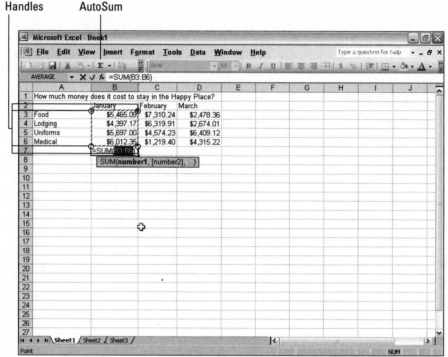

Figure 9-3:
The
AutoSum
function can
make it easy
to add a
column or
row of
numbers.

3. **Move the mouse pointer over the corner handle, hold down the left mouse button, and drag the mouse to highlight more or less cells if necessary.**

   As you highlight more or less cells, Excel automatically updates the formula in the cell to reflect this change.

4. **Press Enter.**

   Excel shows you the result of adding all the numbers you highlighted in Step 3.

The magic of parentheses

The simplest formulas can use two cell references and one operator, such as =B4*C4. However, you'll likely need to create more complicated formulas, involving three or more cell references. With so many cell references, you should use parentheses to organize everything.

For example, suppose you want to add the numbers in cells D3, D4, and D5 and then multiply the total by a number in cell D6. To calculate this result, you may try to use the following formula:

```
=D3+D4+D5*D6
```

Unfortunately, Excel interprets this formula to mean, "Multiply the number in D5 by the number in D6 and then add this result to the numbers in D3 and D4." The reason has to do with *order of operations* — Excel searches a formula for certain operators (such as *) and calculates those results before calculating the rest of the formula.

Say you have the following values stored in the cells:

D3	$45.95
D4	$199.90
D5	$15.95
D6	7.75%

The formula =D3+D4+D5*D6 calculates the number $247.09, which isn't the result you want at all (trust me on this one). What you really want is to add all the numbers in cells D3, D4, and D5 and then multiply this total by the number in D6. To tell Excel to do this, you have to use parentheses:

```
=(D3+D4+D5)*D6
```

The parentheses tell Excel, "Hey, stupid! First add up all the numbers stored in cells D3, D4, and D5 and *then* multiply this total by the number stored in D6." Using the same values for D3, D4, D5, and D6 as in the example without parentheses, Excel now calculates $20.29, which is the result you want.

If you get nothing else from this section (or get a scary flashback to high school algebra), remember that you must always organize multiple cell references in parentheses to make sure that Excel calculates them in the right order.

Referencing two or more cells

Sometimes you may need to reference two or more cells. A group of multiple cells is called a *range*. The two types of cell ranges are

- ✔ Contiguous ranges (cells next to each other), such as D3+D4+D5
- ✔ Noncontiguous ranges (cells that are not next to each other), such as D3+T44+Z89

Specifying a contiguous range

A *contiguous range* of cells is nothing more than a bunch of cells touching each other, such as cells stacked one over the other or side by side. You can specify contiguous cells by using the colon. For example, typing **A2:A5** tells Excel to use the cells A2, A3, A4, and A5.

You can also specify adjacent cells that span two or more columns or rows. For example, typing **D2:E5** tells Excel to use the cells D2, D3, D4, D5 and the cells E2, E3, E4, and E5. This particular contiguous range spans four columns *and* two rows.

Contiguous ranges are handiest when you're using Excel's *functions* — built-in mathematical formulas that act as shortcuts — such as =SUM(D2:D6), which adds together all the numbers stored in cells D2 through D6. Some functions that work with contiguous ranges include AVERAGE, MAX, MIN, and COUNT. To use a function, all you do is pick a cell for the function to live in and then choose a function from the box that appears when you choose Insert⇨ Function. You can find out more about functions in the "Picking a Function to Use" section, later in this chapter.

Suppose you want to use the following formula:

```
=(D3+D4+D5)*D6
```

Cells D3, D4, and D5 are a contiguous range of cells, so you can simplify the formula by just typing the following:

```
=SUM(D3:D5)*D6
```

The D3:D5 reference tells Excel, "Hey, dunderhead! Take all the numbers stored in cells D3 through D5 and sum (add) them all together; then multiply this result by the number in D6."

To specify a contiguous range in a formula, follow these steps:

1. **Click the cell in which you want the results of the formula to appear.**

2. **Type = (the equal sign).**

3. **Type the built-in function that you want to apply to your contiguous range — such as** SUM **or** AVERAGE **and then type the left parenthesis, which looks like this: (.**

4. **Click the cell that contains the first number that you want to use in your formula (for example, cell D3).**

5. **Hold down the left mouse button and drag the mouse to select the entire cell range that you want to include.**

   Excel highlights your selected cell range with a dotted line, as shown in Figure 9-4.

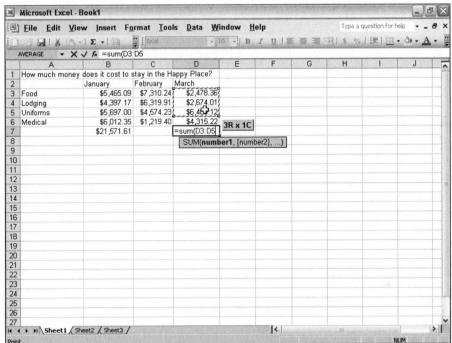

Figure 9-4:
Selecting a
contiguous
range of
cells.

6. **Let go of the mouse button and type the right parenthesis, which looks like this:).**

7. **Type the rest of your formula (if necessary) and press Enter.**

Specifying a noncontiguous range

If you want to include certain numbers in a formula, but they're stored in cells that don't touch each other, you can create a *noncontiguous range* (tech-speak for "a range that includes cells that don't touch each other"). For example, consider the following formula:

```
=SUM(D3,G5,X7)
```

This formula tells Excel, "Take the number stored in cell D3, add it to the number stored in cell G5, and add the result to the number stored in cell X7." Excel salutes smartly and gets to work.

To specify a noncontiguous range in a formula, here's the drill:

1. **Click the cell where you want the results of the formula to appear.**

2. **Type = (the equal sign).**

3. Type the built-in function that you want to apply to your noncontiguous range, such as SUM or AVERAGE, and then type the left parenthesis, which looks like this: (.

4. Click the cell containing the first number that you want to use in your formula (such as cell D3). (Or just type the cell reference you want to use, such as D3.)

5. Type , (a comma).

6. Click the cell containing the next number that you want to use in your formula (such as cell D7). (Or just type the cell reference you want to use, such as D7.)

7. Repeat Steps 5 and 6 as often as necessary.

8. Type a right parenthesis, which looks like this:), and press Enter when you're finished building your formula.

Copying formulas

Just as school was a lot easier when you copied someone else's homework, creating formulas in Excel is much easier if you cheat and just copy an existing formula instead. When you copy a formula and paste it in a new cell, Excel changes the formula cell references automatically for each row or column of numbers.

For example, if you need to add the first five numbers in column A together and want to do the same thing in columns B and C, your formula in cell A6 may look like this:

```
=SUM(A1:A5)
```

When you copy and paste this formula into cells B6 and C6, Excel automatically changes the formula in cell B6 to read

```
=SUM(B1:B5)
```

and changes the formula in cell C6 to read

```
=SUM(C1:C5)
```

Copying an existing formula is especially useful when you have rows or columns of numbers that use the exact same type of formula, such as several columns of numbers that all display a total at the bottom, as shown in Figure 9-5.

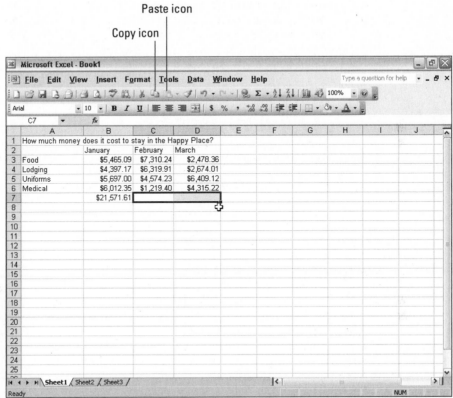

Paste icon

Copy icon

Figure 9-5:
Copying and
pasting a
formula
makes
calculating
easier.

To copy a formula and paste it for other rows or columns to use, follow these
steps:

1. **Type the formula you want to copy.**

   You can skip this step if the formula you want to copy already exists.

2. **Highlight the cell containing the formula you want to copy.**

3. **Press Ctrl+C or click the Copy icon on the Standard toolbar.**

   Excel displays a dotted line around the cell that you highlighted in
   Step 2.

4. **Highlight the cell or range of cells where you want to paste the
   formula.**

5. **Press Ctrl+V or click the Paste icon on the Standard toolbar.**

   Excel displays the results of the formula in your chosen cell or range of
   cells.

For a faster way of copying a formula, click the formula so a tiny black box appears in the lower right-hand corner of that cell. Move the mouse pointer over this tiny box so the mouse pointer turns into a crosshair, and then drag the mouse to highlight neighboring cells. Excel magically copies your formulas into those cells.

Editing Your Formulas

After you type a formula into a cell, you can always go back and edit it later. This capability comes in handy when you type a formula incorrectly (such as when you forget to use parentheses).

Displaying formulas

Before you can edit a formula, you have to find it. A cell with a formula in it looks exactly like a cell with just a regular number in it. That's because a cell with a formula shows the *results* of the formula, not the formula itself — so you may have trouble distinguishing between cells that contain plain old numbers and cells containing formulas.

To display all your formulas in a worksheet, just press Ctrl+` (yep, it's a reverse accent mark). That odd little mark, which you type while holding down the Ctrl key, normally appears on the same key as the tilde symbol (~).

If you have to hunt for your reverse accent (`) key, try looking just to the left of the 1 key on the top row. On some other keyboards, this key appears at the bottom, near the spacebar.

When you press Ctrl+`, Excel displays all the formulas currently hanging out in the worksheet, as shown in Figure 9-6. If you press Ctrl+` a second time, Excel hides the formulas. (As an alternative to pressing Ctrl+`, you can also choose Tools⇨Formula Auditing⇨Formula Auditing Mode.)

Wiping out a formula

The quickest way to edit a formula is to wipe it out completely and start all over again. When you want to exercise your destructive urges and delete a formula for good, follow these steps:

1. **Click the cell containing the formula that you want to delete.**

2. **Press Delete or Backspace.**

   Excel wipes out your formula from the face of the Earth.

Undo icon   Formula Ba

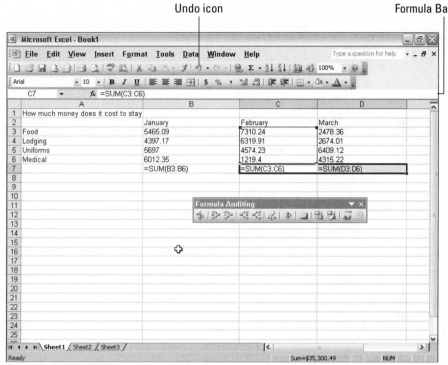

Figure 9-6:
Revealing
the formulas
hidden
behind
numbers.

The preceding steps actually work for deleting the contents of any cell. If you delete something by mistake, you can recover it by immediately pressing Ctrl+Z or clicking the Undo icon.

Changing a formula

If you want to edit a formula by making a minor change — say, typing a parenthesis or adding another cell reference — you can use the Formula bar (refer to Figure 9-6). Each time you click a cell containing a formula, the Formula bar displays the formula you're using so that you can view the whole thing and edit it.

To edit a formula, follow these steps:

1. **Click the cell containing the formula that you want to edit.**

   Excel dutifully displays that formula on the Formula bar (refer to Figure 9-6).

2. **Click in the Formula bar so that a cursor appears in it.**

   Excel highlights all the cells that your chosen formula uses to calculate its result.

3. **Edit your formula as you please.**

   Press Backspace or Delete to erase part of your formula. Use the → and ← keys to move the cursor around; type any corrections.

4. **Press Enter.**

   Excel calculates a new result for that cell, based on your modified formula.

For a faster way to edit a formula in a cell, double-click that cell and type or edit the formula directly in the cell.

Picking a Function to Use

Quick! Write out the formula for calculating the depreciation of an asset for a specified period, using the fixed-declining-balance method. If you have absolutely no idea what the previous sentence means, you're not alone. Of course, even if you *do* know what that sentence means, you may still have no idea how to create a formula to calculate this result.

Well, don't worry. Instead of making you rack your brain to create cumbersome and complicated formulas on your own, Excel provides you with predefined formulas called *functions*.

The main difference between a function and a formula is that a function already has a formula built in. A function just asks you what cell references (numbers) to use; a formula you have to build piece by piece, choosing cell references and telling Excel whether to add, subtract, multiply, or divide. For simple calculations, you can create your own formulas, but for really complicated calculations, you may want to use a built-in function instead.

Just in case you're wondering, you can use functions within any formulas you create. For example, the following formula uses the SUM function but also uses the multiplication operator:

```
=SUM(D4:D5)*D7
```

To help you choose the right function, Excel comes with the Paste Function feature, which guides you step-by-step as you choose a function and fill it with cell references. Relax — you don't have to do it all yourself.

To use the Paste Function feature, follow these steps:

1. **Click the cell where you want to use a function.**

2. **Click the downward-pointing arrow on the AutoSum icon and choose More Functions, choose Insert⇨Function.**

Insert Function icon

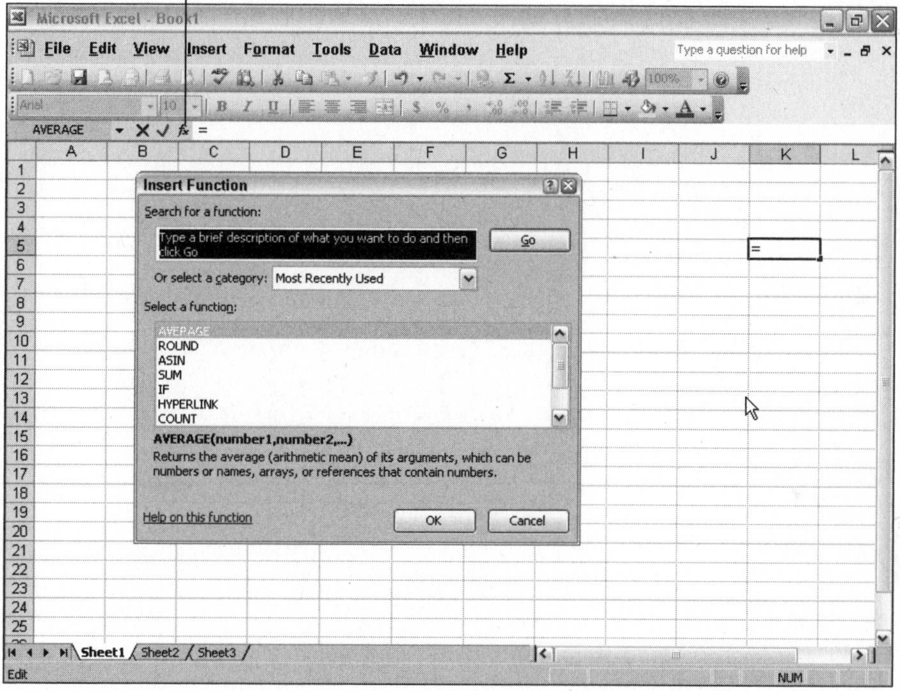

Figure 9-7:
The Insert
Function
dialog box
provides a
variety of
functions
you can use
to calculate
different
results.

The Insert Function dialog box appears, as shown in Figure 9-7.

3. **Click in the Select a category drop-down list box and click the category that contains the type of function you want to use (such as Financial or Statistical).**

4. **Click the function that you want to use in the Select a function box.**

   Each time you click a function, Excel displays a brief explanation of that function at the bottom of the dialog box.

5. **Click OK.**

   Excel displays a Function Arguments dialog box, asking for specific cell references, as shown in Figure 9-8.

   Depending on the function you chose in Step 4, the dialog box that appears after Step 5 may look slightly different.

6. **Click the cells containing the numbers that you want to use (such as cell E3) or type the cell reference yourself.**

   If you click the Shrink Dialog Box icon, the dialog box shrinks so that you can see the rest of your worksheet. You may still need to move the dialog box to get it out of the way.

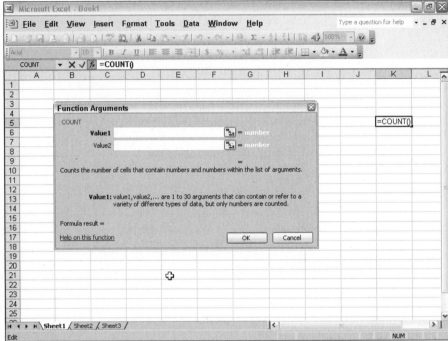

Figure 9-8:
The
Function
Arguments
dialog box
allows you
to specify
the type of
data for
your chosen
function.

7. **Click OK.**

Excel calculates a value based on the function that you chose and the numbers that you told it to use in Step 6.

Although Excel contains several hundred different functions, you may never have to use all of them in your lifetime. Table 9-2 has a short list of the players on the all-star function team; use it as a reference the next time you want to use a common function.

Table 9-2	Common Excel Functions
Function Name	**What It Does**
AVERAGE	Calculates the average value of numbers stored in two or more cells
COUNT	Counts how many cells contain a number instead of text
MAX	Finds the largest number stored in two or more cells
MIN	Finds the smallest number stored in two or more cells
ROUND	Rounds a decimal number to a specified number of digits

Function Name	What It Does
SQRT	(No it isn't what you do with a water pistol.) Returns the square root of a number
SUM	Adds the values stored in two or more cells

Checking Your Formulas for Accuracy

Computers aren't perfect (although they may have fewer faults than some of the people you may work with). Therefore, even if Excel appears to be calculating correctly, you may want to recheck your calculations just to make sure. Some common errors that can mess up your calculations include these little gems:

- **Missing data:** The formula isn't using all the data necessary to calculate the proper result.
- **Incorrect data:** The formula is getting data from the wrong cell.
- **Incorrect calculation:** Your formula is incorrectly calculating a result.

How can you find errors in your worksheets? Well, you could manually check every formula and type in different numbers, just to make sure the formulas are calculating the correct results. But worksheets can contain dozens of formulas (any of which may be interrelated with others) — checking them all manually is impractical unless you've got about a century to spend. As an alternative, Excel comes with built-in *auditing* features for checking your formulas. Using these features, you can

- Make sure your formulas are using data from the correct cells.
- Find out instantly whether a formula could go haywire if you change a cell reference.

Finding where a formula gets its data

Even the greatest whiz-bang formula is no help if it calculates its results using data from the wrong cells. *Tracing* a formula shows you which cells a formula is retrieving data from.

Any cell that supplies data to a formula is called a *precedent*.

To trace a formula, follow these steps:

1. **Click in the cell that contains the formula that you want to trace.**

2. **Choose Tools⇨Formula Auditing⇨Trace Precedents.**

   Excel displays a line showing all the cells that feed data into the formula you chose in Step 1, as shown in Figure 9-9.

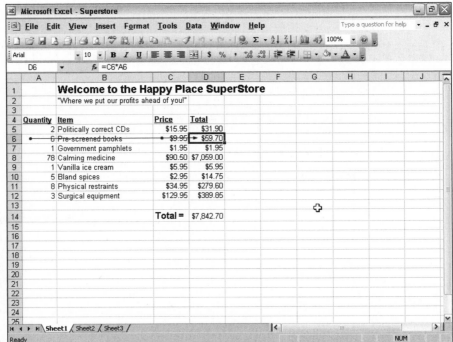

Figure 9-9:
Tracing precedent cells that feed data into a formula.

3. **Choose Tools⇨Formula Auditing⇨Remove All Arrows to make the arrows go away.**

Finding which formula(s) a cell can change

Sometimes you may be curious how a particular cell might affect a formula stored in your worksheet. Although you could just type a new value in that cell and look for any changes, an easier (and more accurate) way is to trace a cell's dependents.

Any formula that receives data is called a *dependent*.

To find one or more formulas that changing a single cell can affect:

1. **Click in a cell that contains a number that you want to check for all the formulas it may affect.**

2. **Choose Tools⇨Formula Auditing⇨Trace Dependents.**

   Excel draws a line showing you the cell containing a formula that depends on the cell that you chose in Step 1, as shown in Figure 9-10.

3. **Choose Tools⇨Formula Auditing⇨Remove All Arrows to make the arrows go away.**

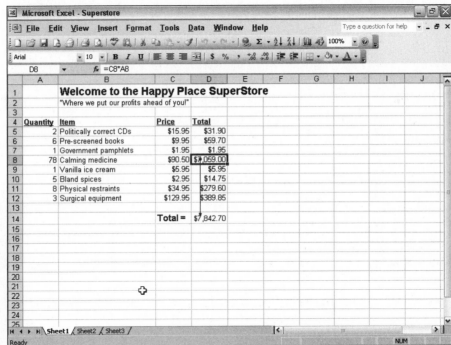

Figure 9-10: Tracing dependent cells shows you which formulas a single cell can change.

Chapter 10

Charting Your Numbers

In This Chapter

▶ Dissecting the parts of a chart

▶ Using the Chart Wizard

▶ Changing your chart

A picture may be worth a thousand words, but unless your picture makes sense, the only words it's likely to evoke are four-letter ones. Because most Excel worksheets consist of nothing but rows and columns full of numbers and labels that mean absolutely nothing to anyone who looks at it, you may want to make your data easier to understand by turning your numbers into charts. Charts can show trends, quantities, or patterns at a glance that may be impossible to understand just by looking at lists of numbers by themselves.

Understanding the Parts of a Chart

Excel can create gorgeous (or ugly) charts that graphically represent the numbers in your worksheets. Of course, to provide maximum flexibility, Excel offers numerous graphing options that may overwhelm you.

But take heart — after you enter your data in a worksheet, creating a chart is just a matter of letting Excel know which information you want to use, what type of chart you want, and where you want to put it. Although you don't need to know much charting lingo to create charts, you should understand a few terms that could be confusing at first.

Most charts contain at least one data series. A *data series* is just a set of numbers that Excel uses to determine how to draw your chart, such as making one slice of a pie chart bigger than another. For example, one data series may be sales results for one particular product sold during January, February, and March. Another data series may be the combined sales of five different products over the same period.

Charts also have an x-axis and a y-axis. The *x-axis* is the horizontal plane (that's left to right), and the *y-axis* is the vertical plane (that's top to bottom).

To help you understand your numbers, a chart may also include a chart title (such as Chart of Our 2008 Losses) and a legend. A *legend* identifies what the different parts of a chart represent, as shown in Figure 10-1.

Some of the more common types of charts include the following, which are shown in Figure 10-2:

- ✔ **Line chart:** One or more lines where each line represents a single item being tracked, such as hot dog buns or transmission failures. You can use a line chart to show trends over time in your data, such as whether sales of different products have been rising (or declining) over a five-year period.

- ✔ **Area chart:** Identical to a line chart except it provides shading underneath each line to emphasize the values being displayed. If you plan to plot more than four items, an area chart can become cluttered and difficult to read.

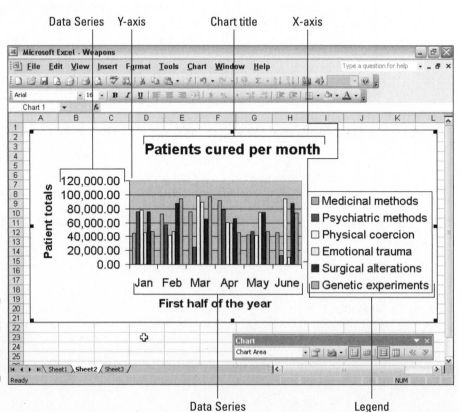

Figure 10-1:
The parts of
a typical
Excel chart.

✔ **Column chart:** Compares two or more items over time (such as sales of white bread versus wheat bread over a six-month period). Columns that represent different items show up side by side, displaying not only how each product is selling month by month, but also how each product sells in comparison to other products.

✔ **Bar chart:** Essentially a column chart tipped on its side, a bar chart displays bars of different lengths from left to right. Bar charts are most useful for comparing two or more items or amounts over time. For example, a bar chart may use five different bars to represent five different products; the length of each bar can represent the profit made from each product.

✔ **Pie chart:** Compares how separate parts make up a whole, such as determining how much money each sales region contributes to (or takes away from) a company's profits each year.

Many charts are also available in 3-D, which gives the chart a different look. Some people find 3-D charts easier to read; others think that 3-D makes the chart look more complicated than it needs to be. (Know your audience.)

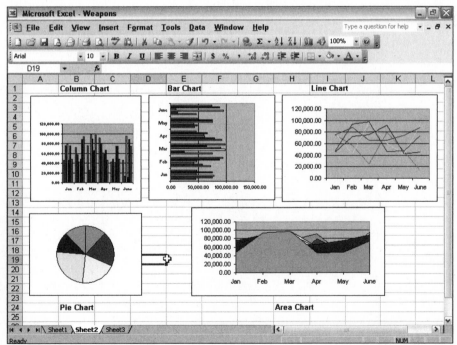

Figure 10-2: Common types of Excel charts you can use to plot your data.

Creating a Chart with the Chart Wizard

To help you create charts (almost) automatically, Excel offers the Chart Wizard, which kindly guides you through the process of creating charts from your data.

Creating Excel charts is easiest when your data is set up in a table format using adjacent rows and columns.

To create a chart with the Chart Wizard, follow these steps:

1. **Highlight all the cells (including the column and row headings) that contain the data that you want to chart.**

   Excel uses column headings for the x-axis title and row headings for the chart legend. (You can always change the headings used in your chart later.)

2. **Click the Chart Wizard icon on the Standard toolbar or choose Insert⇨Chart.**

   The Chart Wizard dialog box appears, as shown in Figure 10-3.

Chart Wizard icon

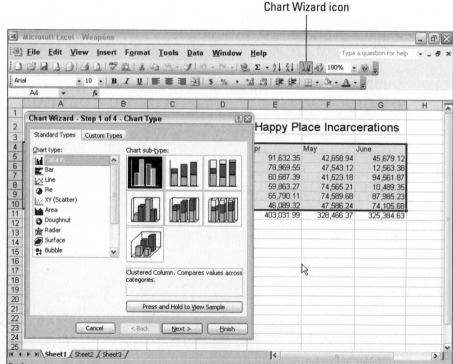

Figure 10-3: The Chart Wizard dialog box guides you through the process of creating a chart.

3. **Click the type of chart you want (such as Line, Pie, or Area) in the Chart type list box.**

4. **Click the variation of the chart you want in the Chart subtype group.**

5. **Click Next.**

   The second Chart Wizard dialog box appears, showing you what your chart looks like, as shown in Figure 10-4.

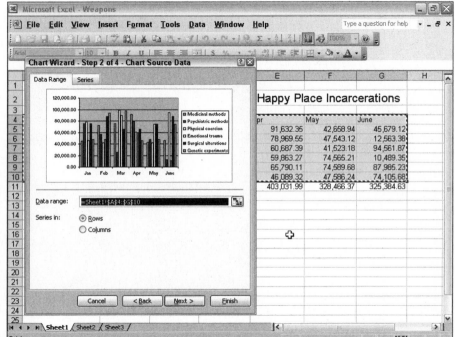

Figure 10-4:
The Chart Wizard dialog box shows you what your chart looks like so you can accept or modify it.

6. **Click either the Rows or Columns radio button to change the way Excel uses your data to create a chart.**

   Choosing the Rows radio button means that Excel uses your row labels (if any) to appear on the x-axis of your chart. Choosing the Columns radio button means that Excel uses your column labels (if any) to appear on the x-axis of your chart.

7. **Click the Collapse Dialog Box icon.**

   The Chart Wizard shrinks to a tiny floating window.

8. **Select the labels and data you want to chart. (You can skip this step if you don't want to change the labels and data you chose in Step 1.)**

   Excel highlights your chosen data with a dotted line.

9. **Click the Expand Dialog Box icon (formerly the Collapse Dialog Box button) and then click Next.**

   The third Chart Wizard dialog box appears, letting you choose a chart title as well as titles for the x-axis and y-axis (see Figure 10-5).

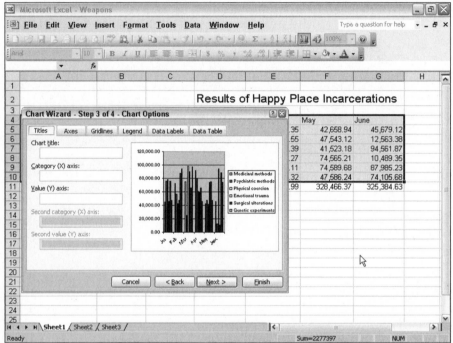

Figure 10-5: The Chart Wizard dialog box where you can type in a title.

10. **Type any titles that you want to add to your chart; then click Next.**

    The fourth Chart Wizard dialog box appears, as shown in Figure 10-6, asking whether you want to place your chart on the same worksheet as your data or on a separate sheet. Sometimes you may prefer keeping the chart on the same worksheet as the data used to create it. Other times, you may want to put the chart on a separate worksheet, especially if the chart is as big as your entire computer screen.

11. **Click either the As New Sheet or the As Object In radio button and choose the worksheet where you want to place the chart.**

    Where you place your chart is a matter of personal preference. If you want to make your chart large, you may want to place it on a separate worksheet so that you can resize it later. If you want to keep your chart near the actual data that you're charting, choose the As Object In radio button and place it near the data you highlighted in Step 1.

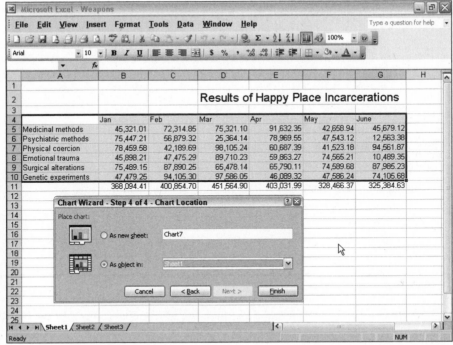

Figure 10-6:
Choosing
whether to
place your
chart on a
separate
sheet or on
an existing
sheet.

12. **Click the Finish button.**

Excel draws your chart for you and places it on your chosen worksheet.

Editing Your Charts

The Chart Wizard helps you create a chart quickly, but afterwards, you may decide to go back and modify your chart a little to make it prettier, move it around, or resize it. Just remember that you can always change any chart you create, so don't be afraid of experimenting and letting your imagination go wild.

When you change the numbers in your worksheet, Excel automatically changes your charts so that you can visually see any changes you made.

Moving, resizing, and deleting an entire chart

Sometimes you may not like where Excel puts your chart. So rather than suffer under the tyrannical rule of Excel, take matters into your own hands and change the chart's position and size yourself.

You can move or resize a chart only if you chose the As Object In radio button in Step 11 in the previous section "Creating a Chart with the Chart Wizard."

To move, resize, or delete an entire chart, follow these steps:

1. **Click the chart that you want to either move, resize, or delete.**

   After you select a chart, little black rectangles, called *handles,* appear on the corners and the sides of the chart's border.

2. **Choose one of the following:**

   • **To move a chart to a new location without changing the size of the chart, click the edge of the chart to select your entire chart.**

   After selecting the chart, place the mouse cursor inside the chart (not on one of the handles) and hold down and move the left mouse button so that the mouse pointer turns into a four-headed arrow. Drag the mouse and notice how Excel shows you an outline of where your chart will appear if you release the mouse button at that point. When you're satisfied with the location, release the left mouse button.

   • **To change the size of a chart, click the edge of the chart and drag a handle.**

   Place the mouse pointer directly over a handle and hold down the left mouse button so that the mouse pointer turns into a two-headed arrow. Drag the mouse and notice how Excel shows you an outline of how your chart looks if you release the mouse button at that point. When you're satisfied with the size, release the left mouse button.

   Note: Middle handles change the location of only one side of the chart; corner handles control two sides at once. If you drag the top-middle handle, for example, you can move the top side of the chart to make the chart taller or shorter (the bottom side stays where it is). If you drag the top-right corner handle, you move both the top side and the right side at the same time.

   • **To delete a chart, press Delete.**

Editing the parts of a chart

In addition to moving, resizing, or deleting the parts of a chart, you can also modify them as well. For example, if you either misspell a chart title, suddenly decide you really want an x-axis title, or don't like the colors in your chart legend, then you can change whatever you don't like.

An Excel chart consists of several objects that you can modify. Most charts include these common parts:

  ✔ **Chart area:** The entire box that contains the plot area plus the legend

  ✔ **Plot area:** The actual chart (such as pie, bar, or line) and its x- and y-axis labels

  ✔ **Legend:** A small box that defines what each color represents on the chart

  ✔ **Chart title:** Text that describes the chart's purpose

Changing titles on your chart

After you create a chart, you may find that you want to modify a title in your chart, such as the chart title. To edit a title, follow these steps:

1. **Click the title that you want to edit.**

   A gray box appears around your text.

2. **Click anywhere inside the title that you want to edit (such as the chart title) so the I-beam cursor appears.**

3. **Type any changes you want to make (or delete the text altogether, if you want).**

   You can use the arrow keys, the backspace key, and delete key to edit your title.

Formatting text

In addition to (or instead of) changing text, you may just want to change the formatting style used to display the text. To change the formatting of text, follow these steps:

1. **Double-click the text that you want to format.**

   A Format dialog box appears.

2. **Choose the font, font style, size, color, and any other formatting options you want to apply to your legend entry.**

3. **Click OK.**

Picking a different type of chart

Some charts look better than others, so if you first pick a chart type (bar, for example) that doesn't visually make your data any easier to understand, try picking a different chart type, such as a pie, line, or scatter chart. To change your chart type, follow these steps:

1. **Click the edge of the chart that you want to change.**

   Handles appear around the chart.

2. **Right-click and click Chart Type.**

   The Chart Type dialog box appears.

3. **Click a chart type that you want to use; then click OK.**

Changing the chart type can change the entire look of your chart, possibly messing up its appearance. If the chart looks really messed up after you change its type, press Ctrl+Z right away to undo your last action.

Using the Chart toolbar

A quick way to modify charts is through the Chart toolbar, which provides several icons that you can click to view and modify the appearance of your chart. The Chart toolbar normally appears when you click a chart

To display (or hide) the Chart toolbar, choose View⇨Toolbars⇨Chart. The Chart toolbar appears, as shown in Figure 10-7, offering commands for modifying your chart.

The Chart toolbar comes packed with the following features:

- ✔ **Chart Objects:** Allows you to select part of your chart, such as the legend or category axis, without having to click it

- ✔ **Format:** Allows you to change the colors, borders, or font of the object you clicked or chose in the Chart Objects list box

- ✔ **Chart Type:** Allows you to quickly choose a different chart type for plotting your data, for example, by switching from a column chart to a pie chart

- ✔ **Legend:** Hides or displays a legend on your chart

- ✔ **Data Table:** Displays the actual data used to create the chart

- ✔ **By Row:** Uses row headings to define your chart

- ✔ **By Column:** Uses column headings to define your chart

- ✔ **Angle Clockwise:** Changes the appearance of text clockwise at an angle

- ✔ **Angle Counterclockwise:** Changes the appearance of text counterclockwise at an angle

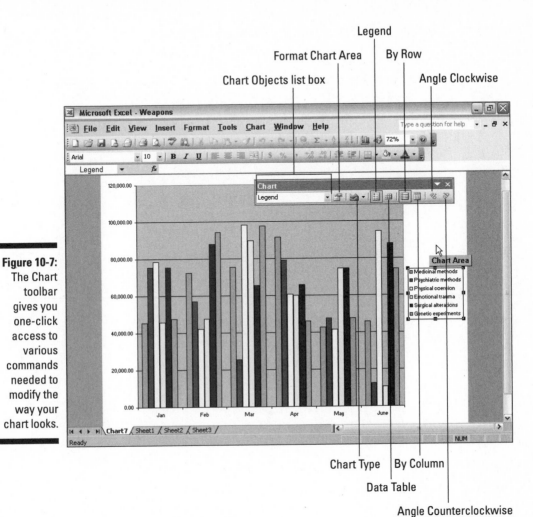

Figure 10-7:
The Chart toolbar gives you one-click access to various commands needed to modify the way your chart looks.

1. **Click the chart that you want to modify.**

   Handles appear around the chart, and the Chart toolbar appears.

2. **Click an icon on the Chart toolbar.**

   Depending on the icon you clicked, Excel may display a dialog box or menu of additional options you can choose.

3. **Click the option you want.**

Part IV
Making Presentations with PowerPoint

The 5th Wave · By Rich Tennant

In this part . . .

The fear of public speaking is the number one fear of most people — with the fear of death running a distant second. Although Microsoft Office 2003 can't help you overcome your fear of death, it can help you overcome your fear of public speaking and giving presentations with the help of Microsoft PowerPoint, which can help you organize and design a presentation that can keep others so amused that they won't even bother looking in your direction.

When you use PowerPoint to create a presentation, you won't need to rely on mere words, pointless hand gestures, or crudely drawn diagrams scribbled on a white board. With PowerPoint, you can give flawless presentations consisting of text, graphics, and even sound effects that people will remember.

The next time you need to dazzle an audience (with facts, rumors, or blatant lies dressed up to look like facts) flip through this part of the book and see how PowerPoint can help you create dazzling slide show presentations and hand-outs that can clarify, emphasize, or entertainingly distort topics for your audience until you have a chance to sneak out of the room and blame the misleading information on a government agency for giving it to you.

Chapter 11

Creating a PowerPoint Presentation

In This Chapter

▶ Making a presentation

▶ Adding text to a slide

▶ Viewing a presentation

▶ Printing a presentation

*T*he number one fear of many people is speaking in public. (The number two fear is wasting time sitting through a boring presentation.) Giving a speech can be terrifying, but displaying a presentation along with your speech can provide an important crutch — visuals. Visuals can take the form of handouts, 35mm slides, black-and-white or color overhead transparencies, or computer images displayed on a monitor or projected on a screen.

Visuals can help structure your presentation so that you don't have to memorize everything yourself. Instead, you can display pretty charts and talk about each one without having the entire audience staring at you all the time.

To help you create presentation slide shows on your computer, Microsoft Office 2003 includes a presentation program called PowerPoint. By using PowerPoint, you can show presentations on your computer or print them out as nifty handouts.

PowerPoint can help you make visually interesting presentations, but all the special visual effects in the world can't save a worthless presentation. Before rushing to create a PowerPoint slide show presentation, take some time to decide what's important to your audience and what you want to accomplish with your presentation (sell a product, explain why dumping oil into the ocean is harmless to the environment, and raise support to sell weapons to unstable Third World countries just for the money, and so on).

Creating a Presentation

A PowerPoint presentation consists of one or more slides where each slide contains text and sometimes graphics. Whether a presentation consists of one slide or dozens of them, every presentation provides information to support a specific point of view, such as explaining why the company plans to lay off hundreds of workers while paying a million dollar bonus to an incompetent CEO.

When you create a presentation, you need to add or define the following four items as shown in Figure 11-1:

- ✔ **Text:** Appears on each slide as a title and a bullet listing.

- ✔ **Graphics:** Can optionally appear on a slide to further illustrate a point, such as displaying a pie or bar chart that shows how profits plummeted last year. Graphics can also include a drawing or a photograph, such as a picture of the CEO, mocking the employees for their peon status.

- ✔ **Layout:** Determines the physical placement of text and graphics on each slide. Every slide can have a different layout.

- ✔ **Design:** Determines the background colors and appearance of every slide in the presentation.

PowerPoint can create the design and layout of your presentation; you just have to supply the actual text and pictures (if any). To create a presentation, you have four choices:

- ✔ Create the presentation one slide at a time.

- ✔ Use the PowerPoint AutoContent Wizard to guide you through the steps of creating a presentation.

- ✔ Use one of the PowerPoint presentation templates so that all you have to do is type in your own information.

- ✔ Create a presentation based on an existing presentation.

The AutoContent Wizard is the fastest way to create a presentation but may require modification to suit your needs. Creating a presentation one slide at a time is the slowest method but offers the most flexibility to design each slide exactly the way you want.

Text (Title)

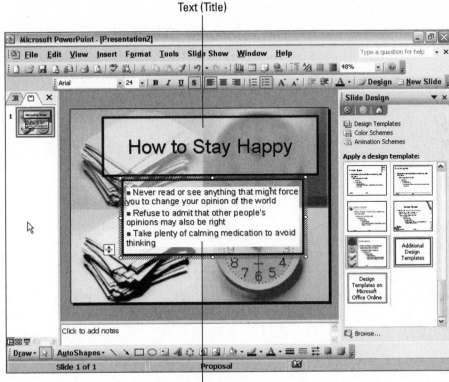

Figure 11-1:
The typical
parts of a
PowerPoint
presenta-
tion.

Text (Bullet listing)

Presenting the AutoContent Wizard

To help you create a presentation quickly, PowerPoint offers the AutoContent Wizard, which lets you put together a presentation almost without thinking, which is the way most people prefer to work anyway. The AutoContent Wizard creates a presentation consisting of several slides with the design and layout already defined. You just type your own text and add pictures that you want.

To use the AutoContent Wizard, follow these steps:

1. **Choose File⇨New.**

   The New Presentation task pane appears.

2. **Click From AutoContent wizard under the New category.**

   An AutoContent Wizard dialog box appears to let you know that it's about to help you create a presentation.

3. **Click Next.**

   Another AutoContent Wizard dialog box appears, asking for the type of presentation you want to give (such as Communicating Bad News or Recommending a Strategy).

4. **Click the desired type of presentation (such as Brainstorming Session or Communicating Bad News) and then click Next.**

   Another AutoContent Wizard dialog box appears, asking how you want to use your presentation.

5. **Click a radio button (such as On-screen Presentation or Web Presentation) and then click Next.**

   Yet another AutoContent Wizard dialog box appears, asking you to name your presentation and type a footer that you want to appear on all your slides.

6. **Type your title and any footer information in the appropriate text boxes and then click Next.**

   The final AutoContent Wizard dialog box appears, letting you know that you're finished answering questions.

7. **Click Finish.**

   PowerPoint displays your first slide along with an outline for your entire presentation, as shown in Figure 11-2.

After you create a presentation with the AutoContent Wizard, you can always modify and edit it later.

Filling in the blanks with a PowerPoint template

As an alternative to using the AutoContent Wizard, you can pick a pre-designed PowerPoint template and just type in your text. By creating a presentation based on a template, you can make a presentation quickly without much effort, thought, or time.

The main difference between the AutoContent Wizard and PowerPoint templates is that the AutoContent Wizard guides you through the creation of your presentation. A PowerPoint template simply contains a predesigned style and layout for your slide that you can modify (just as long as you know what you're doing).

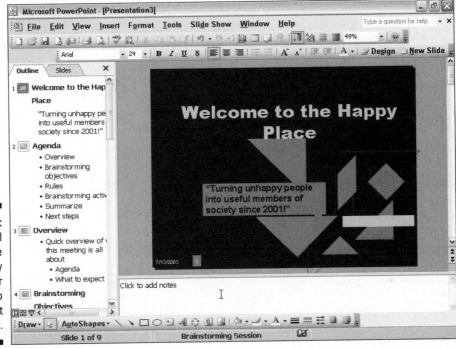

Figure 11-2:
An initial
slide
created by
the Power
Point Auto
Content
Wizard.

To create a presentation with a PowerPoint template, follow these steps:

1. **Choose File⇨New.**

   The New Presentation task pane appears.

2. **Click On my computer under the Templates category.**

   A New Presentation dialog box appears.

   You can find more templates stored on the Microsoft Web site if you click the Templates on Office Online under the Templates category.

3. **Click the Presentations tab.**

   The Presentations tab lists all the predesigned presentations you can choose as shown in Figure 11-3. This list is identical to what you can find if you use the AutoContent Wizard.

4. **Click a template that best describes the kind of presentation you want and then click OK.**

   PowerPoint displays the first slide of the template, ready for you to edit and customize for your own needs.

Figure 11-3:
A list of
available
presen-
tations
displayed in
the New
Presentation
dialog box.

Creating a presentation from an existing presentation

Although templates can make creating a new presentation quick and easy, you may want to save time by basing your new presentation on an existing one instead. For example, if you (or someone else) already created a visually stunning presentation, you may just want to copy that existing file to modify for creating your new presentation.

To copy an existing presentation, follow these steps:

1. **Choose File⇨New.**

   The New Presentation task pane appears.

2. **Click From existing presentation under the New category.**

   A New from Existing Presentation dialog box appears. You may have to switch drives or folders to find the PowerPoint presentation file that you want to use as the basis for your new presentation.

3. **Click the presentation file that you want to copy and then click Create New.**

   PowerPoint creates a copy of your chosen presentation. All you need to do now is edit this presentation and save it under a new name.

Creating a blank presentation

For maximum flexibility, you can create a presentation one slide at a time. That way you can customize the text, graphics, and formatting exactly the way you want (just as long as you want to spend the time doing so).

To create a blank presentation, follow these steps:

1. **Choose File⇨New.**

   The New Presentation task pane appears.

2. **Click Blank presentation under the New category.**

   PowerPoint displays a blank slide along with different slide layouts in the task pane as shown in Figure 11-4.

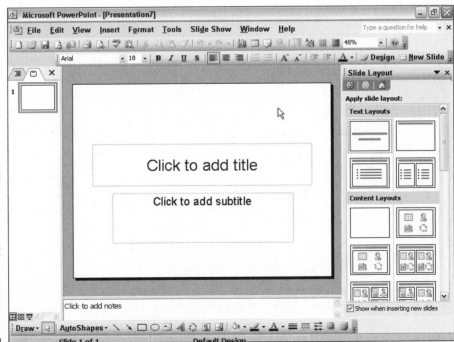

Figure 11-4: The Slide Layout task pane gives you different ways to organize text and graphics on a slide.

3. Click on the slide layout you want to use in the task pane.

PowerPoint creates a blank slide based on the layout you chose. At this point it's up to you to start typing in text, adding colors, and putting in pretty graphics to make your slide look interesting.

Modifying a Presentation

Whether you create a presentation through the help of the AutoContent Wizard or a template, or by creating it one slide at a time yourself, you'll probably need to modify your presentation sometime in the future. Modifying a presentation can mean rearranging your slides in a different order, changing the design that appears on each slide's background, adding new slides, or just deleting an existing slide.

To help you modify your presentations (or just to confuse you even more), PowerPoint divides the screen into several panes where you can to modify your presentation:

- **Slide pane:** Lets you edit the text, graphics, layout, and the design of each slide.

- **Slides tab pane:** Lets you rearrange, delete, and add new slides while also displaying miniature versions of each slide so that you can view your overall presentation, as shown in Figure 11-5.

- **Outline tab pane:** Lets you edit text, rearrange, delete, and add new slides to a presentation, as shown in Figure 11-6.

- **Note pane:** Lets you type text that won't appear on the slide but simply provides more information about each slide.

- **Task pane:** Displays different commands for modifying your presentation.

If you don't like the slides and outline tab pane or the task pane cluttering up your screen, you can hide them by clicking the Close box of each pane. To view the task pane again, choose View⇨Task Pane or press Ctrl+F1. To view the slides and outline tab pane, choose View⇨Normal (Restore Panes).

Viewing a slide

Before you can modify a slide, you need to find it first. PowerPoint provides three ways to find a slide buried in your presentation:

- Click the scroll bars in the Slide pane
- Use the Slides tab pane

✔ Use the Outline tab pane

✔ Use the Slide Sorter view

Using the scroll bars in the Slide pane

Clicking the scroll bars in the Slide pane lets you view your presentation one slide at a time. To view your slides, do one of the following as shown in Figure 11-7:

✔ Drag the scroll box up or down. As you drag the scroll box, PowerPoint displays a tiny window nearby that displays the number of the slide you'll see the moment you release the left mouse button.

✔ Click anywhere above or below the scroll box to view the previous or next slide.

✔ Click the Previous Slide or Next Slide button at the bottom of the scroll bar.

Slides
tab
pane

Slide pane

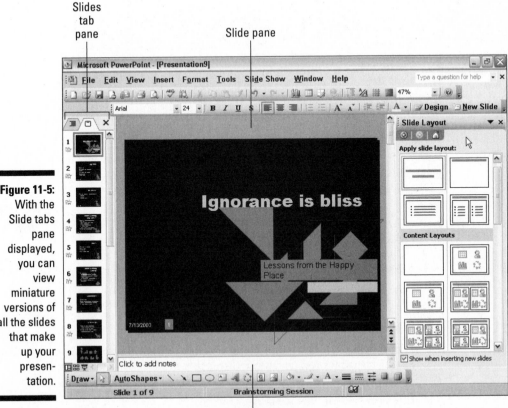

Figure 11-5:
With the
Slide tabs
pane
displayed,
you can
view
miniature
versions of
all the slides
that make
up your
presen-
tation.

Notes pane

Outline
tab
pane

Slide pane

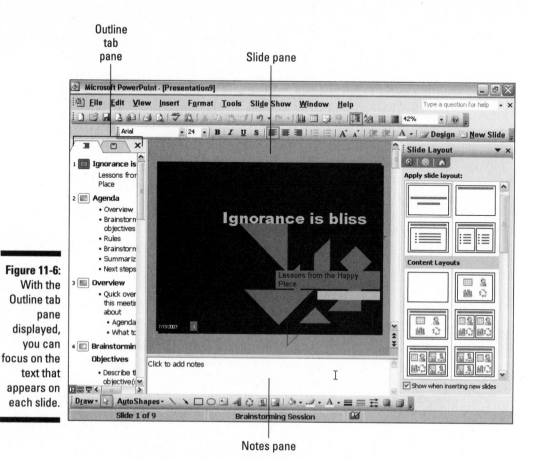

Figure 11-6:
With the
Outline tab
pane
displayed,
you can
focus on the
text that
appears on
each slide.

Notes pane

Using the Outline and Slides tab pane

The Outline and Slides tab pane can be faster when you want to jump from one slide to another quickly. To use the Outline and Slides tab pane, follow these steps:

1. Choose View⇨Normal (Restore Panes).

PowerPoint displays the Outline and Slides tab pane on the left-hand side of the screen.

2. Click the Outline tab or the Slides tab.

If you click the Outline tab, PowerPoint displays the titles of your slides as outline headings. If you click the Slides tab, PowerPoint displays thumbnail views of your slides.

3. Click an outline title or slide.

PowerPoint displays your chosen slide in the Slide pane.

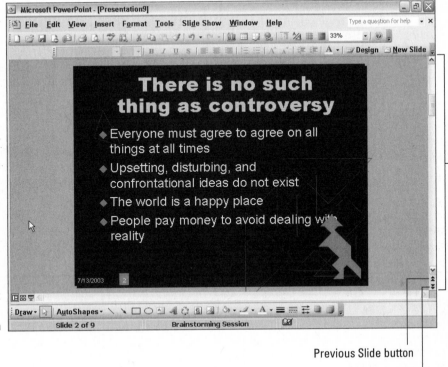

Figure 11-7:
How to use
the Slide
pane to
view a
different
slide.

Previous Slide button

Next Slide button

Scroll bar

Using the Slide Sorter View

The Slide Sorter view replaces the Slide pane with the Slide Sorter pane, which displays all your slides in a miniature version on the screen. To use the Slide Sorter View to choose a slide, follow these steps:

1. **Choose View⇨Slide Sorter or click the Slide Sorter View icon.**

   PowerPoint displays the Slide Sorter view, as shown in Figure 11-8.

2. **Double-click the slide that you want to view.**

   PowerPoint displays your chosen slide in the Slide pane.

Adding a new slide

The most common way to modify a presentation is to add a new slide. When you add a new slide, the slide will use the same design as the rest of the slides in your presentation, but you still need to add text and graphics, and define a layout for your new slide.

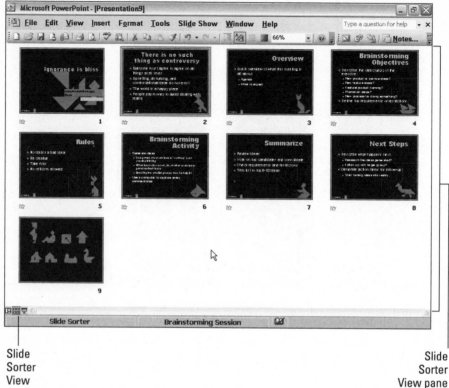

Figure 11-8:
The Slide Sorter View makes it easy to organize all the slides in your presentation.

Slide Sorter View

Slide Sorter View pane

When you add a new slide, PowerPoint inserts it after the slide that currently appears in the Slide pane. To insert a slide, follow these steps:

1. **Choose a slide using one of the methods explained in the previous "Viewing a slide" section.**

   PowerPoint will insert a new slide after any slide you choose in this step.

   If you right-click in the Outline or Slides tab pane, a pop-up menu appears, and you can click New Slide to insert a slide. From within the Outline tab pane, you can also move the cursor to the end of a slide title and press Enter to insert a new slide. If you move the cursor at the front of a slide title and press Enter, you can insert a slide before the slide.

2. **Choose Insert⇨New Slide, press Ctrl+M, or click the New Slide icon on the Formatting toolbar.**

   PowerPoint adds a new slide.

3. **Choose Format⇨Slide Layout.**

   PowerPoint displays the Slide Layout task pane (refer to Figure 11-4).

4. **Click a layout that you want to use.**

   PowerPoint displays your chosen layout on your new slide.

Deleting a slide

Sometimes you may want to delete a slide that you no longer need. To delete a slide, follow these steps:

1. **Choose the slide that you want to delete by using one of the methods explained in the previous "Viewing a slide" section.**

   PowerPoint displays your chosen slide.

2. **Choose Edit⇨Delete Slide.**

   PowerPoint deletes your chosen slide.

From within the Outline tab pane, Slides tab pane, or the Slide Sorter View, you can also right-click a slide that you want to delete. When a pop-up menu appears, click Delete Slide.

If you made a mistake and deleted the wrong slide, press Ctrl+Z or click the Undo icon to recover the slide you just wiped out.

Rearranging slides

Sometimes you may find that a slide might look better in a new position in your presentation. You can rearrange your slides from within the following three locations:

- ✔ The Slide Sorter View
- ✔ The Slides tab pane
- ✔ The Outline tab pane

To rearrange your slides, follow these steps:

1. **Choose one of the following:**

   - Choose View⇨Slide Sorter or click the Slide Sorter View icon.
   - Click the Slides tab
   - Click the Outline tab

2. **Click the slide that you want to move and hold down the left mouse button.**

   PowerPoint highlights your chosen slide.

3. **Drag the mouse (hold down the left mouse button and move the mouse) to a new location.**

   As you drag the mouse, PowerPoint displays a vertical or horizontal line to show you where your highlighted slide will appear if you release the left mouse button.

Editing Text on a Slide

Text can appear as a title or as a bullet listing. You can only put one title on a slide, but you can add as many bullet listings as you want on a slide. To edit text on a slide, you can either do it directly on a slide using the Slide pane or you can edit text in the Outline tab pane.

Editing text

PowerPoint stores text on a slide in a text box. To edit text on a slide, follow these steps:

1. **Choose the slide that contains text that you want to edit.**

   Use one of the methods explained in the "Viewing a slide" section to display a slide in the Slide pane. If you want to edit text within the Outline tab pane, click the Outline tab to display your presentation outline.

2. **Click the text that you want to edit.**

   PowerPoint highlights the text box that holds your chosen text and displays an I-beam cursor.

3. **Type any new text or use the Backspace or Delete keys to delete any text.**

   You can also highlight text with the mouse and then press Delete to erase it.

4. **Highlight any text that you want to format.**

5. **Choose Format⇨Font.**

   A Font dialog box appears that gives you different choices for changing the fonts, font sizes, and bold or italics of your text.

   Rather than use the Font dialog box, you can also click the Formatting toolbar and choose a different font, size, or italics or underlining for your highlighted text, as shown in Figure 11-9.

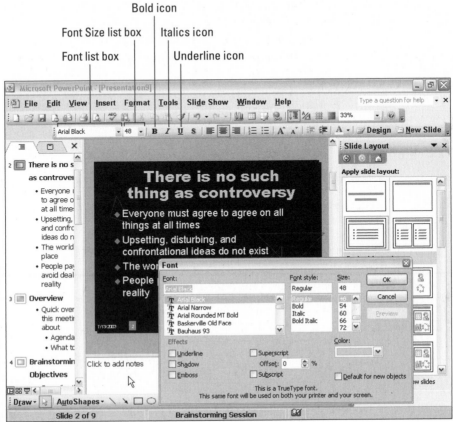

Bold icon

Font Size list box · Italics icon

Font list box · Underline icon

Figure 11-9:
The
Formatting
toolbar
offers
different
options for
formatting
your text.

Moving and resizing a text box

Rather than edit the text inside a text box, you may want to move a text box to a different spot on a slide or change the text box size to display more (or less) text. To modify your text boxes, follow these steps:

1. **Choose the slide that contains the text box that you want to modify.**

   Use one of the methods explained in the "Viewing a slide" section to display a slide in the Slide pane.

2. **Click the text that you want to change.**

   PowerPoint highlights the text box and displays handles around the corners and edges.

3. **Choose one of the following:**

   - To move a text box, move the mouse pointer over the text box edge until the mouse pointer turns into a four-way pointing arrow. Then drag the mouse to move the text box to a new position on the slide.

   - To resize a text box, move the mouse pointer over a text box handle until the mouse pointer turns into a double-pointing arrow. Then drag the mouse to resize the text box.

Adding a new text box

In case you want to create a new text box to display text, you can by following these steps:

1. **Choose the slide where you want to add the text box.**

   Use one of the methods explained in the "Viewing a slide" section to display a slide in the Slide pane.

2. **Choose Insert ⇨Text Box.**

   PowerPoint turns the mouse pointer into a downward-pointing arrow.

3. **Drag the mouse (hold down the left mouse button and move the mouse) to draw your text box.**

4. **Release the left mouse button.**

   PowerPoint displays your text box, ready for you to type something in it.

Adding Notes to a Slide

The Notes pane lets you type notes to go along with each slide. You can refer to these notes during your presentation or pass them out as handouts so that your audience has a handy reference during and after your presentation. (The section "Printing Your Presentation" explains how to print your notes with your slides.)

Text that you type on the Notes portion of a slide doesn't appear on the slide itself. Notes are just a way to keep related text together with your slides.

To type a note for a slide, follow these steps:

1. **Choose the slide that contains the graphic that you want to modify.**

   Use one of the methods explained in the "Viewing a slide" section to display a slide in the Slide pane.

2. **Click in the Notes pane (refer to Figure 11-5) and type any text that you want.**

   If the Notes pane does not appear, choose View ⇨Normal (Restore Panes).

Saving Your Presentations

Unless you enjoy creating everything from scratch over and over again, you should save your work. For extra protection, you should periodically save your work while you're modifying your presentation, as well.

Saving your presentation

To save a presentation, press Ctrl+S or choose File⇨Save. Feel free to choose the Save command as often as possible. That way, if the power goes out or your computer suddenly crashes, you won't lose your valuable data.

If you haven't saved the file before, the Save As dialog box appears, asking you to choose a filename and a directory to store your file in.

Saving PowerPoint presentations to go

Many people create PowerPoint presentations on their desktop computer where they can fine-tune and modify their presentation. Then they pack up their presentation and store it on a laptop computer that they take to another location.

To make this process easier, PowerPoint includes a special Pack and Go feature that crams all the files you need in one location. That way, you minimize the chances of forgetting an important file 3,000 miles away from your desktop computer.

To use PowerPoint's Pack and Go feature, load the PowerPoint presentation that you want to transfer and follow these steps:

1. **Choose File⇨Package for CD.**

   The Package for CD dialog box appears, as shown in Figure 11-10.

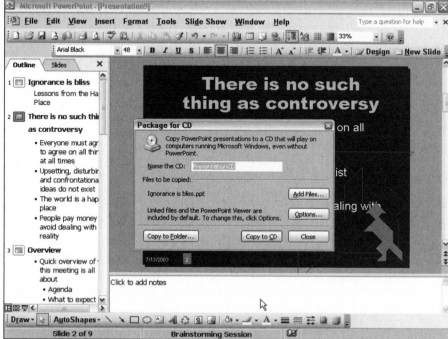

Figure 11-10:
The
Package for
CD dialog
box stores
your
PowerPoint
presentation
on a CD so
that you can
run it on any
computer
that runs
Microsoft
Windows.

2. **Type a name for your CD in the Name the CD text box. (Optional)**

   The name of your CD can simply help you identify which presentation you have stored on it, in case you have several CDs with PowerPoint presentations on them.

3. **Insert a blank CD in your rewritable CD drive.**

   If you don't have a rewritable CD drive, you should click on the Copy to folder button instead.

4. **Click Copy to CD.**

   PowerPoint copies your presentation and all the files you need on to your CD. When it's done, a dialog box appears that asks if you want to copy the same PowerPoint presentation files to another CD.

5. **Click No and then click Close to hide the Package for CD dialog box.**

   Your presentation CD is now ready to be used in another computer.

If you insert your presentation CD into another computer and nothing happens, just run the pptview file stored on your CD; when an Open dialog box appears, click the PowerPoint presentation file stored on your CD.

Printing a Presentation

After you get your presentation in the shape that you want it in, you can print out your hard work so that you can create handouts or wallpaper your office with your wonderfully creative presentations. To print a presentation, follow these steps:

1. **Choose File⇨Print.**

   The Print dialog box appears.

2. **Click the Print What list box and choose one of the following:**

   - **Slides:** Prints one slide per page so that you can see all the text and graphics on each slide

   - **Handouts:** Prints one or more miniature versions of your slides on a page that audience members can take home and study later

   - **Notes Pages:** Prints only your notes for each slide, which you can either hand out to your audience or keep for your own reference

   - **Outline View:** Prints your Presentation Outline so that you can see the overall structure of your presentation without graphics getting in the way

   You can also limit the print job to specific slide numbers by clicking the Current Slide option button or filling in the Slides text box in the Print Range area with the slide numbers you want to print.

3. **Click OK.**

If you click the Preview button, you can see what your presentation will look like before you actually start printing.

Chapter 12

Adding Color and Pictures to PowerPoint

At the simplest level, a PowerPoint presentation can consist of nothing but text. Although functional, such a presentation looks boring. To spice up your presentation, PowerPoint gives you the option of adding colors and pictures on your slides so that people will think your presentation is visually interesting, even if the content may be boring and completely useless.

Color and pictures may look nice, but use them to enhance your presentation and not substitute for a well thought out, clearly organized presentation. If people really want to look at fancy colors or pictures, they can just watch TV instead.

Changing Colors on Your Slides

Color can make your slides look extra special (or extra stupid if you're not careful). The two main parts of your slide that you can color are

✔ Any text that appears on your slide, including your slide title

✔ The background of your slides

Changing the color of text

Text normally appears in black, but you may want to emphasize your text in red, yellow, or any other color you choose. To change color of text:

1. **Click the text that you want to modify.**

   PowerPoint draws a gray border around your chosen text.

2. **Highlight the text that you want to change.**

   PowerPoint highlights your chosen text.

   The Font Color icon displays the last color you chose. If you want to use that color shown on the Font Color icon, just click the Font Color icon and not on the downward-pointing arrow that appears on its right.

3. **Click the downward-pointing arrow next to the Font Color icon on the Formatting toolbar.**

   A drop-down menu appears as shown in Figure 12-1. If you see a color displayed on this pull-down menu that you want to use, click it, and you can skip Steps 4 and 5.

   Instead of clicking the Font Color icon on the Formatting toolbar, you can choose Format⇨Font to display a Font dialog box and then click the Color list box. Besides allowing you to change colors, the Font dialog box also allows you to choose font style, font size, and special effects, such as subscript or superscript, for your text.

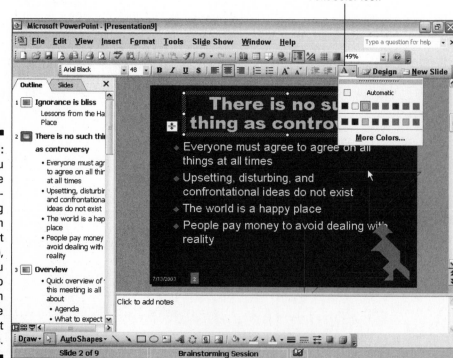

Figure 12-1:
When you
click the
downward-
pointing
arrow on
the Font
Color icon,
a menu
appears so
you can
choose
different
colors.

4. **Click More Colors.**

   A Colors dialog box appears, showing you the entire spectrum of colors available, as shown in Figure 12-2.

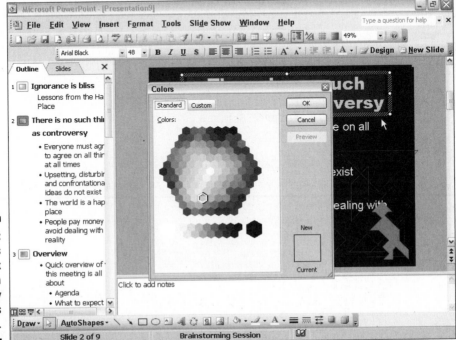

Figure 12-2:
The Colors dialog box offers a wide variety of colors to choose.

5. **Click the color you want for your text and click OK.**

   PowerPoint displays your highlighted text in your chosen color.

Coloring your background

A plain white background for your slides may give your presentation a generic look. So to add a little personality to your presentation, add some color to your background.

If you color your text and your background, make sure the colors compliment each other. Trying to read bright yellow text against a bright yellow background will definitely make your presentation harder to read and understand.

To color the background of your presentation, follow these steps:

1. **Choose a slide using one of the methods explained in the section about viewing a slide in Chapter 11.**

   If you want to change the background color of all your slides, then it doesn't matter which slide currently appears in the Slide pane.

   If you hold down the Ctrl key and click each slide in the Slides tab pane that you want to modify, you can select two or more slides.

2. **Choose Format⇨Background, or right-click your slide in the Slides pane and choose Background.**

   A Background dialog box appears, as shown in Figure 12-3.

3. **Click in the Background Fill list box.**

   A drop-down menu appears.

4. **Click More Colors.**

   A Colors dialog box appears (refer to Figure 12-2).

5. **Click a color you want to use for your background and click OK.**

   PowerPoint displays your chosen color on the background of the Background dialog box.

Background Fill list box

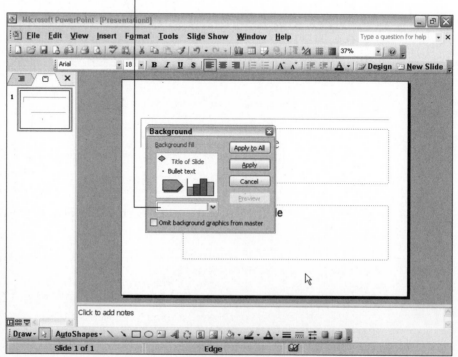

Figure 12-3: The Background dialog box can change the background color of the currently displayed slide or your entire presentation.

6. **Click Apply (to apply your chosen color to the currently displayed slide) or Apply to All (to apply your chosen color to all slides in your presentation).**

   PowerPoint displays your chosen color on the background of your slide or presentation.

If the background color you chose looks hideous, press Ctrl+Z (or click the Undo button) right away to remove the offending colors.

Choosing a color scheme

If wading through individual colors to find a suitable background color sounds too tedious and time-consuming, PowerPoint provides a variety of color schemes that offer colors already chosen for their suitability as a background.

To pick a color scheme, follow these steps:

1. **Choose a slide using one of the methods explained in the section about viewing a slide in Chapter 11.**

   If you want to change the background color of all your slides, then it doesn't matter which slide currently appears in the Slide pane.

   If you hold down the Ctrl key and click each slide in the Slides tab pane that you want to modify, you can select the background on two or more slides.

2. **Choose Format⇨Slide Design, or right-click on a slide in the Slides pane and choose Slide Design.**

   The Slide Design task pane appears.

3. **Click Color Schemes.**

   The Slide Design task pane displays a list of different color schemes as shown in Figure 12-4.

4. **Move the mouse pointer over the color scheme you want to use.**

   A downward-pointing arrow appears to the right of your chosen color scheme.

5. **Click the downward-pointing arrow.**

   A drop-down menu appears.

6. **Choose Apply to All Slides or Apply to Selected Slides.**

   PowerPoint uses your color scheme to color your slides.

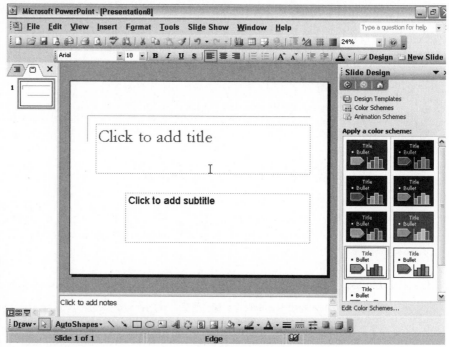

Picking a background pattern

Besides coloring your slides with a solid color, PowerPoint also gives you the option of choosing color gradients or different patterns, such as marble, wood, or striped patterns.

To choose a background pattern, follow these steps:

1. **Choose a slide using one of the methods explained in the section about viewing a slide in Chapter 11.**

    If you want to change the background pattern of all your slides, then it doesn't matter which slide currently appears in the Slide pane.

    If you hold down the Ctrl key and click each slide in the Slides tab pane that you want to modify, you can select two or more slides.

2. **Choose Format⇨Background, or right-click on a slide in the Slides pane and choose Background.**

    A Background dialog box appears (refer to Figure 12-3).

3. **Click in the Background Fill list box.**

    A drop-down menu appears.

4. **Click Fill Effects.**

   A Fill Effects dialog box appears, as shown in Figure 12-5.

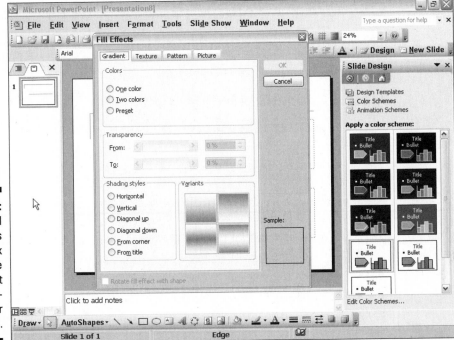

Figure 12-5:
The Fill Effects dialog box can provide different backgrounds for your slides.

5. **Click one of the following tabs:**

   - **Gradient:** Choose one or more colors that gradually fade away to one side of your slide.

   - **Texture:** Choose patterns that resemble marble or wood.

   - **Pattern:** Choose striped, brick, or checkerboard patterns.

   - **Picture:** Use a graphics file of your choice for your background.

6. **Click the choices you want and then click OK.**

   PowerPoint displays your chosen background in the Background dialog box.

7. **Click Apply (to apply your chosen color to the currently displayed slide) or Apply to All.**

   PowerPoint displays your chosen background on your slide or presentation.

If your newly created background looks ugly, press Ctrl+Z right away to remove the background pattern and then start over.

Choosing a design for your slides

The design of your slides consists of the background colors and ornamental graphics. In case you don't like the design currently displayed on all your slides, you can change them at any time.

To change the design of a presentation, follow these steps:

1. **Choose a slide using one of the methods explained in the section about viewing a slide in Chapter 11.**

   If you want to change the design of all your slides, then it doesn't matter which slide currently appears in the Slide pane.

   If you hold down the Ctrl key and click each slide in the Slides tab pane that you want to modify, you can select two or more slides.

2. **Choose Format⇨Slide Design or right-click on a slide in the Slides pane and choose Slide Design.**

   PowerPoint displays the Slide Design task pane.

3. **Click the design you want to use.**

   PowerPoint changes the design on your slides.

If you choose a hideous design, press Ctrl+Z to return to its previous design.

Adding Graphics to a Slide

PowerPoint presentations can display graphics. The two most common types of graphics are charts (such as bar or pie charts) and ordinary pictures.

Adding a chart

A chart can give your slides instant credibility, even though nobody may know what it means. To add a chart to a slide, follow these steps:

1. **Choose the slide where you want to add a chart.**

   Use one of the methods explained in the section about viewing a slide in Chapter 11 to display a slide in the Slide pane.

2. Choose Insert⇨Chart.

PowerPoint displays a column chart and a separate window called a Datasheet, which contains the numbers used to create the column chart, as shown in Figure 12-6.

3. Click in the Datasheet window and type new numbers and labels to define your chart.

4. Choose Chart⇨Chart Type.

PowerPoint displays Chart Type dialog box, which is identical to the dialog box used to choose a different chart in Excel.

5. Click a chart type, such as Bar or Pie, click the variation of that chart that you want, and then click OK.

PowerPoint displays your newly chosen chart.

To change the numbers that define your chart, double-click your chart to display the Datasheet window, then type new numbers in the Datasheet window.

Datasheet window

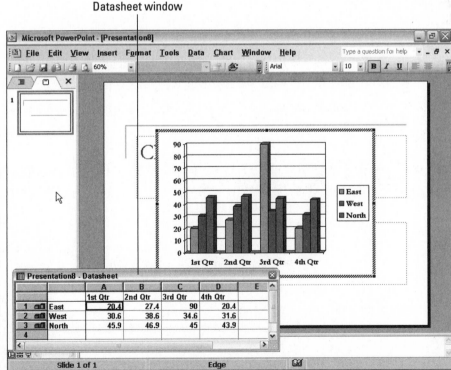

Figure 12-6:
When you add a chart to a slide, you can also modify the numbers in the Datasheet window that defines the chart.

Adding a picture

Sometimes you may just want to add a picture to a slide just to make your slides less boring and monotonous. You can add a picture, such as a clip art image, a digital photograph, or a picture that you scanned in. To add a picture, follow these steps:

1. **Choose the slide where you want to add a chart.**

   Use one of the methods explained in the section about viewing a slide in Chapter 11 to display a slide in the Slide pane.

2. **Choose Insert⇨Picture.**

   PowerPoint displays a pop-up menu that lists different types of pictures you can include, such as Clip Art or From File (in case you have a picture already stored on your computer). Depending on what option you choose, PowerPoint responds differently. For example, if you click From File, an Insert Picture dialog box appears. If you click Clip Art, the Clip Art task pane appears.

Moving and resizing graphics on a slide

After you have a graphic image on a slide, you may want to move, resize, or delete the graphic. To do this, follow these steps:

1. **Choose the slide that contains the graphic that you want to modify.**

   Use one of the methods explained in the section about viewing a slide in Chapter 11 to display a slide in the Slide pane.

2. **Click the graphic that you want to change.**

   PowerPoint highlights the graphic box and displays handles around the corners and edges.

3. **Choose one of the following:**

   • To move a graphic box, move the mouse pointer over the graphic box until the mouse pointer turns into a four-way pointing arrow. Then drag the mouse to move the graphic box to a new position on the slide.

   • To resize a graphic box, move the mouse pointer over a graphic box handle until the mouse pointer turns into a double-pointing arrow. Then drag the mouse to resize the graphic box.

Making your pictures look prettier

After you put a picture or bar chart on your slide, you may want to add a border or modify the appearance of the images on your slide. If so, follow these steps:

1. **Click the picture or bar chart that you want to modify.**

   PowerPoint displays handles around your chosen picture.

2. **Choose Format⇨Object, or right-click and choose Format Object.**

   A Format Object dialog box appears, as shown in Figure 12-7.

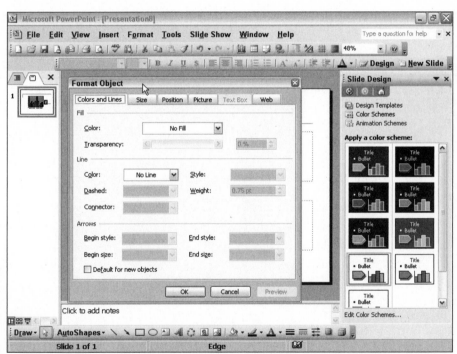

Figure 12-7:
The Format
Object
dialog box.

3. **Click one of the following tabs:**

   • **Colors and Lines:** Adds borders and background colors

   • **Size:** Specifies the width and height of your picture

   • **Position:** Specifies the location of your picture on your slide

   • **Picture:** Adjusts the brightness or contrast of your picture

4. **Make any changes you want to your picture and click OK.**

PowerPoint displays your picture with the options you chose.

Deleting a picture

To get rid of a picture on your slide, delete it by following these steps:

1. **Click the picture or bar chart that you want to delete.**

PowerPoint displays handles around your chosen picture.

2. **Press Delete.**

The first time you press Delete, PowerPoint deletes your chosen picture and displays an empty graphic box. To remove this empty box, press Delete again.

Press Ctrl+Z to retrieve any picture in case you decide you don't want to delete it after all.

Chapter 13

Showing Off Your PowerPoint Presentations

· ·

In This Chapter

▶ Making neat transitions

▶ Preparing your presentation for the public

· ·

After you create a slide show with Microsoft PowerPoint, you'll probably want to show it off like a newborn baby so that people can ooh and ahh over it. Because the appearance of your presentation is often more important than substance (which may explain why your boss gets paid more than you do), Microsoft PowerPoint provides all sorts of ways to spice up your slide show. Some of these ways include Hollywood-style transitions from slide to slide, sound effects to accompany each slide, and scrolling text that makes your slides more entertaining to watch.

Just remember that old saying about too much of a good thing. If you go too far with special effects, you can make your slide show memorable for being obnoxious. Choose your slide show presentation features sparingly so that people don't get distracted by special effects and miss the real message behind your presentation.

Making Nifty Transitions

An informative, inspiring, or just plain interesting slide show that makes the whole audience pay attention and almost regret that the time has passed so quickly.

To help keep your slide show interesting, PowerPoint lets you create special transitions between your slides. Your slides can dissolve into one another on-screen, wipe themselves away from left to right, slide up from the bottom of the screen to cover the previous slide, or split in half to reveal a new slide underneath.

PowerPoint gives you two types of transitions to create for your slides:

- **Visual transitions,** which determine how your slide looks when it first appears
- **Text transitions,** which determine how the text on each slide appears

Creating visual transitions for your slides

A *visual* transition determines how your slide shows itself on-screen (for example, sliding across the screen or popping up right away). To create the visual transition for each slide in your presentation, follow these steps:

1. **Choose a slide using one of the methods explained in the section about viewing a slide in Chapter 11.**

   Your chosen slide appears in the Slide pane.

   If you hold down the Ctrl key, you can click two or more slides that you want to change in the Outline tab pane.

2. **Choose Slide Show⇨Slide Transition.**

   The Slide Transition task pane appears, as shown in Figure 13-1.

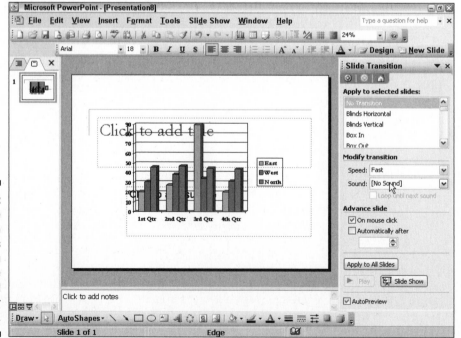

Figure 13-1: The Slide Transition task pane is where you can create visual effects for your slides.

3. **Click a transition in the Apply to Selected Slides list box, such as Box In, Cut, or Wipe Right.**

   PowerPoint shows you the effect of your choice in the Slide pane.

4. **Click the Speed list box and choose the speed of the transition, such as Slow, Medium, or Fast.**

   PowerPoint shows you the effect of the chosen speed.

5. **Click in the Sound list box and choose a sound.**

   Click the Loop Until Next Sound check box if you want your chosen sound to keep playing continuously until the presentation comes to another slide with a different sound assigned to it.

   Use the Loop Until Next Sound option sparingly: Having sound playing continuously may eventually annoy your audience.

6. **In the Advance slide category, choose how the current slide advances to the next.**

   Click the On Mouse Click check box if you want to advance this slide by clicking the mouse. Click the Automatically After check box and, in the Seconds box, type the number of seconds PowerPoint must wait before advancing to the next slide so that your presentation can proceed automatically.

7. **Click the Apply to All Slides button if you want to apply your transition to every slide in your presentation. (Skip this step if you selected multiple slides by holding down the Ctrl key in Step 1.)**

   Click the Play button to review how your slide transition looks.

8. **Repeat Steps 1 through 7 for each slide in your presentation and then click the Close box of the Slide Transition task pane when you're done.**

Creating text transitions for your slides

The whole idea behind text transitions is to make your slide appear without any text at first (or with only a part of its text revealed), and then have each click of the mouse bring a new chunk of text sliding into view. Such dramatics can keep your audience interested in watching your slides, if only to see what unusual and amusing effects you cooked up when you were supposed to be doing some actual work. (Oh well. You can always *pretend* it wasn't fun.)

Text transitions affect an entire text box, whether it contains one word or several paragraphs. If you want different transitions for each word, line, or paragraph, you have to create separate text boxes by choosing Insert⇨ Text Box.

To create a transition for the text on a slide, follow these steps for every slide that you want to display text transitions:

1. **Choose a slide using one of the methods explained in the section about viewing a slide in Chapter 11.**

   Your chosen slide appears in the Slide pane.

2. **Click the text box that you want to modify.**

   PowerPoint highlights your chosen text box with a border and handles.

3. **Choose Slide Show⇨Custom Animation.**

   The Custom Animation pane appears, offering options that you can use to modify the way your text appears on a slide.

4. **Click the Add Effect button.**

   A pop-up menu appears.

5. **Choose one or more of the following:**

   • **Entrance:** Defines how text first appears on the slide

   • **Emphasis:** Defines the appearance of text, such as increasing or decreasing the font size

   • **Exit:** Defines how text disappears off the slide

   • **Motion Paths:** Defines the direction that text moves when appearing or disappearing off a slide

   When you click an option, such as Entrance or Exit, another pop-up menu appears that lists more options for your chosen transition, as shown in Figure 13-2.

6. **Click the transition you want, such as the Diamond transition, within the Entrance pop-up menu.**

   PowerPoint shows you how your text appears with your chosen transition. As you add transitions, PowerPoint displays numbers near every text box that has a transition. The Custom Animation task pane also displays Start, Direction, and Speed list box for you to customize your text transition, as shown in Figure 13-3.

7. **Click the Start, Direction, and Speed list boxes and choose an option to define how your transition behaves.**

8. **Repeat Steps 4 through 7 until you're done picking transition effects for your text.**

9. **Click the Play button.**

   PowerPoint shows you how the different transitions appear on your slide.

10. **Click in the Close box of the Custom Animation task pane when you're done.**

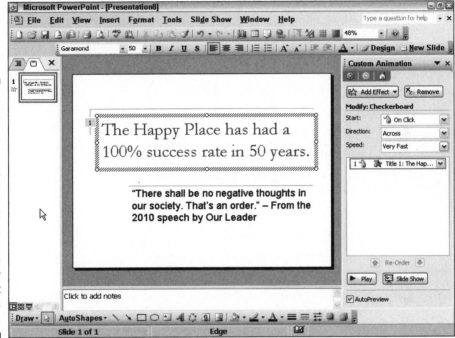

Figure 13-2:
When you click the Add Effects button, you can click on the Entrance option and choose a specific transition to define how your text enters the slide.

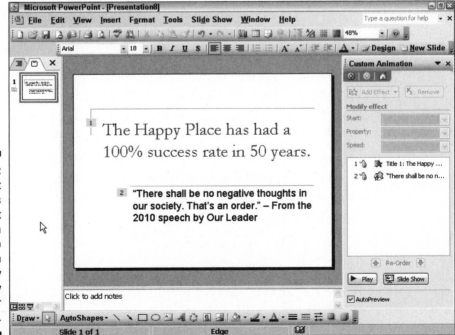

Figure 13-3:
PowerPoint labels all text boxes with numbers so you can quickly identify all your transitions.

Removing transitions

Transitions may be nice, but you may also get tired of seeing the same slides and text whirling around the screen.

To remove a slide transition, follow these steps:

1. **Choose a slide using one of the methods explained in the section about viewing a slide in Chapter 11.**

   Your chosen slide appears in the Slide pane.

   If you hold down the Ctrl key, you can click on two or more slides that you want to change in the Outline tab pane.

2. **Choose Slide Show⇨Slide Transition.**

   The Slide Transition pane appears (refer to Figure 13-1).

3. **Choose No Transition in the Apply to Selected Slides list box.**

4. **Click the Apply to All Slides button. (Skip this step if you want to remove a transition from the currently displayed slide or if you selected multiple slides in Step 1 by holding down the Ctrl key.)**

5. **Click the close box of the Slide Transition task pane to make it go away.**

To remove text transition from a slide, follow these steps:

1. **Choose a slide using one of the methods explained in the section about viewing a slide in Chapter 11.**

   Your chosen slide appears in the Slide pane.

2. **Choose Slide Show⇨Custom Animation.**

   The Custom Animation pane appears. PowerPoint displays a number on the slide next to each text box that contains a transition.

3. **Click the text containing the transition you want to remove.**

   PowerPoint displays a border around your chosen text box.

4. **Click the Remove button in the Custom Animation task pane.**

   PowerPoint removes any transitions from your chosen text box.

5. **Click the Close box of the Custom Animation task pane.**

   The Custom Animation task pane disappears.

Preparing Your Presentation for the Public

After your slide show is perfectly organized, complete, and ready to go, you can reveal it to the unsuspecting public. For maximum flexibility, PowerPoint lets you add different elements to your presentation to help you progress through the presentation manually or display it as a self-running presentation for others to view themselves.

Adding buttons

Most presentations display slides one after another in the same boring order. Keeping a single order is fine sometimes, especially if you're giving the presentation, but it can be too confining if others are going to watch your presentation without your supervision.

Instead of forcing someone to view your slides one after another, you can put buttons on your slides. Clicking a button can display any slide, whether it's the first, last, next, previous, or sixth slide from the last.

Adding buttons (which PowerPoint calls *hyperlinks*) gives your audience the chance to jump from one slide to another. That way, you (or the people controlling your presentation) have greater freedom and flexibility in delivering your presentation.

Creating a hyperlink to another slide

To create a button or hyperlink on a slide, follow these steps:

1. **Choose a slide using one of the methods explained in the section about viewing a slide in Chapter 11.**

   Your chosen slide appears in the Slide pane.

2. **Choose Slide Show⇨Action Buttons.**

   A menu of different buttons appears, as shown in Figure 13-4.

   If you move the mouse pointer over the top of the pop-up menu, the pointer turns into a four-way pointing arrow. Then if you drag the mouse, you can detach the pop-up menu so that it appears on the screen at all times.

3. **Click a button from the menu.**

   The mouse cursor turns into a crosshair.

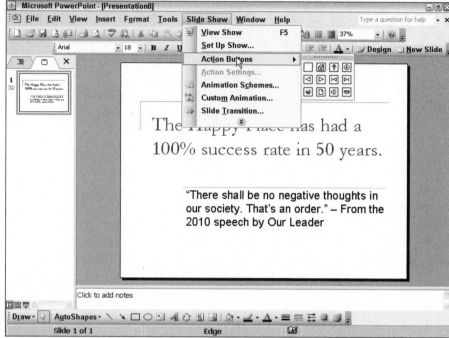

Figure 13-4:
A menu
displaying
the different
types of
hyperlink
buttons you
can put
on a slide.

4. **Place the mouse where you want to draw the button, hold down the left mouse button, drag the mouse to draw your button, and then release the left mouse button.**

   The Action Settings dialog box appears, as shown in Figure 13-5, offering ways to define how your hyperlink button works.

5. **Click the Hyperlink to radio button, click the list box, and then choose a slide such as Next Slide or Last Slide Viewed.**

   When choosing an option in Step 5, such as Next Slide, make sure your option corresponds to the visual appearance of the button that you clicked in Step 3. So if the button you chose looks like a Forward button, you probably don't want to make the action display the previous slide unless you really want to confuse people.

6. **Click OK.**

   To test your button, choose View➪Slide Show or press F5.

After you create a hyperlink button, you may want to change the slide that the button jumps to when it's clicked. To change a button's behavior, right-click the button that you want to change and choose Edit Hyperlink to display the Action Settings dialog box, where you can choose the new destination slide.

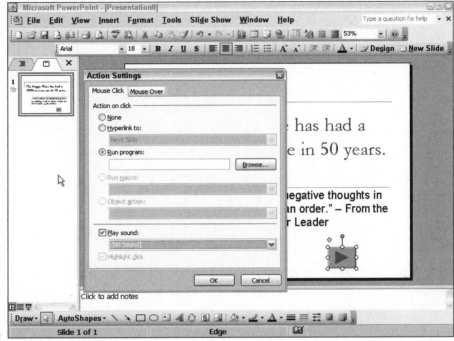

Figure 13-5:
The Action
Settings
dialog box
lets you
define how
a hyperlink
button
works on
your slides.

Deleting a hyperlink button

One day, you may want to remove a certain hyperlink button from your presentation. You can delete a hyperlink button at any time by following these steps:

1. **Choose a slide using one of the methods explained in the section about viewing a slide in Chapter 11.**

   Your chosen slide appears in the Slide pane.

2. **Click the hyperlink button that you want to delete.**

   PowerPoint highlights your chosen hyperlink button.

3. **Press Delete or choose Edit⇨Clear.**

   PowerPoint wipes out your chosen hyperlink button.

Defining how to present your slide show

Many people use PowerPoint to create presentations that they can show like slide shows or lectures, but you can also create self-running presentations for someone else to control. For example, a museum can put a computer in the lobby on which visitors can view a PowerPoint presentation that shows them the main attractions.

To define how to display your presentation, follow these steps:

1. **Choose Slide Show⇨Set Up Show.**

   The Set Up Show dialog box appears, as shown in Figure 13-6.

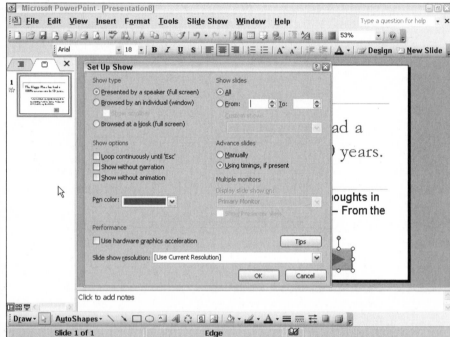

Figure 13-6:
The Set Up Show dialog box lets you define how your presentation runs.

2. **Click one of the following option buttons:**

   • **Presented by a speaker (full screen):** Slides take up the full screen. You can navigate them with a mouse or keyboard.

   • **Browsed by an individual (window):** Slides appear in a window with the PowerPoint menus and toolbars fully visible. You can navigate slides with a mouse or keyboard.

   • **Browsed at a kiosk (full screen):** Slides take up the full screen, but you can only navigate them with a mouse. (To make this option work properly, be sure to put hyperlink buttons on your slides.)

3. **Click one or more of the following check boxes:**

   • **Loop continuous until 'Esc':** Keeps repeating your entire presentation until someone presses the Esc key.

- **Show without narration:** Eliminates any narration that you may have recorded using the Slide Show⇨Record Narration command. (The Record Narration feature lets you add your own voice or other sounds through a microphone. To find out more about this feature, look at *PowerPoint 2003 For Dummies* by Doug Lowe, published by Wiley Publishing, Inc.)

- **Show without animation:** Eliminates all the fancy text and slide transitions you may have painstakingly created.

4. **In the Advance slides group, click either the Manually or Using Timings If Present radio button.**

5. **Click OK.**

If you click the Browsed at a Kiosk radio button in Step 2 and Using Timings If Present radio button in Step 3, choose Slide Show⇨Slide Transition and make sure that all your slides have the Automatically After check box chosen. Otherwise you won't be able to advance through your slide show presentation.

Testing your slide show

Before showing your presentation during that crucial business meeting, you should test your slide show. That way, if you find any mistakes or annoying visual effects, you can edit them out, and they won't detract from your presentation.

Besides making sure that your text and slide transitions work, make doubly sure that your spelling and grammar are correct. Nothing can make you look dumber than spelling your own company's name wrong.

To test your slide show, follow these steps:

1. **Choose Slide Show⇨View Show or press F5.**

   PowerPoint displays your first slide.

2. **Press any key or click the left mouse button to see the next slide.**

3. **Press Esc to end the slide show at any time.**

Part V
Getting Organized with Outlook

The 5th Wave   By Rich Tennant

"...so if you have a message for someone, you write it on a piece of paper and put it on their refrigerator with these magnets. It's just until we get our e-mail system fixed."

In this part . . .

After a few days on the job, most people's desks disappear under a pile of memos, reports, and papers. If you actually want to use the top of your desk as a writing surface rather than a filing cabinet or garbage bin, you may need the help of Microsoft Outlook to save the day — a combination e-mail program and a personal information organizer.

In addition to helping you create, send, receive, and sort through your e-mail, Outlook also organizes your appointments, tasks, and important contacts. With the help of Outlook, you can track meetings and appointments you'd rather avoid, store the names of people you might forget, and organize e-mail in a single location so that you don't have to search frantically all over your hard drive for an important message that could determine the future of your career or your business.

Outlook can handle all your personal information so you can focus on doing the work that really needs to get done. Who knows? If Outlook makes you productive enough at work, you just may find that you have enough time to relax and take that extended lunch break you've needed for so long.

Chapter 14

Organizing Your E-Mail

*N*early everyone has an e-mail account nowadays — some people have several. If you're using multiple e-mail accounts, your messages may be scattered in different places, so you have a hard time sorting out who just sent what to whom.

With Outlook, you can not only write, send, and read e-mail, but also funnel all your e-mail from your Internet accounts into a central mailbox. That way, when you want to organize your e-mail, you can do it all from within a single program quickly and easily.

Chapter 20 shows how to reduce that pesky spam e-mail.

Setting Up Outlook to Work with E-Mail

When you install Microsoft Office 2003, Outlook guides you through the process of setting up an e-mail account. However, you may later add or cancel an Internet account, so you need to know how to tell Outlook about these changes to your e-mail.

Defining an e-mail account for Outlook requires technical details, such as knowing your Internet's POP3 or SMTP information. If you don't have the faintest idea what this might be, call your Internet service provider for help or ask a knowledgeable friend to help you out.

Adding an e-mail account to Outlook

To add an e-mail account to Outlook, follow these steps:

1. **Choose Tools⇨Options.**

   The Options dialog box appears.

2. **Click the Mail Setup tab.**

   The Mail Setup tab appears, as shown in Figure 14-1.

3. **Click the E-Mail Accounts button.**

   The E-Mail Accounts dialog box appears.

4. **Click the Add a New E-Mail Account radio button and then click Next.**

   An E-Mail Accounts dialog box asks for your server type, as shown in Figure 14-2.

   If you're connecting to an Internet account that forces you to dial through your phone line, click the POP3 radio button. If you want to connect to a Hotmail, Yahoo!, or another Web-based e-mail account, click the HTTP radio button. Talk to a computer expert (preferably someone nearby) to help you use the other options, which are often used to connect Outlook to a corporate e-mail account on a local area network.

5. **Click a Server Type option (such as POP3) and click Next.**

   Depending on the option you chose, another dialog box appears, asking you to type in technical details about your e-mail account, such as your mail server name.

6. **Type the information required in the User Information text boxes.**

   Typical user information includes the following:

   - **Your Name:** Your name

   - **E-mail address:** Your actual e-mail address, for example, yourname@isp.net

   - **Incoming mail server (POP3):** Your Internet service provider's POP3 information, for example pop.yourisp.net

   - **Outgoing mail server (SMTP):** Your Internet service provider's SMTP information, for example smtp.yourisp.net

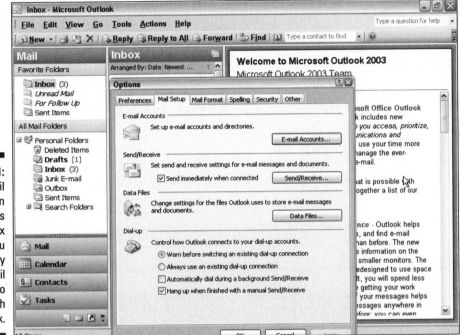

Figure 14-1:
The Mail Setup tab in the Options dialog box lets you specify an e-mail account to use with Outlook.

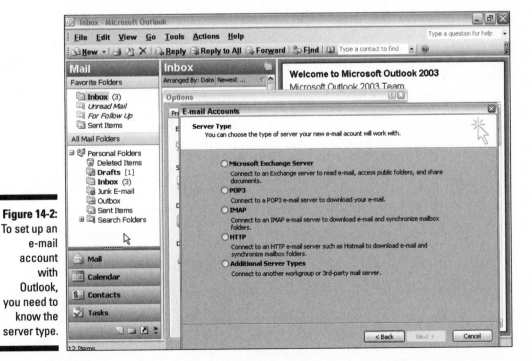

Figure 14-2:
To set up an e-mail account with Outlook, you need to know the server type.

- **User Name:** The name of your Internet account, usually the first portion of your e-mail address, such as `Jsmith` if your e-mail address is `Jsmith@meISP.net`

- **Password:** The password that magically lets you access your account

You may want to click the Test Account Settings button to make sure you correctly typed in all the information about your e-mail account. Even one typo can prevent your e-mail account from working correctly.

7. Click Next.

Another dialog box appears, informing you that you have successfully created an e-mail account to work with Outlook.

8. Click Finish.

The Options dialog box appears again.

9. Click OK.

Deleting an e-mail account from Outlook

If you move to a different company or switch Internet service providers, your old e-mail account may no longer be valid. Rather than keep this obsolete information lodged in Outlook, delete it to keep Outlook from trying to send and retrieve e-mail from a dead e-mail account. To delete an e-mail account from Outlook, follow these steps:

1. Choose Tools⇨Options.

The Options dialog box appears. (Refer to Figure 14-1.)

2. Click the Mail Setup tab.

3. Click the E-Mail Accounts button.

The E-Mail Accounts dialog box appears.

4. Click the View or Change Existing E-Mail Accounts radio button and click Next.

A list of e-mail accounts appears, as shown in Figure 14-3.

5. Click the Internet e-mail account that you want to delete and then click the Remove button.

A dialog box appears asking whether you're sure you want to delete your e-mail account.

As an alternative to deleting an entire e-mail account, you may want to click the Change button instead of the Remove button. That way you can edit your current e-mail account settings.

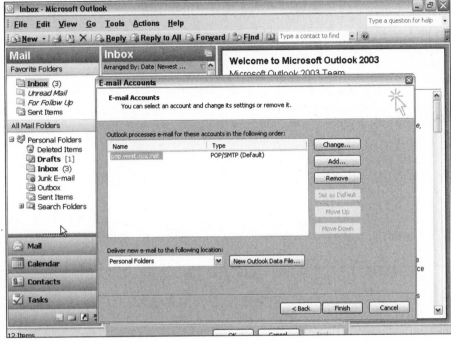

Figure 14-3:
Viewing a
list of
existing
e-mail
accounts in
Outlook.

6. **Click Yes.**

7. **Click Finish.**

The Options dialog box appears again.

8. **Click OK.**

Storing e-mail addresses in Outlook

The trouble with e-mail addresses is that they look cryptic, as if a cat made them by walking across your keyboard. Typical Internet addresses consist of letters separated by periods and that silly at-sign character (@), as in yourname@yourisp.net.

Type one character wrong and Outlook won't know how to send e-mail to the correct destination. In a desperate attempt to make computers less user-hostile, Outlook lets you store names and e-mail addresses in the Address Book. That way, you need only type the e-mail address right *once*. After that, you can just choose an address by clicking a name from the Address Book list.

Outlook gives you two ways to store an e-mail address:

- ✔ Typing the e-mail address manually
- ✔ Copying an e-mail address from a message you received

Stuffing e-mail addresses in Outlook

Sometimes you may get an e-mail address from someone and you may want to store that e-mail address before you lose it. To store a name and e-mail address in Outlook, follow these steps:

1. **Choose Tools⇨Address Book or press Ctrl+Shift+B.**

   The Address Book window appears

2. **Click the New Entry icon or choose File⇨New Entry.**

   A New Entry dialog box appears, as shown in Figure 14-4.

3. **Choose File⇨New Entry or click the New Entry icon.**

   The New Entry dialog box appears.

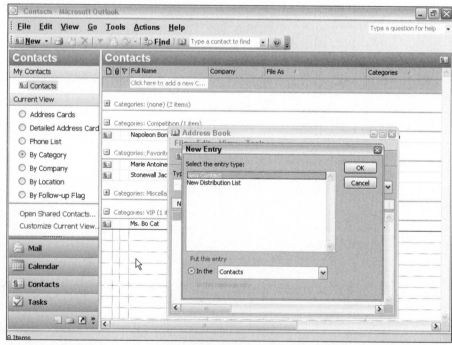

Figure 14-4:
The New Entry dialog box lets you decide where to store your e-mail addresses.

4. **Click OK.**

   A Contact window appears, as shown in Figure 14-5.

5. **Type the person's name and e-mail address in the appropriate text boxes.**

6. **Click Save and Close.**

   Outlook displays your entry in the Address Book window.

7. **Choose File⇨Close.**

Storing e-mail addresses from an e-mail message

If someone sends you an e-mail message and you actually want to keep the e-mail address for future use, it's a lot easier to tell Outlook, "See that e-mail address of that message that I just received? Store that e-mail address for me so I don't have to do any more typing than necessary."

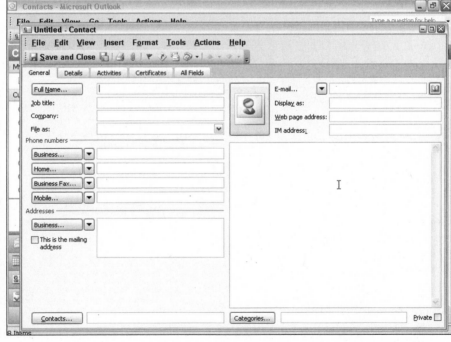

Figure 14-5: The Contact Window lets you type in a person's name and e-mail address along with any other relevant information such as a phone number.

To store an e-mail address from an e-mail message, follow these steps:

1. **Choose Go⇨Mail, or press Ctrl+1.**

   The Inbox pane appears.

2. **Click on an e-mail message.**

   Your chosen e-mail message appears in a separate pane.

3. **Right-click on the name of the person who sent you the e-mail message.**

   A pull-down menu appears, as shown in Figure 14-6.

4. **Click Add to Outlook Contacts.**

   A Contact window appears, as shown in Figure 14-7.

5. **Type any additional information you want to store (such as a telephone number) and click Save and Close.**

   Outlook stores your address in the Outlook Contacts Address Book.

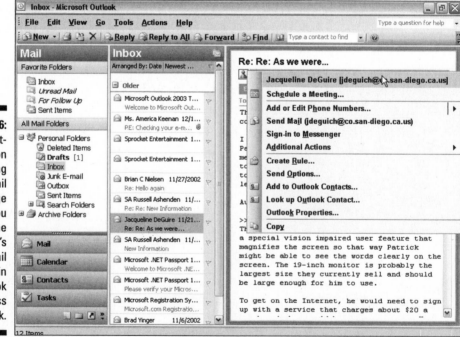

Figure 14-6: Right-clicking on an existing e-mail message lets you store the sender's e-mail address in your Outlook address book.

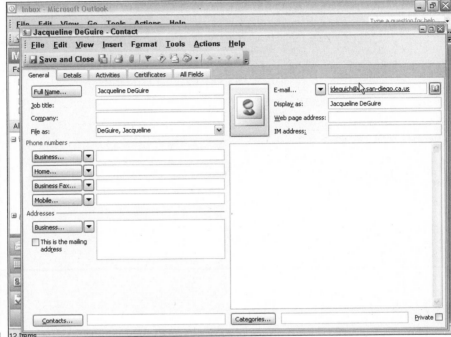

Figure 14-7:
The Contact window lets you save additional information about a person besides their name and e-mail address.

Creating an E-Mail Message

You can write e-mail in Outlook when you're online (connected to the Internet) or when you're offline (not connected to the Internet).

You don't need to connect to the Internet to write e-mail, but you eventually have to connect to the Internet to send your e-mail.

To create an e-mail message, follow these steps:

1. **Choose Go⇨Mail, or press Crl+1.**

   The Inbox pane appears.

2. **Click the New icon on the toolbar, choose Actions⇨New Mail Message, or press Ctrl+N.**

   A Message window appears, as shown in Figure 14-8.

   The Message window is actually Microsoft Word in disguise. This gives you all the options from Word for creating an e-mail message, including spell-checking, tables, and macros.

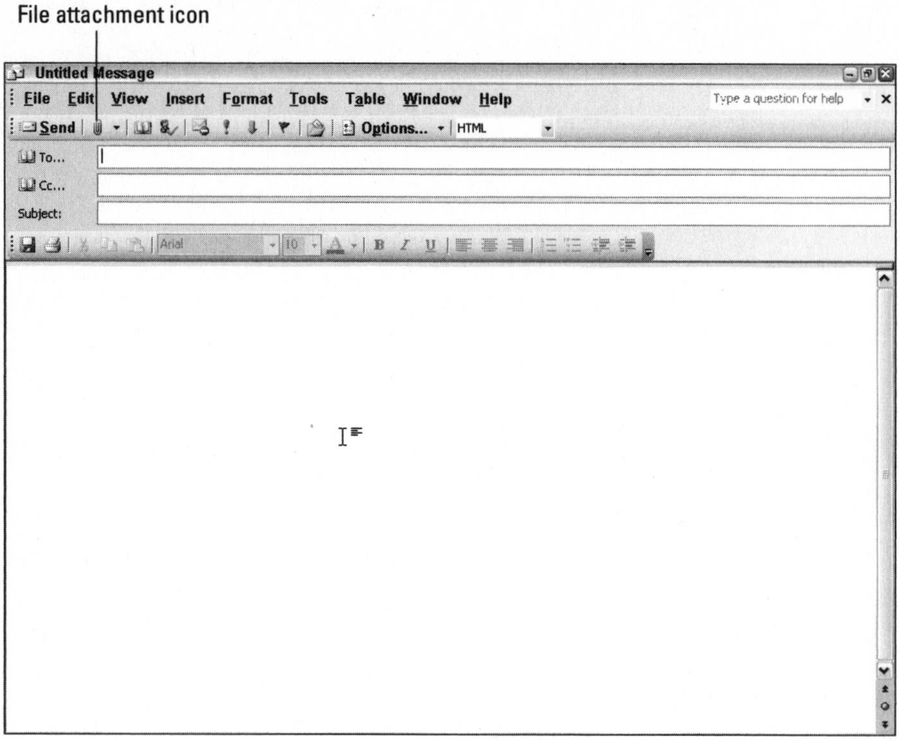

File attachment icon

Figure 14-8:
The
Message
window
where you
can type an
e-mail
address and
your
message
to send.

3. **Click in the To text box and type the e-mail address where you want to send your message.**

Click the To button to display a Select Names dialog box and then double-click the name of the recipient. Then click OK.

To send the same e-mail to two or more people, you can type multiple e-mail addresses, separated by a semicolon, in the To text box, such as **john@doe.com; jane@doe.com**.

To send a *carbon copy* (twentieth-century-speak for *identical message*) of the e-mail to other people, you can type an e-mail address directly in the Cc text box.

Although clicking the To and Cc buttons can send e-mail to two or more people, the Cc button is meant more to send e-mail to someone so that they can stay informed on your correspondence without necessarily having to respond to it.

4. **Click in the Subject text box and type a subject for your message.**

For example, type **Secret plans for eliminating gravity from the planet**.

5. **Click in the big text box at the bottom of the Message window and type your message.**

If you want to send a file along with your e-mail, don't follow Step 6 just yet. Instead, follow the instructions in the following section, "Attaching files to e-mail," and then return to Step 6.

Choose Tools⇨Spelling and Grammar or press F7 to check the spelling in your message.

6. **Click the Send button.**

Outlook sends your e-mail right away if you're currently connected to the Internet. Otherwise, Outlook stores your message in the Outbox folder.

Attaching files to e-mail

Rather than just send plain text, you can also send music, programs, word processor documents, photographs, or any other type of file you care to send.

Try not to send massive files larger than one megabyte. The larger the file, the longer it will take for someone else to download it. To compress files, consider a file compression program, such as WinZip (www.winzip.com).

To attach a file to your e-mail, follow these steps:

1. **Create your e-mail following Steps 1 through 5 in the previous section, "Creating an E-Mail Message."**

2. **Choose Insert⇨File or click the Insert File icon (it looks like a paper-clip) on the toolbar.**

An Insert File dialog box appears.

3. **Click the file you want to send with your e-mail.**

You may have to switch drives or folders to find the file you want to send.

4. **Click Insert.**

Outlook displays an icon and your chosen file in an Attach text box directly underneath the Subject text box. At this point, you're ready to send your e-mail.

You can attach multiple files to an e-mail message. Just repeat Steps 2 through 4 for each additional file you want to attach.

5. **Click the Send button.**

Outlook sends your e-mail along with your attached file.

Using the Outbox folder

Until you connect to the Internet, Outlook stores any e-mail messages that you have not yet sent in the Outbox folder. As soon as you connect to the Internet, Outlook empties your Outbox folder by sending your messages on their way.

Viewing and editing messages in the Outbox folder

To view all the messages trapped temporarily in your Outbox folder, follow these steps:

1. **Choose Go⇨Mail or press Ctrl+1.**

   The Mail window pane appears.

2. **Click the Outbox icon in the All Mail Folders group.**

   Outlook displays a list of e-mail messages waiting to be sent.

3. **Double-click the e-mail message you want to view.**

   A Message window appears where you can edit your e-mail message.

4. **Choose File⇨Save to store your e-mail back in the Outbox folder.**

To send e-mail stored in your Outbox folder, follow the steps in the following section.

Sending e-mail from the Outbox folder

Messages stored in the Outbox folder remain there until one of two conditions occurs:

- ✔ You manually send them on their way.
- ✔ You configure Outlook to send all e-mail stored in the Outbox automatically the moment you connect to the Internet (or local area network).

To manually send e-mail from the Outbox folder, follow these steps:

1. **Choose Go⇨Mail or press Ctrl+1.**

   The Mail window pane appears.

2. **Click the Outbox icon in the All Mail Folders group.**

   Outlook displays a list of e-mail messages waiting to be sent.

3. **Click the e-mail message you want to send.**

   To choose more than one e-mail message, hold down the Ctrl key and click each message you want to send. To select a continuous range of e-mail messages, click the first message you want to send, hold down the Shift key, and then click the last message you want to send.

4. **Choose Tools➪Send/Receive➪Send/Receive All or Send All, or press F9.**

   If you aren't connected to the Internet, a dialog box appears, asking for the user name and password to your Internet account so that Outlook can connect and send your e-mail.

In case manually sending e-mail from your Outbox seems troublesome, make Outlook send e-mail automatically instead. To configure Outlook to send e-mail automatically from your Outbox folder, follow these steps:

1. **Choose Tools➪Options.**

   The Options dialog box appears. (Refer to Figure 14-1.)

2. **Click the Mail Setup tab.**

3. **Click the Send Immediately When Connected check box that appears under the Send/Receive category. (If a check mark already appears in the check box, skip this step.)**

4. **Click OK.**

   From now on, Outlook automatically sends all e-mail from your Outbox as soon as you connect to the Internet.

Retrieving and Reading E-Mail

Outlook can retrieve and organize e-mail from most Internet accounts with the exception of America Online. Think of Outlook as a super organizer on your computer that you can't misplace anywhere (unless you misplace your laptop computer).

Retrieving e-mail

To retrieve e-mail, follow these steps:

1. **Choose Go➪Mail or press Ctrl+1.**

   The Mail window pane appears.

2. **Choose Tools➪Send/Receive.**

   A pop-up menu appears, listing all the Internet accounts you've defined for Outlook.

   To retrieve e-mail for all your accounts, choose Send/Receive All.

3. **Click the Internet account you want to retrieve mail from.**

   If Outlook finds e-mail for you, it kindly stores your e-mail in the Inbox folder.

Reading an e-mail message

To read an e-mail message, follow these steps:

1. **Choose Go⇨Mail or press Ctrl+1.**

   The Mail window pane appears.

2. **Click the Inbox icon under the All Mail Folders group.**

   Outlook displays all the messages stored in your Inbox, divided into categories according to how long ago you received them. Unread messages appear in bold.

3. **Click the e-mail message that you want to read.**

   The contents of your chosen message appear in a pane on the right side of the screen.

4. **After you finish reading the message, click another message.**

   If you want to reply to an e-mail message, follow the steps listed in the next section, "Replying to an e-mail message."

Replying to an e-mail message

You often need to reply to someone who has sent you an e-mail message, either out of courtesy or because you want something from them. Replying to e-mail is easy because Outlook automatically knows where to send your reply without making you retype that cryptic e-mail address. To reply to an e-mail message, follow these steps:

1. **Follow Steps 1 through 3 in the previous section, "Reading an e-mail message."**

2. **Choose Actions⇨Reply, press Ctrl+R, or click the Reply icon on the toolbar.**

   If you want your reply to go to everyone who received the original message, choose Actions⇨Reply to All, press Ctrl+Shift+R, or click the Reply to All icon on the toolbar.

   The Message window appears with a copy of the original message in the message window and the recipient's e-mail address (or recipients' e-mail addresses) already typed for you.

3. **Type your reply and then click the Send button.**

Forwarding e-mail

Rather then reply to an e-mail, you may want to pass an e-mail message on to someone else, which can be an amusing way to distribute jokes while you are at work. Passing along an e-mail message is known (in stuffier, more technical circles) as *forwarding* it. To forward an e-mail message, follow these steps:

1. **Follow Steps 1 through 3 in the section, "Reading an e-mail message," earlier in this chapter.**

2. **Choose Actions⇨Forward, press Ctrl+F, or click the Forward icon on the toolbar.**

   The Message window appears with the original e-mail message already typed in for you.

3. **Type an address, in the To text box, to whom you want to send the e-mail.**

   If you want to send e-mail to an address stored in your Address Book, click the To button and then click the recipient's name. If you want to send the message to someone who isn't in your Address Book, then you have to type the e-mail address in the To box.

4. **Type any additional message that you want to send along with the forwarded message.**

5. **Click the Send button.**

Deleting Old E-Mail

If you don't watch out, you may find your Inbox overflowing with ancient e-mail messages that you no longer need. Rather than waste valuable hard disk space storing useless e-mail messages, take some time periodically to clean out your Inbox.

Besides the Inbox, another folder that may get cluttered is the Sent Items folder, which contains copies of every e-mail message you've sent out. Although you may like to keep a record of these messages for future reference, you'll probably want to wipe out at least some of your sent messages at some point.

Deleting e-mail

To delete an e-mail message stored in any folder, follow these steps:

1. **Choose Go➪Mail or press Ctrl+1.**

   The Mail window pane appears.

2. **Click a folder that contains the e-mail messages you want to delete, such as the Inbox folder.**

   When you click a folder, a separate pane appears, listing all the messages stored in that particular folder.

3. **Click the message that you want to delete.**

   If you want to delete multiple messages, hold down the Ctrl key and click each message you want to delete. If you want to delete a range of messages, hold down the Shift key, click the first message you want to delete, and then click the last message you want to delete.

4. **Choose Edit➪Delete, press Ctrl+D, or click the Delete icon on the toolbar.**

   Outlook deletes your chosen messages.

When you delete messages, Outlook stores them in the Deleted Items folder to give you one last chance to recover any e-mail messages that you want to save before you permanently delete them. (See "Recovering e-mail from the Deleted Items folder," up next.)

Recovering e-mail from the Deleted Items folder

If you delete a message and suddenly decide that you need it after all, you can still get it out of your Deleted Items folder. To recover e-mail from your Deleted Items folder, follow these steps:

1. **Choose Go➪Mail or press Ctrl+1.**

   The Mail window pane appears.

2. **Click the Deleted Items icon under the All Mail Folder group.**

   A separate pane displays all the messages stored in the Deleted Items folder.

3. **Click the e-mail message that you want to recover.**

   If you want to recover a number of messages, you can select multiple messages by holding down the Ctrl key and clicking each message.

4. **Choose Edit↪Move to Folder or press Ctrl+Shift+V.**

The Move Items dialog box appears, as shown in Figure 14-9.

The Move Items dialog box isn't just limited to moving messages out of the Deleted Items folder. You can use the Move Items dialog box to move messages from any folder to another one.

5. **Click the Inbox icon and then click OK.**

The message appears in your Inbox in its original condition. (If you want, you can choose a folder other than Inbox.)

Deleting e-mail for good

Until you delete your e-mail messages from the Deleted Items folder, those messages can be retrieved and read by others. At the very least, your unwanted messages still just sit around and take up space on your hard disk until you get rid of them for good.

After you delete e-mail from the Deleted Items folder, you can never recover the message. So you'd better make sure you mean it.

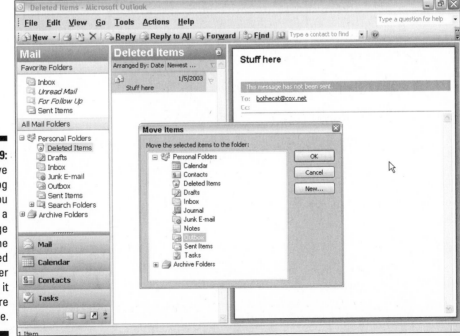

Figure 14-9: The Move Items dialog box lets you retrieve a message from the Deleted Items folder and store it somewhere else.

To delete e-mail from your computer forever, follow these steps:

1. **Choose Go⇨Mail or press Ctrl+1.**

   The Mail window pane appears.

2. **Click the Deleted Items icon under the All Mail Folder group.**

   A separate pane lists all the messages stored in your Deleted Items folder.

3. **Click the e-mail message that you want to delete.**

   If you want to delete a number of messages at one time, you can select multiple messages by holding down the Ctrl key and clicking each message.

4. **Choose Edit⇨Delete, press Ctrl+D, or click the Delete icon on the toolbar.**

   A dialog box appears, warning you that you are about to permanently delete the e-mail messages.

5. **Click the Yes button.**

   Kiss your chosen e-mail messages good-bye. (It's quieter than a maniacal laugh.)

If you're in a hurry and want to dump all the e-mail stored in your Deleted Items folder, choose Tools⇨Empty "Deleted Items" Folder.

Chapter 15

Setting Tasks and Making Contacts

*B*esides letting you read and write e-mail messages, Microsoft Outlook also lets you organize the rest of your life outside the Internet. With the magical features of Outlook, you can create your own to-do lists (so you don't have to waste money buying special paper labeled "Things to do today") and store valuable names, addresses, phone numbers, and other important information about people who may be able to further your career.

For more information about using Outlook's wonderful features, pick up a copy of *Outlook 2003 For Dummies,* by Bill Dyszel (published by Wiley Publishing, Inc.).

Organizing Contact Information

Most folks have business cards that they can hand out to people who may be useful to them in the future. People stuck in the Dark Ages store their business card collection in a Rolodex file, but you can progress to the twenty-first century by storing names and addresses in Outlook instead. By using Outlook, you can quickly copy your valuable business contacts and share them with others or just get rid of your cumbersome Rolodex file and put a much more cumbersome computer on your desk instead.

Storing contact information

To store information about a contact in Outlook, follow these steps:

1. **Choose Go⇨Contacts or press Ctrl+3.**

   The Contacts pane appears.

2. **Choose Actions⇨New Contact or press Ctrl+N.**

   The Contact dialog box appears, as shown in Figure 15-1.

3. **Type the name, address, phone number, and any other information you want to store about the contact in the appropriate boxes.**

   If you type a company name, make sure you type it consistently. Don't type it as "Communist Propaganda Publishing Inc." one time and just "Communist Propaganda Inc." another time, or Outlook won't consider those names to mean the same company.

   • If you click the Full Name button, a Check Full Name dialog box appears. In it, you can specify a title (such as Dr. or Ms.); first, middle, and last name; and a suffix (such as Jr. or III).

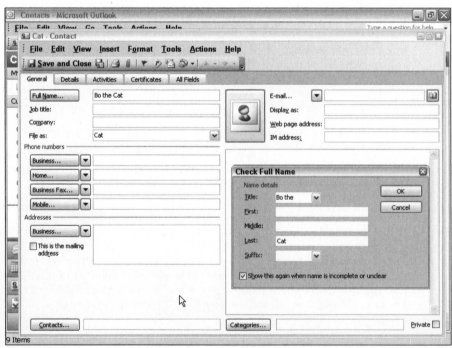

Figure 15-1: The Contacts window lets you store all the important information you need about a person.

- If you click the Address button, a Check Address dialog box appears. Here, you can specify a street name, city, state or province, postal code, and country.

- If you click the downward-pointing arrow button that appears in the Addresses category, you can specify two or more addresses for each person, such as a business address and a home address.

- The This Is the Mailing Address check box lets you specify which address to use when sending postal mail.

- If you click the button that looks like an open book, which appears to the right of the E-Mail list box, a list of e-mail addresses that you have previously stored for all your contacts appears.

- If you click the Add Picture icon, you can store a digital picture of your contact if you have a picture of that person already stored on your computer.

4. **Click Save and Close to save your information.**

You don't have to fill in every single box. For example, you may just want to store someone's name and phone number. In this case, you don't need to type in the address or any other irrelevant information.

Changing your point of view

The real power of your computer and Outlook comes into play in sorting and displaying different views of your information to help you find just the information you need. You have seven ways to display your contacts in Outlook:

- ✔ **Address Cards:** Displays names (sorted alphabetically by last name), addresses, phone numbers, and e-mail addresses.

- ✔ **Detailed Address Cards:** Displays every piece of information about a person, such as company name, fax number, and job title.

- ✔ **Phone List:** Displays names and phone numbers (including business, home, fax, and mobile phone numbers) in row-and-column format for easy viewing.

- ✔ **By Category:** Displays information according to categories, such as Business, Hot Contacts, Key Customer, and Suppliers. (You can learn how to organize your contacts into categories in the "Categorizing your contacts" section, later in this chapter.)

- ✔ **By Company:** Displays names grouped according to company name. (Useful for finding multiple names belonging to the same company.)

✔ **By Location:** Displays information by country, city, and state/province.

✔ **By Follow-Up Flag:** Displays contacts identified with a follow-up flag, which you can add to a contact by pressing Ctrl+Shift+G or by choosing Actions➪Follow-Up.

To choose a different view to display your contact information, just click the appropriate radio button displayed in the Current View category in the Contacts pane on the far left side of the screen as shown in Figure 15-2. (As an alternative, you can also choose View➪Arrange By➪Current View and then click on a view such as Phone List or By Category.)

Searching your contacts

After you start using Microsoft Outlook, you may wind up storing globs of information that you may have trouble finding again. So to help you search for a specific contact stored in Outlook, follow these steps:

1. **Choose Go➪Contacts or press Ctrl+3.**

   The Contacts pane appears.

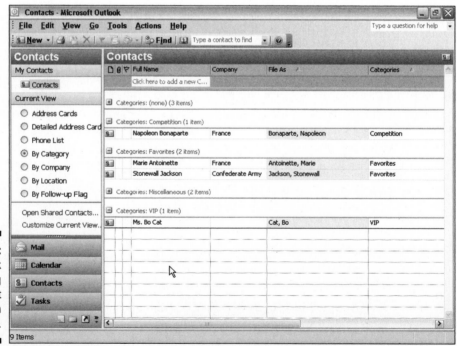

Figure 15-2:
Outlook
displaying
your contact
information
by category.

TIP

If you choose Go➪Mail or press Ctrl+1 in Step 1, you can search your e-mail messages for the name of a person who sent you e-mail or who you sent e-mail to.

2. **Choose Tools➪Find➪Find, press Ctrl+E, or click the Find icon on the toolbar.**

   Outlook displays a Look for and Search in list box near the top of the screen as shown in Figure 15-3.

3. **Click in the Look For box and type the phrase (such as first name or last name) that you want to find.**

   To make the search faster, type as much as you can of the phrase that you want to find. For example, instead of typing **F** to search for everyone with a first name that begins with F, make it more specific and type as much of the name as possible, such as **FRAN**.

REMEMBER

Make sure you spell a name correctly or else Outlook won't be able to find it.

Look for   Search In
text box   list box

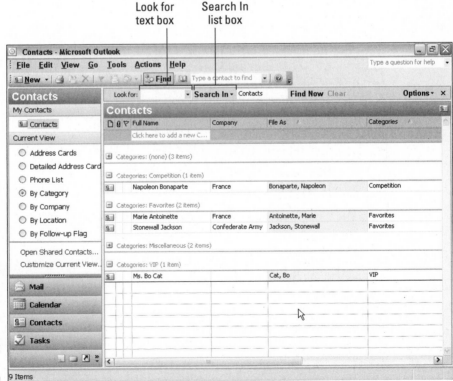

Figure 15-3:
Before you
can find a
name in
Outlook, you
specify the
name and
the address
book name
where you
stored that
name.

4. **Click the Find Now button that appears to the right of the Search In list box.**

   Outlook displays the contacts that match your search criteria. You can double-click the contact that you want to view.

5. **Click the Clear button that appears to the right of the Search In list box.**

   Outlook displays all your contacts again.

Categorizing your contacts

If you're a busy person (or just a pack rat who can't resist storing every possible name and address that you find), you may find your Outlook contact list so full of names that trying to find any single name is cumbersome.

To solve this problem, you can organize your contacts into categories, such as personal or customer contacts. When you want to see information for just a particular group of contacts, you can tell Outlook to sort your contact list by the appropriate category.

Defining a category for a contact

Before you can ask Outlook to organize your contacts by category, you need to put each contact in one or more categories. To define a category for each contact, make sure you're in the Contacts view and then follow these steps:

1. **Choose Go⇨Contacts or press Ctrl+3.**

   The Contacts pane appears and displays your list of contacts.

2. **Click a contact that you want to categorize.**

3. **Choose Edit⇨Categories.**

   The Categories dialog box appears, as shown in Figure 15-4.

4. **Click the check box for each category that your contact belongs in.**

   Many contacts may logically belong in multiple categories, such as under the Business, Hot Contacts, and Key Customer categories.

5. **Click OK.**

As a faster method for categorizing your contacts, right-click a contact and click Categories from the pop-up menu. Then follow Steps 4 and 5 in the preceding steps list.

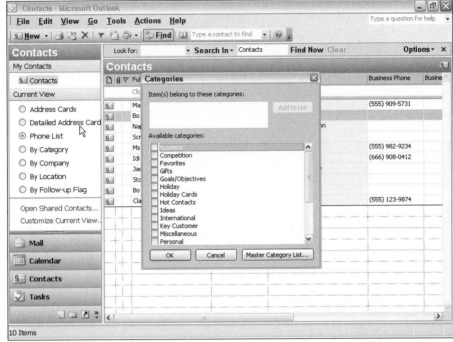

Figure 15-4:
The
Categories
dialog box
allows you
to group
your
contacts.

In case you want another way to define a category for a contact, or if you want to organize multiple contacts into a category, follow these steps:

1. **Choose Tools➪Organize.**

   The Ways to Organize Contacts window appears, as shown in Figure 15-5.

2. **Click the contacts you want to add to a category.**

   You can choose multiple contacts by holding down the Ctrl key and clicking on the contacts you want to include.

3. **Click in the Add Contacts list box, choose a category (such as Business or Hot Contacts) and click the Add button.**

   To create a new category, type the category name in the Create a New Category Called text box and click the Create button.

4. **Click the Close box of the Ways to Organize Contacts window.**

Sorting contacts by categories

After you assign your contacts to different categories, you can have Outlook show you only those contacts within a given category. That way, you can quickly find business-related contacts, personal contacts, or top-secret contacts. To view your contacts by category, follow these steps:

Figure 15-5:
The Ways to
Organize
Contacts
window
helps you
organize
multiple
contacts
into
categories.

1. **Choose Go⇨Contacts or press Ctrl+3.**

   The Contacts pane appears and displays your list of contacts.

2. **Click in the By Category radio button in the Current View category, or choose View⇨Arrange By⇨Current View⇨By Category.**

   Outlook displays all the categories you checked, as shown in Figure 15-6.

   If you have too many categories cluttering up your screen, you can collapse a category by clicking the collapse button (minus sign) that appears to the left of a category name. To expand a previously collapsed category, click the expand button (plus sign) that appears to the left of a category.

3. **Double-click the contact that you want to view.**

   The Contact window appears, displaying all the information for your chosen contact.

4. **Click Save and Close when you're done viewing or editing the contact.**

Expand button   Collapse button

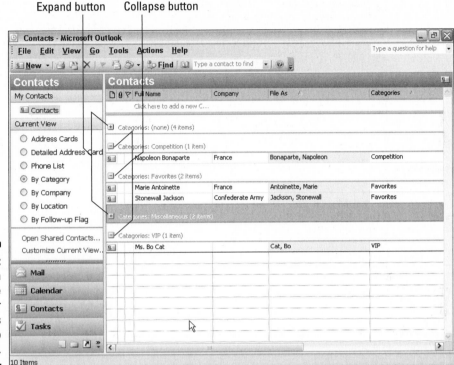

Figure 15-6:
Outlook can
organize
your
contacts
according to
categories.

Managing Your Tasks

To keep from wasting your days doing trivial tasks and forgetting all your important ones, you can create a daily to-do list in Outlook and check off your tasks as you complete them.

Creating tasks for a to-do list

To create a to-do list, follow these steps:

1. **Choose Go⇨Tasks or press Ctrl+4.**

   The Tasks view appears, as shown in Figure 15-7.

2. **Click the Click Here to Add a New Task text box and type a task.**

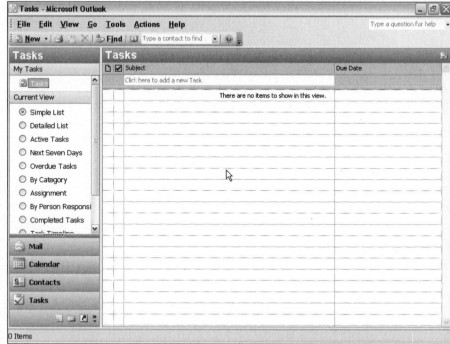

Figure 15-7:
The Tasks
view lists all
the tasks
you need to
accomplish
today (or
whenever
you get
around to it).

3. **Click the Due Date box. (Skip Steps 3 through 5 if you don't want to choose a due date.)**

   A downward-pointing arrow appears.

4. **Click the downward-pointing arrow.**

   A calendar appears.

5. **Click a due date and press Enter.**

   Outlook displays your task with your chosen due date.

Editing a task

After you create a task, you can edit it later to set a reminder or track how much of the task you've completed. To edit a task, follow these steps:

1. **Choose Go⇔Tasks or press Ctrl+4.**

   The Tasks view appears (refer to Figure 15-7).

2. **Double-click a task (or click the task and then press Ctrl+O).**

   The Task window appears, as shown in Figure 15-8.

3. **Choose one or more of the following:**

   - **Click in the Due Date or Start Date list boxes and choose a new date.**

   - **Click the Status list box and choose a status for your task, such as In Progress, Completed, Deferred, or Waiting on Someone Else.**

     A task's status shows you how each task is progressing (or not progressing); this feature helps you manage time more effectively.

   - **Click the Priority list box and choose Low, Normal, or High.**

     Categorizing tasks by priority, you can identify the ones that really need to get done and the ones that you can safely ignore and hope they go away.

   - **Click the % Complete list box to specify how much of the task you've already completed.**

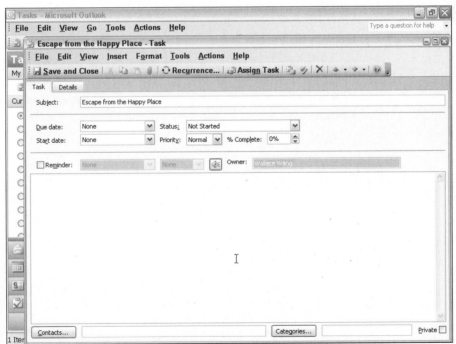

Figure 15-8:
The Task window lets you edit your task.

- Click the Reminder check box and specify a date and time for Outlook to remind you of this particular task.

  If you click the Alarm button (it looks like a megaphone), you can specify a unique sound that Outlook plays to remind you of your task.

  - Type your task in more detail in the big text box at the bottom of the Task dialog box.

4. **Click Save and Close.**

Moving a task

Normally, Outlook organizes your tasks in the order that you created them. Because this order isn't always the most efficient way to organize tasks, take some time to move tasks around. To move a task, follow these steps:

1. **Choose Go⇨Tasks or press Ctrl+4.**

   The Tasks view appears (refer to Figure 15-7).

2. **Click the task that you want to move.**

3. **Hold down the left mouse button and drag the mouse up or down.**

   Outlook displays a red horizontal line showing you where it will move your task the moment you let go of the left mouse button.

4. **Release the left mouse button when the task appears where you want it.**

Organizing your tasks

After you've created several tasks, you may have trouble knowing which ones are due when or who may be responsible for any given task. So to help you organize your tasks in categories, follow these steps:

1. **Choose Go⇨Tasks or press Ctrl+4.**

   The Tasks view appears (refer to Figure 15-7).

2. **Click on a radio button in the Current View category, such as Overdue Tasks or Next Seven Days, or choose View⇨Arrange By⇨Current View and then click a category, such as Active Tasks or By Person Responsible.**

   Outlook organizes your tasks by the categories you checked, as shown in Figure 15-9.

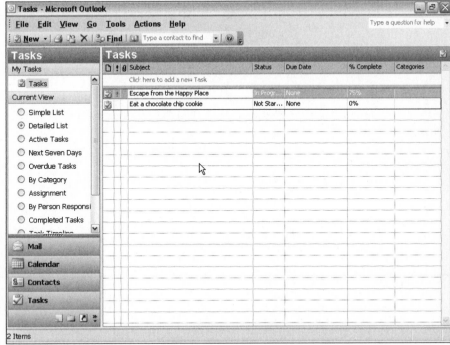

Figure 15-9:
Outlook can
organize
your tasks
according to
categories.

3. **Double-click the task that you want to view.**

   The Task window appears, displaying all the information for your chosen task.

4. **Click Save and Close when you're done viewing or editing the contact.**

Finishing a task

To tell Outlook that you've completed a task, click its check box. Outlook shows a check mark in the check box, dims the task, and draws a line through the task.

Deleting a task

After you complete a task (or just decide to ignore it permanently), you can delete it from Outlook so that it doesn't clutter up your screen. Here's how:

1. **Choose Go⇨Tasks or press Ctrl+4.**

   The Tasks view appears (refer to Figure 15-7).

2. **Choose Edit⇨Delete, press Ctrl+D, or click the Delete icon on the task dialog box toolbar.**

   Outlook deletes your chosen task.

If you delete a task by mistake, press Ctrl+Z right away. Outlook retrieves it.

Chapter 16

Scheduling Your Time

In This Chapter

▶ Making an appointment

▶ Changing an appointment

▶ Printing your schedule

*B*esides organizing your e-mail messages and contact information, Microsoft Outlook can also act like an electronic version of a day planner. By tracking your appointments on your computer, you are always sure to remember your daily, weekly, monthly, and even yearly tasks (unless you don't turn on your computer).

Making an Appointment

You can overload yourself with so many appointments that you never have time to do any work. To help you sort out your appointments and keep them handy, Outlook keeps track of your busy and free time.

Making a new appointment

Outlook lets you schedule appointments for tomorrow or (if you prefer the long view) decades in advance. To make an appointment in Outlook, follow these steps:

1. **Choose Go⇨Calendar or press Ctrl+2.**

   The Calendar view appears.

2. **Click the day on the calendar on which you want to schedule an appointment.**

   Outlook highlights the current day in a red box in the calendar. If you click another day (such as tomorrow or a day three weeks from today), Outlook highlights your newly chosen day in gray but still displays a red box around the current day.

3. **Click Day icon that appears in the toolbar.**

   Outlook displays your appointment list for that day, divided into half-hour time increments, as shown in Figure 16-1.

4. **Click the time on the Appointment list that you want your appointment to begin, such as 11:00 or 3:00.**

   If you want to set an appointment in the morning, make sure you click a time slot in the AM. Likewise, if you want to set an appointment in the afternoon or evening, make sure you click on a time slot in the PM.

   Outlook highlights your chosen time.

5. **Type a short description for your appointment, such as** Lunch with mistress **or** Dinner at Boring Office Banquet.

   Outlook displays your text in the Appointment list with a border.

6. **Move the mouse pointer over the bottom edge of the border surrounding your appointment.**

   The mouse pointer turns into a double-pointing arrow.

7. **Hold down the left mouse button and drag the mouse down to the time when you hope the appointment will end, such as 12:30.**

   Congratulations! You just stored an appointment in Outlook.

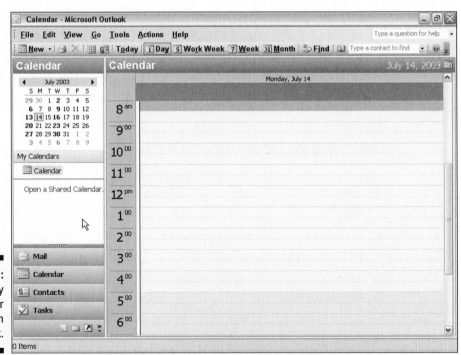

Figure 16-1:
The daily Calendar view in Outlook.

Editing an appointment

After you create an appointment, you may want to edit it to specify the appointment location, the appointment subject, the exact starting and ending times, and whether Outlook should beep a reminder before you risk missing the appointment altogether.

To edit an appointment in Outlook, follow these steps:

1. **Choose Go⇨Calendar or press Ctrl+2.**

   The Calendar view appears (see Figure 16-1).

2. **Click the calendar day that contains the appointment you want to edit.**

3. **Open the appointment by doing one of the following:**

   • Double-click the appointment.

   • Click the appointment and press Ctrl+O.

   • Right-click the appointment and click Open.

   The Appointment window appears, as shown in Figure 16-2.

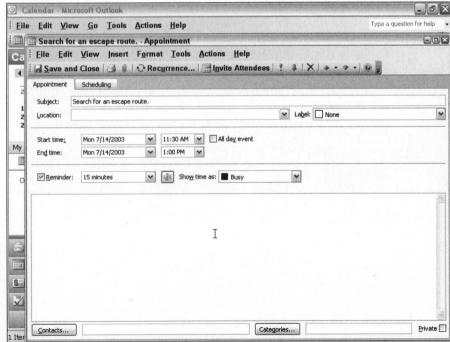

Figure 16-2:
The
Appointment
window
lets you
edit your
appointment.

4. **Click in the Subject text box to edit your appointment description.**

   For example, type **Turn in two-week notice, flee job, streak naked through parking lot during lunch hour, etc.**

5. **Click in the Location text box and type the location of your appointment.**

   If you have typed locations for other appointments, you can click the downward-pointing arrow and click a location you've used before (such as a specific meeting room, restaurant, convention center, or secret headquarters).

6. **Click in the Start Time list boxes to specify the date and time when the appointment begins.**

7. **Click in the End Time list boxes to specify the date and time when the appointment ends.**

8. **Click the Reminder list box to specify when you want Outlook to remind you of your appointment.**

   The Reminder list box tells Outlook to remind you when your appointment is coming up (such as 15 minutes or one hour beforehand). As long as Outlook is running on your computer (even if minimized or hidden), it can remind you of an appointment — no matter what other program you're using at the time.

9. **Click the Show Time As list box and choose Free, Tentative, Busy, or Out of Office.**

   If you're on a network, you can signal coworkers to let them know whether they can bother you during your appointment. Choosing Out of Office, for example, sends a pretty clear I-am-not-here-so-don't-bug-me message.

10. **Click the Save and Close button to save your edited appointment.**

    Outlook displays your appointment on-screen.

When you set a reminder for an appointment, that appointment appears on the Appointment list with an alarm bell icon next to it. When the time comes to remind you of an appointment, Outlook displays the Reminder box, as in Figure 16-3.

To have Outlook repeat the reminder in a little while, click the Snooze to Be Reminded Again In list box, specify how long Outlook must wait to remind you again, and then click the Snooze button. If you don't want to be reminded again, click the Dismiss button.

The Reminder feature works only when Outlook is running (you can minimize the program so it doesn't clutter your screen). If you want to be reminded of appointments, don't exit Outlook. If it's shut down, it can't do *anything* for you.

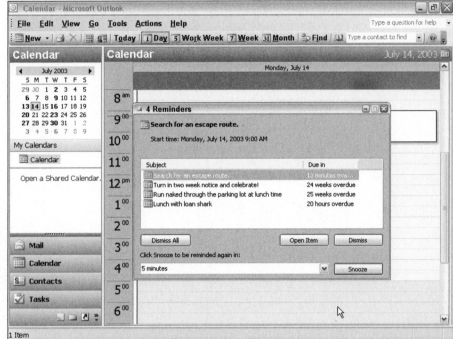

Seeing the big picture of your appointments

Outlook offers several different ways to display your appointments:

- ✔ **Day:** Shows a single day, hour by hour (refer to Figure 16-1), so you can see what appointments you may have already missed today.

- ✔ **Work Week:** Shows all appointments for a single week (see Figure 16-4) except Sundays and Saturdays.

- ✔ **Week:** Shows all appointments for a single week, including weekends (see Figure 16-5) so you won't forget that Saturday golf game.

- ✔ **Month:** Shows all appointments for a calendar month (see Figure 16-6) so you can keep track of appointments for several weeks in advance.

To switch to a particular view in Outlook, follow these steps:

1. Choose Go⇨Calendar or press Ctrl+2.

The Calendar view appears (refer to Figure 16-1).

2. **Click one of the following icons in the Outlook toolbar:**

   • **Today:** Displays the appointments for the current day.

   • **Day:** Displays the day currently highlighted in the calendar.

   • **Work Week:** Displays appointments for the week that contains the day currently highlighted in the calendar.

   • **Week:** Displays appointments for the week that contains the day currently highlighted in the calendar, including weekends.

   • **Month:** Displays appointments for the month shown by the calendar.

Changing an appointment

Because appointments can always change or get cancelled, you may need to edit an appointment by following these steps:

1. **Choose Go⇨Calendar or press Ctrl+2.**

   The Calendar view appears (refer to Figure 16-1).

2. **Click the appointment that you want to edit.**

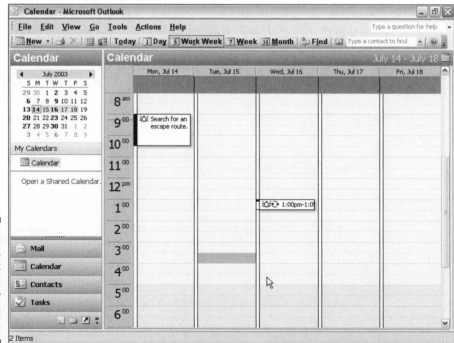

Figure 16-4:
The Outlook Work Week view: Monday through Friday.

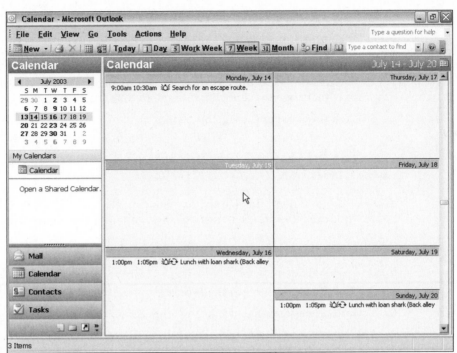

Figure 16-5:
The Outlook
Week view.

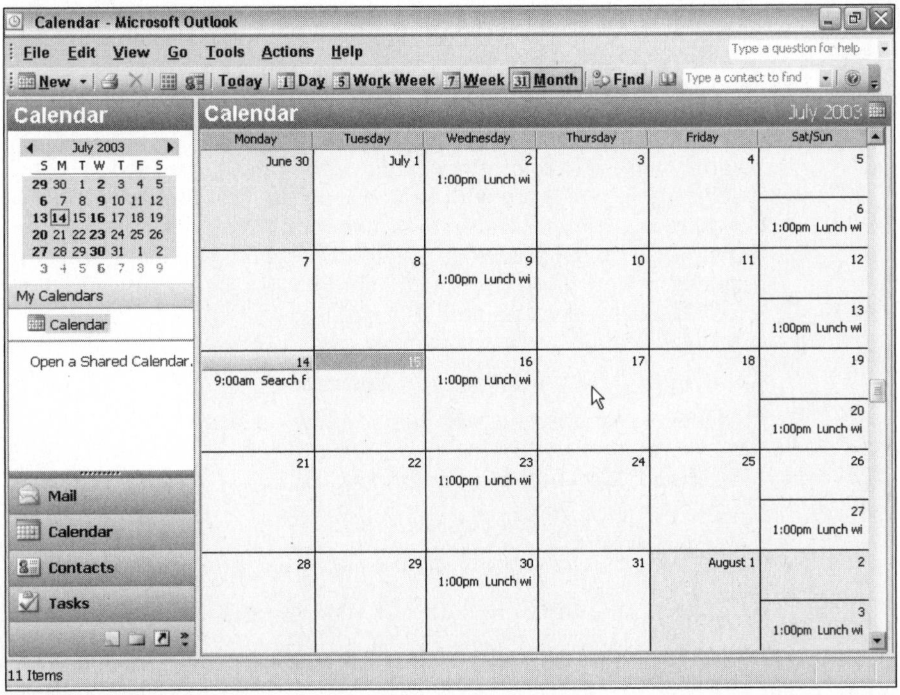

Figure 16-6:
The Outlook
Month view.

3. **Press Ctrl+O or double-click the appointment that you want to modify.**

   The Appointment dialog box appears (refer to Figure 16-2).

4. **Make your changes to the appointment.**

   For example, click the Start Time or End Time list box and type a new time to change the start or end time or date for your appointment.

5. **Click the Save and Close button.**

Deleting an appointment

After an appointment has passed or been canceled, you can delete it to make room for other appointments. To delete an appointment, follow these steps:

1. **Choose Go⇨Calendar or press Ctrl+2.**

   The Calendar view appears (refer to Figure 16-1).

2. **Click the appointment that you want to delete.**

   Outlook highlights your chosen appointment.

3. **Choose Edit⇨Delete, press Ctrl+D, or click the Delete icon in the Outlook toolbar.**

If you delete an appointment by mistake, press Ctrl+Z to recover it.

Defining a recurring appointment

You may have an appointment that occurs every day, week, month, or year (such as going to lunch with the boss on the first Monday of the month or checking into a motel that rents by the hour every Friday evening). Instead of typing recurring appointments again and again, you can enter them once, then define how often they occur. Outlook automatically schedules those appointments unless you tell it not to.

Creating a new recurring appointment

To define a recurring appointment, follow these steps:

1. **Choose Go⇨Calendar or press Ctrl+2.**

   The Calendar view appears (refer to Figure 16-1).

2. **Choose Actions⇨New Recurring Appointment.**

   The Appointment Recurrence window appears, as shown in Figure 16-7.

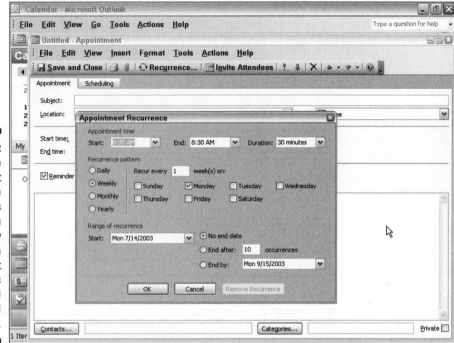

Figure 16-7:
The
Appointment
Recurrence
window is
where you
specify how
often an
appointment
occurs
again and
again and
again.

3. **Click the Start list box and enter the start time for your recurring appointment by clicking the down-pointing arrow until the right time shows up.**

   You can also type a time, such as **8:13 AM**, in the Start list box.

4. **Click the End list box and enter the end time for your recurring appointment.**

5. **Click the Duration list box and choose the length of your appointment.**

6. **Click one of the following radio buttons to specify the frequency of the appointment: Daily, Weekly, Monthly, or Yearly (or choose a specific day, such as Sunday or Tuesday).**

7. **In the Range of Recurrence area, click the Start list box and click the date that corresponds to the first instance of your recurring appointment.**

8. **Click one of the radio buttons in the Range of Recurrence area to define when you want the appointments to stop recurring.**

   You can specify a number of occurrences (End after), an end date (End by), or no ending at all (No end date).

9. **Click OK.**

   The Appointment window appears for you to define your recurring appointment.

10. **Type your appointment in the Subject box (for example,** leave work early**).**

11. **Type the location of your appointment in the Location box.**

12. **Click the Reminder list box and choose how early you want Outlook to remind you of your appointment.**

13. **Click the Show Time As list box and choose Free, Tentative, Busy, or Out of Office.**

    Step 9 in the "Editing an appointment" section has information about these options.

14. **Click the Save and Close button.**

    Outlook displays your appointment on-screen, as shown in Figure 16-8. Recurring appointments show revolving arrows next to the descriptions.

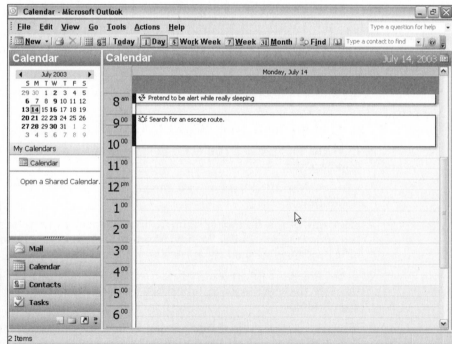

Figure 16-8:
Outlook
identifies a
recurring
appointment
with a
circular
indicator.

You can make any existing appointment recur by double-clicking it and then clicking the Recurrence icon on the toolbar. (Logical, isn't it?)

Editing a recurring appointment

To edit a recurring appointment, follow these steps:

1. **Choose Go⇨Calendar or press Ctrl+2.**

   The Calendar view appears (refer to Figure 16-1).

2. **Double-click the recurring appointment that you want to edit, press Ctrl+O, or right-click and choose Open.**

   The Open Recurring Item dialog box appears.

3. **Click one of the following radio buttons:**

   - **Open This Occurrence:** You can edit just this specific appointment (for example, just the instance that occurs on October 18).

   - **Open the Series:** You can edit all the recurring appointments (for example, all your "leave work early on Friday" appointments).

   Outlook displays the Appointment Recurrence dialog box, as in Figure 16-7.

4. **Make any changes to your recurring appointment (such as changing start time or day of occurrence), and then click the Save and Close button.**

Printing Your Schedule

You may occasionally need to print your appointment schedule on paper so that you can look at it without using electricity or copy it for all your fans and relatives.

Previewing your schedule

Before you waste paper to find out that Outlook didn't print what you really wanted, check a print preview of your schedule. For a preview, follow these steps:

1. **Choose Go⇨Calendar or press Ctrl+2.**

   The Calendar view appears (see Figure 16-1).

2. **Choose File⇨Print Preview.**

   Outlook displays a schedule, as shown in Figure 16-9.

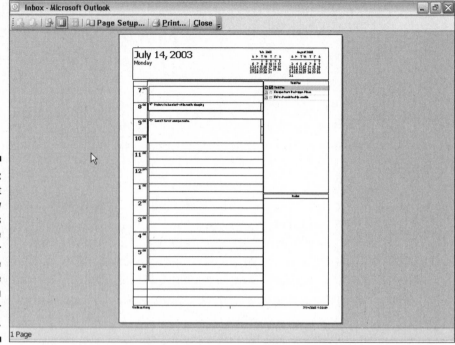

Figure 16-9:
The Print Preview feature lets you see what your schedule looks like before you waste paper printing it.

3. **Click Print to print it or click Close to exit the Print Preview window.**

   If you click Print, a Print dialog box appears, as explained in the following section, "Printing your schedule."

Printing your schedule

To print your appointment schedule, follow these steps:

1. **Choose Go⇨Calendar or press Ctrl+2.**

   The Calendar view appears (refer to Figure 16-1).

2. **Choose one of the following:**

   • Choose File⇨Print.

   • Press Ctrl+P.

   • Click the Print icon on the Standard toolbar.

   The Print dialog box appears, as shown in Figure 16-10.

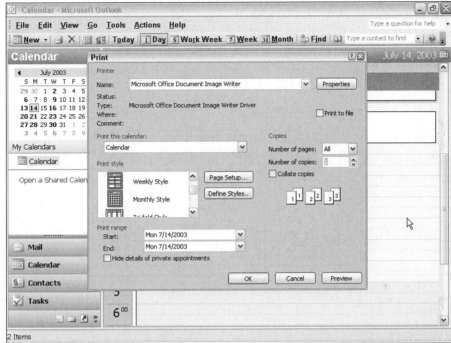

Figure 16-10:
The Print
dialog box
lets you
specify a
print style.

If you click the Print icon on the Standard toolbar, Outlook prints your entire appointment schedule without giving you a chance to do Steps 3 through 5.

3. Click a style in the Print Style box (such as Weekly Style or Monthly Style).

This is where you can define the time frame for printing your schedule.

4. Click the Preview button to preview your printed schedule.

To specify a printout size for your day planner, click the Page Setup button, click the Paper tab, and choose an option in the Size list box — booklet, a Day-Timer page, a Day-Runner page, or a Franklin Day Planner page.

5. Click the Print button to start printing.

Part VI
Storing Stuff in Access

In this part . . .

Personal computers provide an excellent tool for storing large chunks of information in databases so you don't have to store this same information in filing cabinets. Databases cannot only store huge amounts of data, but they can also sort and search through that data as well, which makes them particularly valuable to businesses that need to track their customers, inventories, or assets. So it's no surprise that the more advanced (and expensive) versions of Microsoft Office 2003 include a special database program called (what's in a name?) Access.

For those of you who enjoy deciphering computer terminology, Access is a relational database. For those of you who prefer English, the previous sentence means that Access lets you store lots of stuff in a variety of different ways so you can find it again — fast — when you need it.

This part of the book gets you started storing stuff in Access. The goal is to get you feeling comfortable enough to create databases with Access so you can store great huge stockpiles of useful (or if you're at work, useless) information in your computer.

Chapter 17

Using a Database

In This Chapter

▶ Understanding database basics

▶ Entering your data

▶ Viewing your data

Despite the power of personal computers, many people still store important names, addresses, and phone numbers in Rolodex files, on index cards, or on sheets of paper stuffed into folders. Although sometimes convenient, paper is terrible for retrieving and analyzing information. Just look at a typical file cabinet and ask yourself how much time you need to find the names and phone numbers of every customer who lives in Missouri *and* ordered more than $5,000 worth of your products in the past six months. (Frightening isn't it?)

Instead of racking your memory or hunting for slips of paper, try using Microsoft Access to organize your information. Access enables you to store, retrieve, sort, manipulate, and analyze information — making trends or patterns in your data easier to spot (so you can tell whether your company is losing money). The more you know about your information, the better off you are when dealing with less knowledgeable competitors, coworkers, or supervisors.

If you just need to store names and addresses, you may find Outlook much easier and faster than Access. (For more on Outlook, check out Part V.) If you need to store more complicated information, such as customer invoices or inventory part numbers, use Access.

Database Basics 101

Access is a *programmable relational database,* which may sound intimidating (or stupid), but it boils down to a simple idea: Access is nothing more than a fancy virtual file cabinet. You dump information in and yank it back out again, almost instantly, without squashing your fingers. Before you can perform this feat, however, you have to tell the program what type of information you want to store. A typical Access file (stored on your hard disk with the funny file extension .mdb, which stands for *Microsoft database*) consists of the following elements:

- ✔ **One or more fields:** A *field* contains one chunk of data, such as a name, fax number, or a telephone number.

- ✔ **One or more records:** A *record* contains two or more related fields. For example, each employee record could contain one person's name, address, phone number, and employee ID number.

- ✔ **One or more database tables:** A *database table* stores your information and displays it as one or more records in rows and columns, much like a spreadsheet. Database tables are convenient for viewing multiple records at one time, such as sorting all records alphabetically by last name.

- ✔ **One or more forms:** A *form* typically displays one record at a time, such as showing one person's name, address, and phone number. Forms provide a convenient way to enter and view data for a single record stored in a database table.

- ✔ **One or more reports:** A *report* contains predefined ways to display your data either on-screen or in print. (For example, you could print out a list of employees who earn more than $50,000 a year and work in Iowa.) Reports help you make sense of the data stored in your database.

At the simplest level, you can use Access just for storing data, such as the names of your friends, their addresses, their mobile phone numbers, and their birthdays.

On a more complicated level, you can write miniature programs in Access to fit a specific purpose, such as managing inventory in an electronics company or creating a mailing list program for charities.

This book focuses mostly on the simpler uses for Access in storing data and getting it back out again. If you want to learn more about designing custom databases, pick up a copy of *Access 2003 For Dummies,* by John Kaufeld (published by Wiley Publishing, Inc).

Creating a new database file with a Wizard

Think of a database as a file cabinet devoted to holding one type of data — say information related to taxes or to tracking the inventory in your business. When you want to create a database, Access gives you two choices.

✔ **You can create an entire database from scratch,** defining the fields (such as name, phone number, part number, or birth date) that describe the type of information you want the database to hold.

✔ **You can use the Access Database Wizard** to help speed you through the process of creating a database. When you create a database using the Access Database Wizard, Access creates a special window for your database called the *Main Switchboard window*. The Main Switchboard window provides a list of actions you can use with your database data (such as adding new data), so you don't have to use an Access form or table yourself.

Most of the time, the Access Database Wizard is the easier way to create a database. Remember, you can always modify a database after you create it with the wizard. Leave starting from scratch to those with too much time on their hands.

To create a new database file by using the Database Wizard, follow these steps:

1. **Choose File➪New.**

   The New File task pane appears, as shown in Figure 17-1, giving you a choice of creating a new database or opening an existing one.

   If you click Templates Home Page under the Templates on Microsoft.com category, you can view more predefined Access templates that you can use to create your database file.

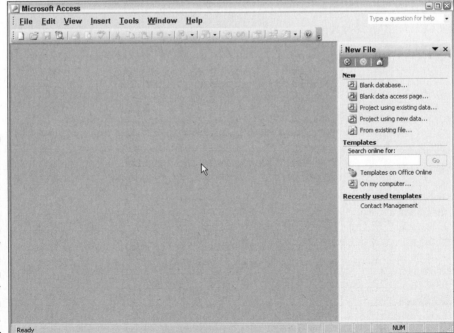

Figure 17-1: The New File task pane where you can create a new database from scratch or from a template.

2. **Click the On My Computer option under the Templates category.**

   The Templates dialog box appears.

3. **Click the Databases tab.**

   Access shows you a list of predefined databases that you can customize, as shown in Figure 17-2.

4. **Click the type of database that you want to use (such as Asset Tracking, Inventory Control, or Contact Management) and then click OK.**

   Note: Depending on which database you choose, what Access shows you differs slightly from what you see in this book. The figures in this chapter show what happens when you choose the Contact Management Database Wizard.

   The File New Database dialog box appears.

5. **Type a name for your database in the File Name box and click the Create button.**

   If you want to store your database in a specific folder, click the Save In list box and choose the folder.

   After a few seconds, the Database Wizard dialog box appears, letting you know the type of information that the database will store.

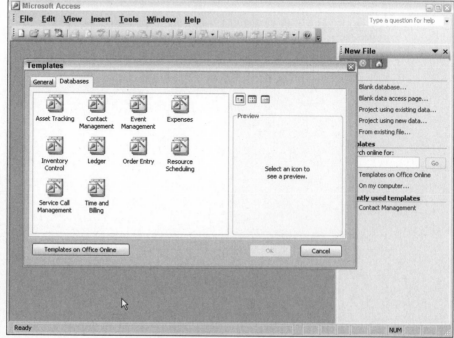

Figure 17-2:
The Templates dialog box lets you choose one of many predesigned databases.

6. **Click Next.**

   Another Database Wizard dialog box appears, listing the tables and fields that it's ready to create, as shown in Figure 17-3.

7. **Click the check boxes of the additional fields that you want to store in your database (or clear any check boxes of fields that you don't want to include in your database) and then click Next.**

   If your database consists of two or more tables, you may have to click each table on the left side of the Database Wizard dialog box and then repeat Step 6 to choose any additional fields to add for each database table.

   Still another Database Wizard dialog box appears, giving you the chance to select a background picture for your database forms, as shown in Figure 17-4.

8. **Choose a screen display style (choose Standard if you don't like fancy backgrounds) and click Next.**

   Another Database Wizard dialog box appears, asking what style you want to use for printed reports, as shown in Figure 17-5. A *report* is a printed copy of your database information. A style makes your report look interesting (even if you have nothing important to say).

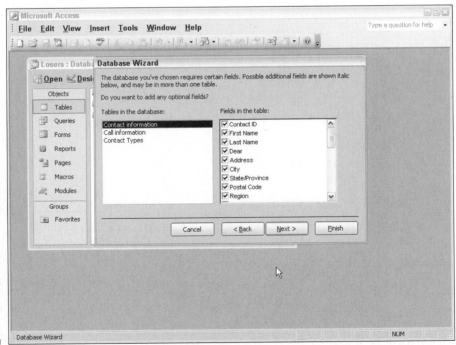

Figure 17-3: The Database Wizard lists the tables and fields it will create for your database.

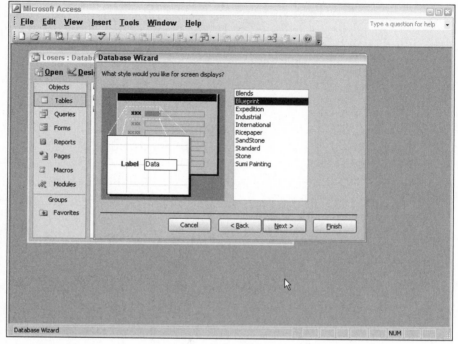

Figure 17-4:
You can
choose
different
back-
grounds
for your
database.

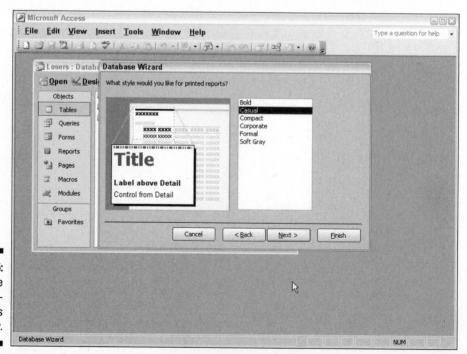

Figure 17-5:
Styles make
your data-
base reports
look fancy.

To help you pick the style best suited to your needs, click several different styles, one at a time, and check out the left window to see what each
style looks like.

9. **Choose a style and then click Next.**

One more Database Wizard dialog box appears, asking you for a database title and if you want to add a picture on your reports. (Access displays the database title on the Main Switchboard window. The database
title is purely decorative; it doesn't affect the design or organization of
your database at all.)

10. **Type a title for your database (such as Valuable Names or People
I Have to Deal With) and then click Next.**

The last Database Wizard dialog box appears, letting you know that it's
finished asking you annoying questions. If you want to start using your
database right away, make sure the Yes, Start the Database check box is
selected.

11. **Click Finish.**

Access creates your database and displays the Main Switchboard
window (a simple user interface for accessing your database), as shown
in Figure 17-6.

After you create a database, you can open it again if you choose File➪Open
or press Ctrl+O.

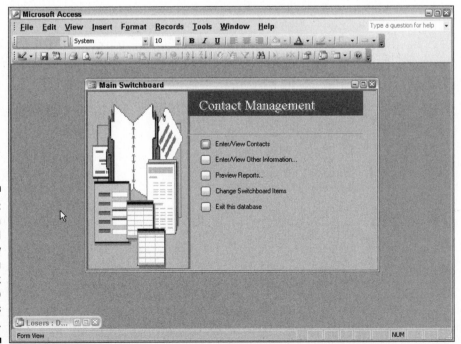

Figure 17-6:
The Main
Switchboard
window
gives you
one-click
access to
your Access
database.

Looking at the parts of your database

When Access uses a wizard to create a database, the database actually consists of two separate windows:

✔ The Main Switchboard window

✔ The Database window

The Main Switchboard window provides a simple one-click method of using your database so you can view, edit, and print your database information. (Refer to Figure 17-6.)

If you create a database without using the Access Database Wizard, your database won't have a Main Switchboard window.

The Database window shows all the separate parts (reports, modules, forms, tables, and macros) that make up your entire database, as shown in Figure 17-7.

A report allows you to print or view specific data from your database.

Figure 17-7: The Database window shows the different parts that make up your Access database.

To switch between the Main Switchboard window and the Database window, choose Window⇨Main Switchboard or Window⇨Database.

The whole purpose of the Main Switchboard window is to hide the ugly details of managing a database. If you really want to get involved with creating, modifying, and programming Access, switch to the Database window. If you just want to use a database and couldn't care less about the fine details, use the Main Switchboard window instead.

Putting Information into a Database

After Access creates a database, the new database is completely empty (and also completely useless) until you start stuffing your own information into it.

As you type data into a database, Access automatically saves it to disk. (In other Office 2003 programs, such as Word or Excel, you have to manually save your data by pressing Ctrl+S.) When you choose File⇨Save in Access, you save the design and structure of your database, not just the data itself.

Entering data through the Main Switchboard

The easiest way to stuff data into a new or existing database is from the Main Switchboard window. To use the Main Switchboard window to add new data, follow these steps:

1. **Open the database that you want to use and choose Window⇨Main Switchboard.**

   The Main Switchboard window appears.

2. **Click one of the Enter/View buttons on the Main Switchboard window.**

   For example, if you want to add a new contact in the database displayed in Figure 17-6, click Enter/View Contacts.

   Access displays a form, showing the first record in your database and the fields where you can type information, as shown in Figure 17-8.

3. **Click the field where you want to add data (such as First Name or Address); then type the data.**

4. **To type data for the next record, choose Insert⇨New Record, press Ctrl++ (plus sign), click the New Record icon that appears on the Form View toolbar, or click the Next Record button on the form.**

   Access displays a blank record.

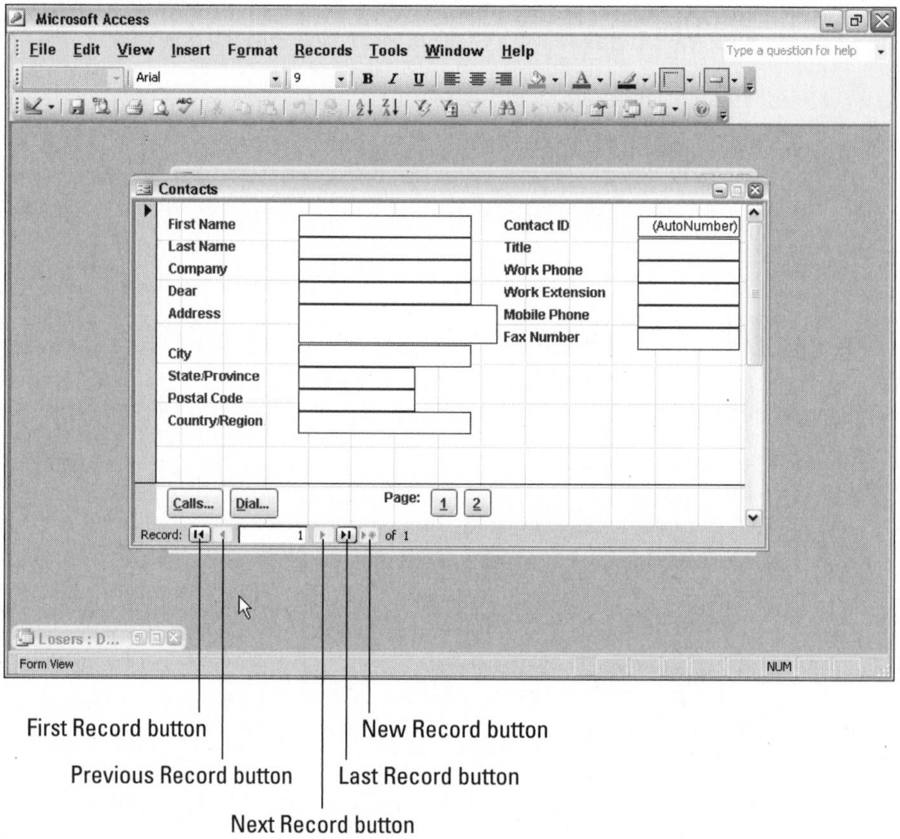

Figure 17-8:
A typical
form for
typing
information
into a
database.

First Record button

Previous Record button

Next Record button

New Record button

Last Record button

5. **Repeat Steps 3 and 4 for each new record that you want to add to your database.**

6. **After you enter the data you want, click the Close box of the form window.**

If you have several records in a database, you can view them by clicking one of the following buttons that appear on the database form:

✔ **First Record button:** Displays the first record of the database

✔ **Previous Record button:** Displays the record that comes before the one you're currently viewing

✔ **Next Record button:** Displays the record that comes after the one you're currently viewing

✔ **Last Record button:** Displays the last record of the database

Entering data through a table or form

If you don't use the Main Switchboard, you can enter data using the Database window. When you use the database window, you can either enter data through a table or through a form. Entering data in a table lets you see multiple records at once in rows and columns like a spreadsheet. Entering data in a form lets you see one record at a time in a window that resembles a paper form.

Access doesn't care whether you enter data in a form or a table, because forms and tables are just different ways of viewing the same data anyway.

Entering data into a form is equivalent to using the Main Switchboard to enter data.

To enter data in a table or form, follow these steps:

1. **Open an existing database.**

2. **Choose Window⇨Database.**

   Access displays the Database window (refer to Figure 17-7).

3. **Click the Tables icon or Forms icon in the Objects panel (the left panel) of the Database window.**

4. **Double-click the table or form that you want to use to enter data.**

   Access displays your chosen table or form, as shown in Figure 17-9.

5. **Type your data in the appropriate fields.**

   To move from one field to another, use the mouse, press Tab, or press Shift+Tab.

6. **When you finish, click the Close box of the Table or Form window.**

Deleting data

Eventually, you may want to delete individual field data or even entire records. For example, you may have a record in your database containing information about someone who you never want to speak to again, such as a former spouse or roommate. Rather than have that person's name and address constantly haunt you by their existence in your database, you can delete that record and (figuratively) eliminate that person's name from the face of the earth — or at least the face of your computer.

Delete Record icon

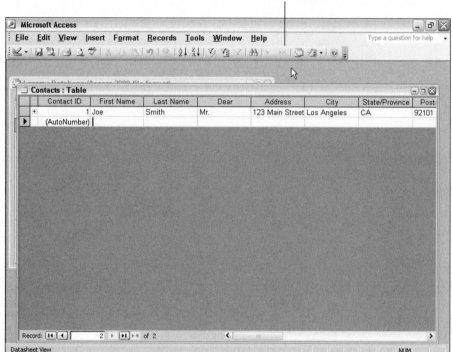

Access provides two ways to delete data:

- ✔ Just delete the information stored in a field (useful for editing a single field, such as the address of someone who has moved).

- ✔ Delete all the information stored in an entire record (useful for wiping out all traces of a single record, which can be handy to completely obliterate all information about a person who no longer works for your company).

Deleting data in a field

To delete data stored in a field, follow these steps:

1. **Follow the steps in the "Entering data through the Main Switchboard" section or "Entering data through a table or form" section until you find the record containing data that you want to delete.**

2. **Click the field that contains the data that you want to delete.**

3. **Choose one of the following methods to delete the data:**

   • Press Delete or Backspace to delete one character at a time.

   • Drag the mouse to select the data; then press Delete or Backspace to delete the entire selection.

Deleting an entire record

Deleting a single field or two can be useful for editing your records. But if you want to wipe out an entire record altogether, follow these steps:

1. **Follow the steps in the "Entering data through the Main Switchboard" section or "Entering data through a table or form" section until you find the record containing data that you want to delete.**

2. **Choose Edit⇨Select Record.**

   Access highlights your chosen record.

3. **Choose Edit⇨Delete, press Delete, or click the Delete Record icon on the Form View toolbar.**

   A dialog box appears, warning that if you continue, your deleted record will be lost for good.

4. **Click the Yes button (but only if you're sure that you want to delete your chosen record forever). Otherwise click the No button.**

Make sure that you really want to delete the entire record. You won't be able to retrieve your deleted data afterwards.

Modifying the Structure of a Database

Although Access provides predefined databases that you can use, you may want to create a database from scratch or modify an existing database. The two most common parts of a database that you may need to add, delete, or modify are tables and forms.

Tables display data in row and column format, much like a spreadsheet. *Forms* display data like a paper form on the screen.

Adding a table

To add a table to an existing Access database file, follow these steps:

1. **Open an existing database.**

2. **Choose Window⇨Database.**

   Access displays the Database window (refer to Figure 17-7).

3. **Click the Tables icon in the Object panel of the Database window.**

4. **Double-click the Create Table by Using Wizard icon.**

   The Table Wizard dialog box appears, as shown in Figure 17-10.

5. **Click the Business or Personal radio button.**

   Access displays a list of common fields for Business or Personal databases.

6. **Click the Sample Tables list box and choose the table that most closely matches the table you want to create (such as Contacts or Mailing List).**

7. **Click the Sample Fields list box and click the field that most closely matches the field you want to create (such as LastName or City).**

8. **Click the right arrow (>) button.**

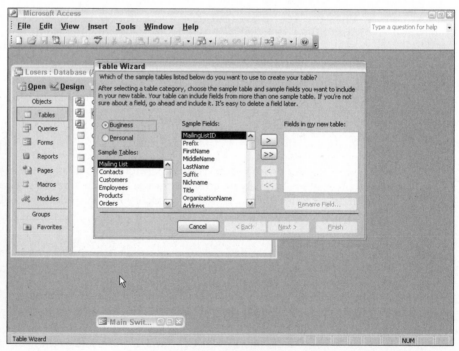

Figure 17-10: The Table Wizard dialog box can guide you through the steps in creating a new table for your database file.

Access displays your chosen field in the Fields in My New Table list box. If you click the Rename Field button, you can (guess what?) rename a field.

9. **Repeat Steps 7 and 8 for each field you want to add.**

10. **Click Next.**

Another Table Wizard dialog box appears.

11. **Type a name for your table and click Next.**

Still another Table Wizard dialog box appears, asking you whether your new table contains records related to other tables stored in your database. Multiple tables can share the same fields, such as a Customer ID or a Company Name field. When two tables share the same field, you only need to type the data in that particular field once, and it shows up in multiple places.

12. **Click Next.**

A final Table Wizard dialog box appears, asking whether you want to modify the design of your table or start entering data right away.

13. **Click one of the options (such as Enter Data Directly into the Table) and click Finish.**

If you click the Enter Data Into the Table Using a Form the Wizard Creates for Me radio button, Access creates a plain-looking form where you can start typing in data.

What the heck is a relational database?

Sometimes people refer to Access as a *relational database*. This term means that one database table stores information that's identical to information stored in another database table.

The reason for doing this is partly out of laziness but mostly out of usefulness. For example, you might have one database table that stores employee ID numbers, names, addresses, and phone numbers. Then you might have a second database table that lists employee ID numbers along with the current salaries for each person. Obviously, some of the same employee ID numbers need to be appear in each database table,

so rather than force you to type this same information twice, the two database tables share this identical information between themselves, hence the term "relation" or "relational").

By sharing identical information between database tables, you can reduce typing identical information over and over again and store data separately so one database table doesn't have to list everything (such as cramming employee address information in the same database table as employee salary information).

Deleting a table

You may want to delete a table if you don't need to save the information stored in it.

Deleting a table wipes out any information, such as names and addresses, stored in that table. So make sure you really want to delete a table and all the data in it. If you delete a table, any forms you created to display that data will be useless. If you're deleting a table, you should delete any forms that display data stored in that table.

To delete a table, follow these steps:

1. **Open an existing database.**

2. **Choose Window➪Database.**

   Access displays the Database window (refer to Figure 17-7).

3. **Click the Tables icon in the Object panel of the Database window.**

4. **Click the table that you want to delete.**

5. **Choose Edit➪Delete, press Delete, or click the Delete icon in the Database toolbar.**

   A dialog box asks whether you really want to delete your chosen table. If your table contains data related to other tables, Access displays a dialog box alerting you to this fact and giving you a chance to delete your table anyway.

6. **Click Yes.**

Press Ctrl+Z if you suddenly decide you don't want to delete your table after all.

Modifying a table

After you create a table, you may want to modify the table (but not the data stored in the table). You may have forgotten to create a field to store a person's employee IDLikewise, you may suddenly decide that you don't want to store phone numbers, so you can delete that field.

Adding a new field to a table

To add a field to a table, follow these steps:

1. **Open an existing database.**

2. **Choose Window➪Database.**

   Access displays the Database window (refer to Figure 17-7).

3. **Click the Tables icon in the Object panel of the Database window.**

4. **Click the table where you want to add a new field.**

5. **Click the Design icon in the Database toolbar or right-click the table and choose Design View.**

   A Table window appears, as shown in Figure 17-11.

6. **Click the row where you want to insert your new field.**

   Access doesn't care where you insert your new field. The location of a field is for your convenience, such as listing the First Name and Last Name fields next to each other.

7. **Choose Insert⇨Rows, or click the Insert Rows icon on the Table Design toolbar.**

   Access inserts a blank row in your table.

8. **Type your field name under the Field Name column.**

9. **Click the Data Type column.**

   A downward-pointing arrow appears in the Data Type cell, and a Field Properties pane appears at the bottom of the screen.

Insert Rows icon   Delete Rows icon

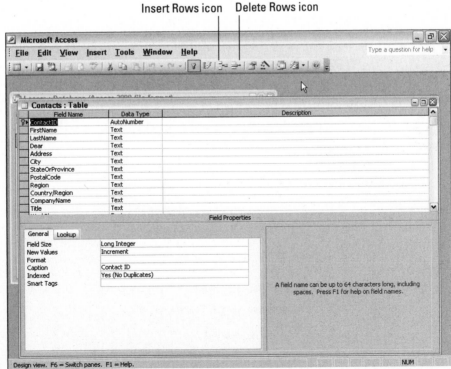

Figure 17-11:
The Table window shows you all the fields used to store data.

10. **Click the downward-pointing arrow in the Data Type column and choose the type of data you want to store, such as Text or Date/Time.**

    Depending on the data type, you can define the maximum number of characters or the values the field can accept.

11. **Click the Close box of the Table window.**

    A dialog box appears, asking if you want to save the changes to your table.

12. **Click Yes.**

Modifying a field in a table

After you create a table, define various fields (such as Name, Phone, or Employee Nickname), and type actual data (such as Bob, 555-1234, or LoserBoss), you may realize that a field needs modification. You may have initially defined a field so small that data appears cut off. Or you may want to display numbers as currency instead of in scientific notation. To modify a field in a table, follow these steps:

1. **Open an existing database.**

2. **Choose Window⇨Database.**

    Access displays the Database window (refer to Figure 17-7).

3. **Click the Tables icon in the Object panel of the Database window.**

4. **Click the table where you want to modify an existing field.**

5. **Click the Design icon in the Database toolbar or right-click the table and choose Design View.**

    A Table window appears (refer to Figure 17-11).

6. **Click the field that you want to modify and type or edit the field name.**

7. **Click the Data Type column.**

8. **Click the downward-pointing arrow in the Data Type column and choose the type of data you want to store, such as Text or Date/Time.**

    Depending on the data type you choose, you can modify the field properties by defining the maximum number of characters or the acceptable values the field can accept.

    Changing the field name or the data type to store won't change any data already stored in those fields. Changing the data type simply modifies the way the data looks.

9. **Click the Close box of the Table window.**

    A dialog box appears, asking if you want to save the changes to your table.

10. **Click Yes.**

Deleting a field from a table

To delete a field from a table, follow these steps:

1. **Open an existing database.**

2. **Choose Window⇨Database.**

   Access displays the Database window (refer to Figure 17-7).

3. **Click the Tables icon in the left panel of the Database window.**

4. **Click the table where you want to delete an existing field.**

5. **Click the Design icon in the Database toolbar or right-click the table and choose Design View.**

   A Table window appears (refer to Figure 17-11).

6. **Click the gray box to the left of the field (row) that you want to delete.**

   Access highlights the entire row.

7. **Choose Edit⇨Delete, or press Delete.**

   If the field contains data, a dialog box appears, asking whether you really want to delete the field and any data that may be stored in that field. If the field is empty, no dialog box appears, and you can skip to Step 9.

8. **Click Yes.**

9. **Click the Close box of the Table window.**

   A dialog box asks if you want to save the changes that you made to your table.

10. **Click Yes.**

Adding a form

A form mimics a paper form by providing an organized way to view and enter data. Because a form can display your data in different ways, you may later find that all your current forms display too much (or too little) data for certain uses. For example, you may need one form to display the names and medical insurance numbers of people, and a completely different form to display those same people's names, addresses, phone numbers, and contact information.

Multiple forms can customize the viewing and adding of data to your Access database for specific tasks. To add a form to your database file, follow these steps:

1. **Open an existing database.**

2. **Choose Window⇨Database.**

   Access displays the Database window (refer to Figure 17-7).

3. **Click the Forms icon in the Object panel of the Database window.**

4. **Double-click the Create Form by Using Wizard icon.**

   A Form Wizard dialog box appears (as shown in Figure 17-12), offering you a choice of which fields to display on your form.

5. **Click the Tables/Queries list box and choose a table containing the data you want to display on your form.**

6. **Click the Available Fields list box and choose the field you want to add to your form.**

   You can choose fields from two or more database tables if you select a different database table in Step 5 and then choose fields from that database table in Step 6.

7. **Click the right arrow (>) button to add fields to the Selected Fields list.**

8. **Repeat Steps 6 and 7 for each field you want to display on your form.**

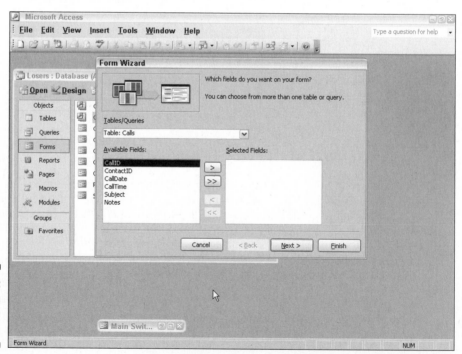

Figure 17-12:
The Form Wizard dialog box.

9. **Click Next.**

   A Form Wizard dialog box appears and asks how you want to view your data. (If you only chose fields in Step 6 from a single database table, you won't see this dialog box, and you can skip to Step 11.)

10. **Click one of the displayed options for displaying your data and click Next.**

    Another Form Wizard dialog box asks you to choose a layout for your form. If you chose to display fields from two or more database tables, the Form Wizard dialog box appears and asks how you want to view your data.

11. **Click one of the options (such as Tabular or Justified) and click Next.**

    Yet another Form Wizard dialog box asks you to choose a style for your form.

12. **Click a form style such as Blueprint or Sandstone and click Next.**

    A final Form Wizard dialog box asks for a title for your form.

13. **Type a name for your form and click Finish.**

    Access displays your form as shown in Figure 17-13.

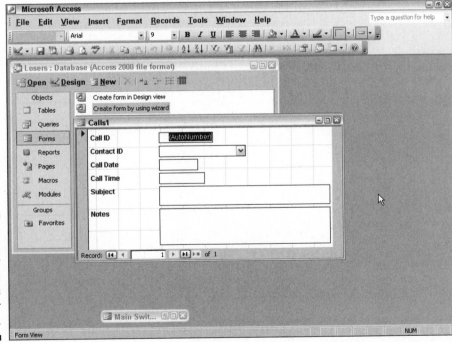

Figure 17-13: A typical form for displaying the contents of your database.

Deleting a form

If you delete a form, you can't recover it again. Make sure you really want to delete the form before you do so.

When you delete a form, you do not delete any data that the form displays. (If you want to delete the actual data stored in Access, you have to delete the table containing that data. Refer to the earlier section "Deleting data.")

When you want to delete a form, just follow these steps:

1. **Open an existing database.**

2. **Choose Window⇨Database.**

   Access displays the Database window. (Refer to Figure 17-7.)

3. **Click the Forms icon in the Object panel of the Database window.**

4. **Click the form that you want to delete.**

5. **Choose Edit⇨Delete, press Delete, or click the Delete icon in the Database toolbar.**

   A dialog box asks whether you really want to delete your chosen table.

6. **Click Yes.**

   Access deletes your chosen form for good.

Modifying a form

Forms display data on the screen, making it easy for people to view or type in new information. The most common items to modify on a form are labels and text boxes.

Labels are purely decorative but are often used to describe what type of information appears in a text box, such as a First Name or Telephone Number. *Text boxes* provide a blank box where actual data appears.

There are many ways to modify a form, but the most common way is to add or delete a new field that appears on a form. For more information on the different ways to modify a form, pick up a copy of *Access 2003 For Dummies*, by John Kaufeld (published by Wiley Publishing, Inc).

Adding a new field to a form

If you want to add a new field, you need to add a text box (to hold the actual data) and a label (to describe the type of information that someone should type in the text box). To add a text box (field) to a form, follow these steps:

1. **Open an existing database.**

2. **Choose Window⇨Database.**

   Access displays the Database window (refer to Figure 17-7).

3. **Click the Forms icon in the Object panel of the Database window.**

4. **Click the form that you want to modify.**

5. **Click the Design icon in the Database toolbar or right-click the table and choose Design View.**

   Access displays your form and a Form toolbox, as shown in Figure 17-14.

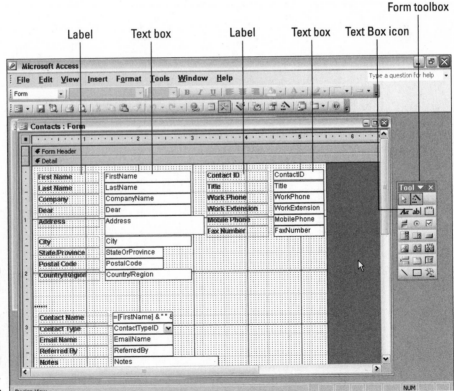

Figure 17-14:
When you add fields to a form, you need to add a label and a text box.

6. **Click the Text Box icon in the Form toolbox.**

   The mouse cursor changes into a crosshair with a Text Box icon attached to it.

7. **Move the mouse to the spot on the form where you want to draw your text box.**

8. **Hold down the left mouse button and drag the mouse to draw the text box.**

9. **Release the left mouse button when the text box is the size you want it.**

   Access draws the text box and automatically draws an accompanying label to go along with your newly drawn text box.

10. **Right-click the text box and choose Properties.**

   A Text Box properties dialog box appears, as shown in Figure 17-15.

11. **Click the Control Source box.**

   A downward-pointing arrow appears.

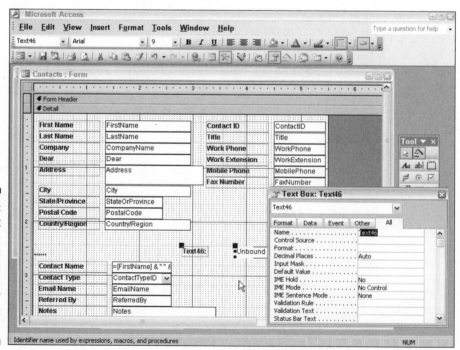

Figure 17-15: The Text Box properties dialog box lets you define how your text box behaves.

12. **Click the downward-pointing arrow.**

    A list of fields stored in your database appears.

13. **Click a data source, such as FirstName or Address.**

    The data source tells Access what type of data to display in your newly created text box.

14. **Click the Close box of the Text Box properties dialog box.**

15. **Double-click the Field label.**

    A Label Properties dialog box appears.

16. **Click the Caption box and type a caption for your new field (such as Employee ID or Marital Status).**

    Whatever you type in the Caption box appears on your form.

17. **Click the Close box of the Label Properties dialog box.**

18. **Click the Close box of the Form window.**

    A dialog box appears, asking if you want to save changes to your form.

19. **Click Yes.**

Modifying a field on a form

After you create a field, you may need to resize or move the field so it looks nice and pretty on your form. To resize a field, follow these steps:

1. **Open an existing database.**

2. **Choose Window⇨Database.**

    Access displays the Database window (refer to Figure 17-7).

3. **Click the Forms icon in the Object panel of the Database window.**

4. **Click the form that you want to modify.**

5. **Click the Design icon in the Database toolbar or right-click the table and choose Design View.**

    Access displays your form along with a Form toolbox.

6. **Click the field or its accompanying caption.**

    Access highlights the field or caption with black handles around its border.

7. Move the mouse over a handle so the mouse cursor turns into a double-pointing arrow.

8. Hold down the left mouse button and drag the mouse to resize the field or caption.

9. Release the left mouse button when the field or caption is the size you want it.

10. Click the Close box of the Form window.

   A dialog box appears, asking if you want to save changes to your form.

11. Click Yes.

To move a field, follow these steps:

1. Open an existing database.

2. Choose Window⇨Database.

   Access displays the Database window (refer to Figure 17-7).

3. Click the Forms icon in the left panel of the Database window.

4. Click the form that you want to modify.

5. Click the Design icon in the Database toolbar or right-click the table and choose Design View.

   Access displays your form along with a Form toolbox.

6. Click the field or its accompanying caption.

   Access highlights the field or caption with black handles around its border. Notice that the biggest handle is in the upper-left corner.

7. Move the mouse over the big handle in the upper-left corner, hold down the left mouse button, and drag the mouse.

   Access shows you the outline of your field or caption as you move it.

8. Release the left mouse button when the field or caption is in the location you want.

9. Click the Close box of the Form window.

   A dialog box appears, asking if you want to save changes to your form.

10. Click Yes.

Deleting a field from a form

To delete a field from a form, follow these steps:

1. **Open an existing database.**

2. **Choose Window⇨Database.**

   Access displays the Database window (refer to Figure 17-7).

3. **Click the Forms icon in the left panel of the Database window.**

4. **Click the form that you want to modify.**

5. **Click the Design icon in the Database toolbar or right-click the table and choose Design View.**

   Access displays your form along with a Form toolbox.

6. **Click the field or its accompanying caption.**

   Access highlights the field or caption with black handles around its border.

7. **Press Delete.**

8. **Click the Close box of the Form window.**

   A dialog box appears, asking if you want to save changes to your form.

9. **Click Yes.**

Saving Your Database

Access gives you two different ways to save your database:

- ✔ As an Access database file (recommended for most cases)
- ✔ As a foreign database file (good for sharing data stored in an Access database with people who use other database programs, such as Paradox or dBASE)

As you edit, delete, and add new data, Access automatically saves the data you type into your database file. However, if you add or delete fields or tables in your database, you must save the design of your database file, which includes any reports, forms, or tables you may have created and modified.

Saving your database as an Access file

To save changes to your database file as an Access file, you need to choose one of the following three methods:

  ✔ Choose File⇨Save.

  ✔ Press Ctrl+S.

  ✔ Click the Save icon on the Standard toolbar.

Exporting to another file format

Despite Microsoft's best efforts to dominate the world without raising the ire of antitrust legislators, not everyone uses Access to store data. In the old days, many people used a slow, cumbersome program called dBASE. Some people eventually graduated to a faster, cumbersome program called Paradox while others defected to rival cumbersome programs with odd names, such as FileMaker or FoxPro.

If you your data with people who don't use Access, export your data from an Access table into a file format that other programs (such as Paradox or FoxPro) can read.

Many people actually use their spreadsheets to store data, so Access can also save its databases as a Lotus 1-2-3 or Excel spreadsheet.

Almost every database program in the world can read dBASE III files. So if you want to share your files with other database programs, such as FileMaker, save your files to dBASE III format. If you want to use one of the newer standards for sharing data, save your files to XML format.

To export an Access database table into a different file format, follow these steps:

1. **Open an existing database.**

2. **Choose Window⇨Database.**

   The Database window appears.

3. **Click Tables in the Object panel of the Database window.**

   Access displays a list of tables in your database.

4. **Click a database table.**

5. **Choose File⇨Export.**

   The Export Table To dialog box appears.

6. **Type a name for your file in the File Name text box.**

7. **Click the Save As Type list box and choose a file format to use, such as dBASE III or Paradox 5.**

8. **Click Save.**

Whenever you have two copies of the same data stored in different files, make sure that any change to one copy of your data is also in the second copy of your data. Otherwise you could wind up with different versions of the same data and then you won't know which copy of your data is the most current and reliable one to use.

Chapter 18

Searching, Sorting, and Making Queries

● ●

In This Chapter

▶ Searching a database

▶ Sorting information in your database

▶ Making and using database queries

● ●

*T*he real power of a computer database comes from its superfast capability to search, sort, and retrieve information that would be too tedious, boring, or frustrating to do with a paper database. Want to know which products are selling the fastest (and which ones deserve to be dropped like a lead anchor)? Access can tell you at the touch of a button. Need to know which of your salespeople are generating the most commissions (and business expenses)? Access can give you this information pronto, too. Knowledge may be power, but until you use the power of a computer database, your information may be out of reach.

Searching a Database

Typical paper databases, such as filing cabinets, Rolodex files, and paper folders, are designed for storing and retrieving information alphabetically. By contrast, Access can find and retrieve information any way you want: by area code, by ZIP code, alphabetically by last name or first name, by state, by date, or whatever.

Access provides two basic ways to search a database:

✔ You can search for a specific record.

✔ You can find one or more records by using a filter.

Access also provides a third way to search a database. You can ask it specific questions called *queries,* which you can find out about in the "Querying a Database" section, later in this chapter.

Finding a specific record

To find a specific record in a database file, you need to know part of the information you want. Because Access can't read your mind, you have to give it clues, such as "Find the name of the person whose fax number is 555-1904" or "Find the phone number of some guy named Bill Gates."

The more specific the data you already know, the faster Access can find the record you want. Asking Access to find the phone number of someone who lives in California takes longer (for example) than asking Access to find the phone number of someone whose last name is Bangladore and lives in California. You may have stored the names of several hundred people who live in California, but how many people in your database have the last name Bangladore?

To find a specific record in a database, follow these steps:

1. **Open the form that displays the information you want to search.**

   For example, if you want to find a customer's phone number, you must first open a form that displays customer phone numbers. You can open a form by clicking one of the Enter/View buttons on the Main Switchboard window, or by choosing Window⇨Database, clicking the Forms icon, and double-clicking the form that you want to display.

2. **Choose Edit⇨Find or press Ctrl+F.**

   The Find command won't appear on the Edit menu until you open a form first.

   The Find and Replace dialog box appears, as shown in Figure 18-1. If you haven't stored any information in your database, Access scolds you with a dialog box to let you know you can't use the Find command.

3. **In the Find What text box, type the data that you want to find (such as Jefferson).**

4. **Click the Look In list box and choose the field that you want to search (such as First Name or Phone Number).**

5. **Click the Match list box and choose one of the following options:**

   • **Any Part of Field:** The text can appear anywhere in the field (a search for Ann would find both Maryanne and AnnMarie).

   • **Whole Field:** The text must appear by itself, not as part of another word. (A search for Ann finds records containing just Ann by itself; it doesn't find Maryanne or AnnMarie.)

• **Start of Field:** The text appears at the beginning of the field. (A search for Ann finds AnnMarie and Ann but not Maryanne).

6. **Click the Search list box and choose Up, Down, or All.**

• **Up:** Searches your database starting with the currently displayed record up to the first record.

• **Down:** Searches your database starting with the currently displayed record down to the last record.

• **All:** Searches your entire database.

If you choose the Up or Down option in the Search list box and Access can't find the data you're looking for, that could mean either the data doesn't exist or that it's hiding out in part of the database that you didn't search. So if you chose the Up option and couldn't find your data, your data could be stored near the end of your database.

7. **Click the Match Case check box if you want to choose this option.**

The Match Case option tells Access to find only those records that exactly match the capitalization of what you typed in the Find What box. Choosing this option means that if you search for AnN, Access finds records containing AnN but not records containing Ann, ann, or aNN.

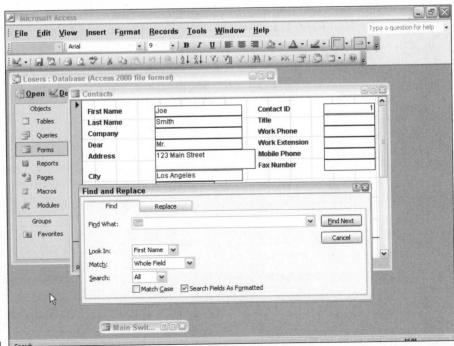

Figure 18-1: The Find and Replace dialog box can help you search your database.

8. **Click the Find Next button.**

   Access highlights the first record that contains your chosen data. You may have to move the Find and Replace dialog box so you can see the record that Access finds. If Access can't find a match, a dialog box pops up to inform you that the search item wasn't found in your database.

9. **Click Close to close the Find and Replace dialog box. (Or click Find Next if you want to see the next record that contains your chosen data.)**

   Access shows you the record it found in Step 8 or searches for the next matching record.

Finding one or more records by using a filter

When you use a filter, Access displays only those records that contain the information you're looking for. That way, you can concentrate on viewing only the information you want to see without the rest of your database getting in your way.

Think of the difference between the Find command and a filter in this way: Suppose you want to find a pair of green socks. The Find command forces you to look through an entire pile of laundry just to find a pair of green socks. A filter simply separates all your non-green socks from your pile of laundry, leaving your green socks behind.

When you want to use a filter, use the Filter dialog box to specify several options:

- ✔ **Field:** Tells Access which fields you want to search. You can choose one or more fields.

- ✔ **Sort:** Tells Access to sort records in alphabetical order (ascending), to sort records in reverse alphabetical order (descending), or not to bother sorting at all (not sorted). We describe sorting records later in the section imaginatively titled "Sorting a Database."

- ✔ **Criteria:** Tells Access to look for specific criteria. Instead of simply listing addresses (for example), Access can find addresses of people who own homes in Oregon *or* California or those of people who own homes in both Oregon *and* California.

Sorting a database just reorganizes your data, but you can still see all the data stuffed in your database. Filtering by criteria only displays records that match specific criteria, which means some data may be hidden from view.

Filtering with a form

Forms can display one entire record on the screen. If a filter finds multiple records, the form displays the total number of records found (such as 1 of 6). To view all the records found by a filter, click the Next or Previous Record buttons on the form.

To find one or more records by using a filter, follow these steps:

1. **Open the form containing the information you want to search.**

2. **Choose Records➪Filter➪Filter by Form, or click the Filter by Form icon on the Standard toolbar, as shown in Figure 18-2.**

   A Filter by Form dialog box appears, which looks strangely similar to the form you opened in Step 1.

Filter by Form icon

Filter by Selection icon

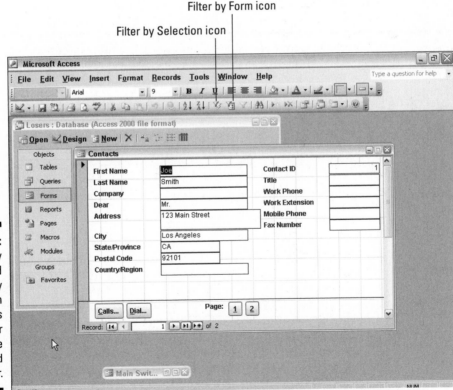

Figure 18-2: The Filter by Form and Filter by Selection icons appear on the Standard toolbar.

3. Click the field that you want to use as your filter.

For example, if you want to find all the people who live in Illinois, click the State/Province field.

A downward-pointing arrow appears to the right of the field that you click.

4. Click the downward-pointing arrow.

A list appears, as in Figure 18-3, containing all the data (such as all the states stored in your database) available in that particular database field.

5. From this pull-down list, click the data that you want to find (such as TX to find Texas).

6. Repeat Steps 3 through 5 for each field that you want to use for your filter.

The more filters you use, the narrower the search — which means you have fewer records to wade through before you find the ones you really want. You could end up filtering out and not seeing records that you actually want to include, so be selective when creating filters.

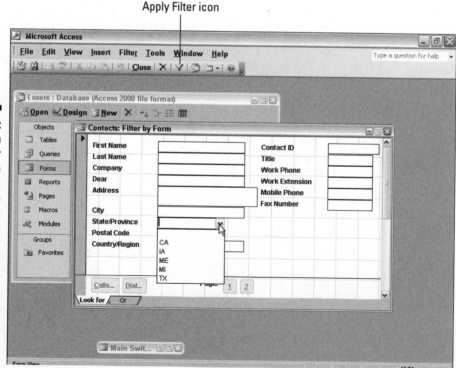

Figure 18-3: When you filter your database through a form, you can define the data to look for by clicking on the downward-pointing arrow next to a specific field.

7. **Choose Filter⇨Apply Filter/Sort or click the Apply Filter icon on the toolbar.**

   Access displays only those records matching your search criteria. Just to remind you that you're looking at a filtered version of your database, Access politely displays the word (Filtered) near the bottom of the form. You may have to click the Next or Previous Record buttons to see other records that your filter found for you.

8. **When you're ready to see your whole database again (not just the results of the search), choose Records⇨Remove Filter/Sort, or click the Remove Filter icon on the Standard toolbar, as shown in Figure 18-4.**

   Choosing this command displays all the information in your database once more.

After using a filter, make sure that you remove the filter by using the Remove Filter/Sort command; otherwise, Access displays only those records matching your last search, and you may think that the rest of your data is gone.

Sort Descending icon

Sort Ascending icon | Remove Filter icon

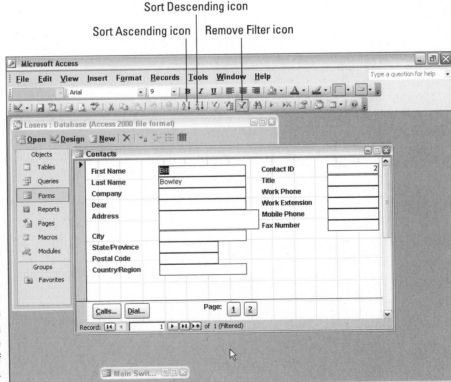

Figure 18-4: When you're viewing a filter through a form, the word (Filtered) appears near the bottom of the form.

Filtering with a table

Rather than use a filter with a form, you may prefer using a filter with a table. The main advantage of using a filter through a table is that you can see multiple records at once, while a form can display only one record at a time. To find one or more records by using a filter with a table, follow these steps:

1. **Open the table containing the information you want to search.**

2. **Click the field that you want to use as your filter.**

   For example, if you want to find all people with the last name of Doe, click in any Last Name field that contains the name *Doe*.

3. **Choose Records⇨Filter⇨Filter by Selection, or click the Filter By Selection icon on the Standard toolbar.**

   Access immediately displays only those records that meet your criteria.

   To select multiple criteria to filter your data, repeat Steps 2 and 3 as often as necessary.

4. **When you're ready to see your whole database again (and not just the results of the search), choose Records⇨Remove/Filter/Sort, or click the Remove Filter icon on the Standard toolbar.**

Sorting a Database

To sort a database, you have to tell Access which field you want to sort by and how you want to sort it (in ascending or descending order).

For example, you can sort your database alphabetically by last name, country, or city. Unlike searching, which shows only part of your database, sorting simply shows your entire database with all your data rearranged.

When you sort a database, you can always restore the original order by choosing Records⇨Remove Filter/Sort.

To sort a database, follow these steps:

1. **Open the form or table containing the information you want to search.**

2. **Click the field that you want to sort by.**

   If you want to sort by last names, for example, click the field that contains last names.

3. **Choose Records⇨Sort⇨Sort Ascending (or Descending) or click the Sort Ascending or Sort Descending icon on the Standard toolbar.**

   The Sort Ascending option sorts from A to Z (or 0 to 9). Sort Descending sorts in reverse, from Z to A (or 9 to 0).

Access obediently sorts your records.

4. **When you're ready to restore the original order to your database, choose Records⊅Remove Filter/Sort.**

Because a table can display multiple records at once, you may find sorting a database through a table easier to see.

Querying a Database

Storing information in a database is okay, but the real fun comes when you use the data that you entered. After all, storing all the names and addresses of your customers is a waste if you don't use the information to help you make more money (which is what business is really all about).

To help you use your stored information effectively, Access provides different ways to analyze your data. When you store information on Rolodex cards, in address books, or on paper forms, the information is static. When you store data in Access, the data can be molded, shaped, and manipulated like Silly Putty.

Asking questions with queries

A *query* is a fancy term for a question that you ask Access. After you store information in a database, you can use queries to get the information back out again — and in different forms. A query can be as simple as finding the names and phone numbers of everyone who lives in Arkansas, or as sophisticated as making Access retrieve the names and quantities of all products your company sold between November 2 and December 29.

The secret to creating effective queries is to know what you want and to get the hang of telling Access how to find it.

What's the difference between a query and the Find command?

Both a query and the Find command tell Access to retrieve and display certain data from your database. Queries have an advantage, however: You can save them as part of your database file and use them over and over without having to define what you're looking for each time. (You always have to define what you want to look at each time you use the Find command.)

Think of a query as a way of storing filters that you can use over and over again to find specific information.

Use the Find command when you need to search through one or more fields only one time. Use queries when you need to search through one or more fields on a regular basis.

Creating a query

When you create a query, you must specify *search criteria,* attributes that tell Access the specific type of data you want to find.

Queries can get fairly complicated. For example, you can ask Access to find the names of all the people in your database who earn less than $75,000 a year, live in either Seattle or Detroit, have owned their own houses for over six years, work in sales jobs, own personal computers, and subscribe to more than three but fewer than six magazines a year.

Just remember that the quality of your answers depends heavily on the quality of your queries (questions). If you create a poorly designed query, Access probably won't find all the data you really need and may overlook important information that can affect your business or your job.

To create a query, follow these steps:

1. **Choose Window⇨Database.**

   The Database window appears.

2. **Click the Queries icon in the Object panel of the database window.**

3. **Double-click the Create Query by Using Wizard icon.**

   The Simple Query Wizard dialog box appears, as shown in Figure 18-5.

4. **Click the downward-pointing arrow to the right of the Tables/Queries list box and click the table that you want to search.**

   A database table simply contains related information, such as names, addresses, and phone numbers of students. When you choose a database table, you're telling Access to search only in one particular table, not to search your entire Access database file, which may consist of one or more tables.

5. **Click the Available Fields list box and click a field that you want to display in the query result.**

   For example, if you want to display the FirstName and PhoneNumber fields, click one of them (then come back after Step 6 to click the other one).

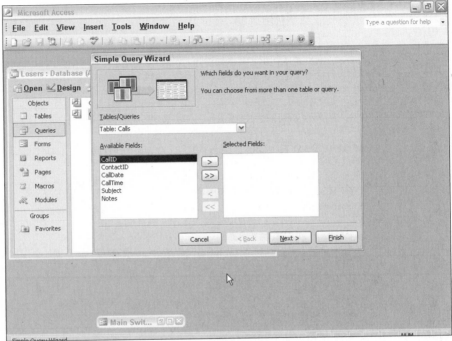

Figure 18-5:
The Simple
Query
Wizard
dialog box.

6. **Click the single right arrow button that appears between the two big boxes.**

   Access displays your field in the Selected Fields box. Repeat Steps 5 and 6 for each field that you want to use in your query.

7. **Click Next.**

   Access asks what title you want to give your query.

8. **Type a name for your query in the What Title Do You Want for Your Query text box.**

   Give your query a descriptive name, such as *Track low-selling products* or *List of employees I plan to fire*.

9. **Click Finish.**

   Access displays the result of your query in a Select Query window. Any time you need to use this query, just double-click the query name in the Database window.

10. **Click the close box of the Select Query window to make it go away.**

Using a query

After you create and save a query, you can use that query as many times as you want, no matter how much you add, delete, or modify the records in your database. Because some queries can be fairly complicated ("Find all the people in North Dakota who owe over $10,000 on their credit cards, own farms, and have sold their crops in the past thirty days"), saving and reusing queries saves you time, which is the purpose of computers in the first place.

Queries are most useful if you need to reuse the same query on a regular basis.

To use an existing query, open the database file containing your query and then follow these steps:

1. **Choose Window⇨Database.**

2. **Click the Queries icon in the Object panel in the database window.**

   A list of your available queries appears.

3. **Double-click the query name that you want to use.**

   Access displays the results of your query in a window. At this point, you can view your information, or you can print it out by pressing Ctrl+P.

4. **Click the Close box to remove the window displaying your query result.**

Deleting a query

Eventually, a query may no longer serve its purpose as you add, delete, and modify the data in your database. To keep your Database window from overflowing with queries, delete the ones you don't need.

Deleting a query doesn't delete data. When you delete a query, you're just deleting the criteria that you used to search your database with that query.

To delete a query, follow these steps:

1. **Choose Window⇨Database.**

2. **Click the Queries icon in the Object panel in the database window.**

   A list of your available queries appears.

3. **Click the query that you want to delete.**

4. **Choose Edit➪Delete, press Delete, or click the Delete icon in the toolbar.**

   A dialog box appears, asking whether you really want to delete your chosen query.

5. **Click Yes.**

   Your query disappears from the Database window.

If you suddenly realize that you deleted a query by mistake, don't cringe in horror. Immediately choose Edit➪Undo Delete or press Ctrl+Z. Access undoes your last command and restores your query to its original state.

Chapter 19

Making Reports

In This Chapter

▶ Creating a database report

▶ Printing your reports

▶ Making your reports look beautiful in Word

*A*ccess can store gobs of useful (or useless) information within the silicon brains of your computer. However, you may want to print your data once in a while so that other people don't have to crowd around your computer screen to see your information.

Fortunately, you can print any data stored in an Access database file. But rather than just print a random jumble of names, addresses, and phone numbers (or whatever data you have in the database), you can design reports so that other people can actually understand your data.

For example, you may use Access to keep track of all your customers. At the touch of a button (and with a little help from this chapter), you can create a report that prints out a list of your top ten customers. Touch another button, and Access can spit out a list of your top ten products. A report is simply a way for Access to print out and organize information so that you can make sense of it.

Making a Report

A report can selectively display data and make it look so pretty that people forget that your data doesn't make any sense. To make a report from your database, follow these steps:

1. **Choose Window⇨Database.**

   The Database window appears.

2. **Click the Reports icon in the Objects panel in the database window.**

3. **Double-click the Create Report by Using Wizard icon.**

   The Report Wizard dialog box appears, as shown in Figure 19-1.

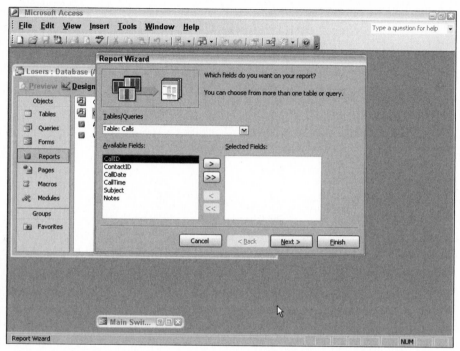

Figure 19-1:
The Report
Wizard
dialog box.

4. **Click the Tables/Queries list box to select a database table to use.**

   For example, if you want to print a report that shows the results of each salesperson in your company, look for the database table that contains this type of information, such as Sales People or Sales Results.

5. **Click the Available Fields list box and choose the fields that you want to print on your report.**

   The Available Fields list box lists all the fields used in the table or query that you select in the Tables/Queries list box. Be selective in choosing fields to appear on the report — not every field has to appear on a report.

6. **Click the single right arrow button, between the Available Fields and Selected Fields boxes.**

   Access displays the chosen field in the Selected Fields box. Repeat Steps 5 and 6 for each field that you want to use in your report.

7. **Click Next.**

   Another Report Wizard dialog box, shown in Figure 19-2, appears and asks whether you want any grouping levels. A *grouping level* tells Access to organize your printed data according to a specific field. For example, if you want to organize the data in your report by state or province, choose the StateOrProvince field for your grouping level. With this grouping level, your report may group all the people in Alabama, Michigan, and Texas in separate parts of your report, letting you find someone in a specific state more easily.

8. **If you want to group the information, click the field that you want to group by, and then click the right arrow button.**

   Access shows you what your report will look like if you group a level. Grouping levels can help you organize your report by a specific field, such as date or last name. That way you can flip through the report and see only records that are based on a certain date or name.

9. **Click Next.**

   Another Report Wizard dialog box, shown in Figure 19-3, appears and asks what sort order you want for detail records. This is Access's confusing way of asking how you want it to sort the data on your report.

   For example, if you defined a grouping level in Step 8, Access can alphabetically sort names within each grouping level by first or last name.

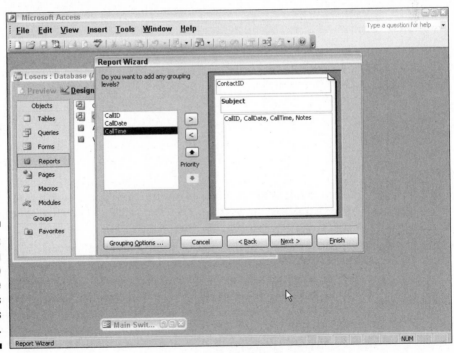

Figure 19-2:
Grouping levels help organize how Access displays your data.

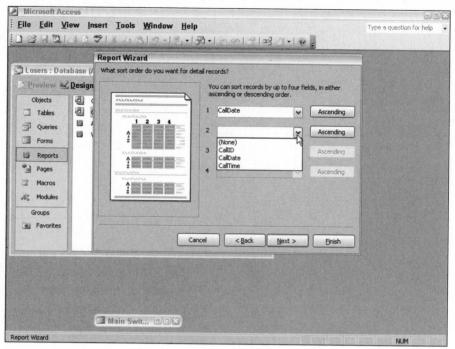

Figure 19-3:
Access
sorts your
data on a
report.

10. **Click the downward-pointing arrow of the 1 list box and choose a field that you want to sort by (if any). If you want to sort by more than one field, choose fields in the 2, 3, and 4 list boxes. Then click Next.**

    Still another Report Wizard dialog box appears and asks, "How would you like to lay out your report?"

11. **Click an option under Layout and an option under Orientation to specify the design of your report.**

    Different layout options simply print your report in different ways, depending on what you like best. Each time you click a layout option, Access politely shows you what your report will look like, on the left side of the Report Wizard dialog box.

12. **Click Next.**

    Another Report Wizard dialog box appears, asking you to specify a *style* — a definition of the fonts used to print out your report. Each time you click a style, Access shows you an example of your chosen style at the left of the Report Wizard dialog box.

13. **Click a style in the list box and then click Next.**

    Another Report Wizard dialog box appears, asking, "What title do you want for your report?"

14. **Type a title for your report and then click Finish.**

    Your report title should be something descriptive, such as "Profits made in March" or "How much money we lost because of Bob's stupid mistake."

    Access displays your report on-screen.

15. **Choose File⇨Close (or click the Close box of the report window).**

    Access displays the Database window again and automatically saves your report in the Reports section of the Database window. The next time you need to use that report, just double-click the report name.

Using a Report

After you create and save a report, you can add or delete as much data as you want. Then when you want to print that data, use the report that you already designed.

To use an existing report, open the database file containing your report and then follow these steps:

1. **Choose Window⇨Database.**

2. **Click the Reports icon in the Objects panel in the database window.**

   A list of your available reports appears.

3. **Double-click the report name that you want to use.**

   Access displays your chosen report in a window. At this point, you can print the report by choosing File⇨Print or pressing Ctrl+P.

4. **Click the Close box (the X in the upper-right corner) to remove the window displaying your report.**

Deleting a Report

As you add, delete, and modify the data in your database, you may find that a particular report no longer serves its purpose, because you no longer need the information it prints out, or because you changed the design of your database. To keep your database window from overflowing with useless reports, delete the ones you don't need.

Deleting a report does not delete data. When you delete a report, you're just deleting the way you told Access to print your data.

After you delete a report, you can't retrieve it again, so make sure that you really don't need it anymore before you decide to delete it. To delete a report, follow these steps:

1. **Choose Window⇨Database.**
2. **Click the Reports icon in the Objects panel in the database window.**

   A list of your available reports appears.

3. **Click the report that you want to delete.**
4. **Choose Edit⇨Delete, press Delete, or click the Delete icon on the Database window toolbar.**

   A dialog box appears, asking whether you really want to delete your chosen report.

   If you delete a report, you can't undelete it later, so make sure you really want to delete a particular report.

5. **Click Yes.**

   Your report disappears from the Database window.

Giving Your Access Data a Facelift

Instead of using Access's rather feeble report-generating abilities, you can create better-looking reports if you combine the professional report-making capabilities of Access with the wonderful writing, formatting, and publishing features available in Word.

Of course, you can't work with your Access data in Word until you copy your work from Access into Word. To use Word to make your Access data look better, follow these steps:

1. **Choose Window⇨Database.**
2. **Click the Tables icon in the Objects panel in the database window.**
3. **Double-click the database table containing the data that you want to copy into Word.**

   Access displays your database table and any data stored inside it.

4. **Choose Tools⇨Office Links⇨Publish It with Microsoft Word.**

   Word loads and displays your chosen Access database table in a Word document as a series of rows and columns.

5. **Make any changes you want to your Access data or type additional text around the Access data.**

   For example, you can change the font and size of the type. (For more information about using Word, see Part II of this book.) At this point you can print or save your Word document.

When you work with an Access database table in a Word document, Microsoft Office 2003 simply copies the data from Access and pastes it into Word. Any changes you make to your data in Word won't affect data stored in Access, and vice versa.

If your database contains a lot of numbers that you would like to use to calculate new results, you can take your Access data and load it into Microsoft Excel. To use Excel to analyze your Access data, follow these steps:

1. **Choose Window⇨Database.**

2. **Click the Tables icon in the Objects panel in the database window.**

3. **Double-click the database table containing the data that you want to copy into Excel.**

   Access displays your database table and any data stored inside it.

4. **Choose Tools⇨Office Links⇨Analyze It with Microsoft Excel.**

   Excel loads and displays your chosen Access database table in an Excel worksheet as a series of rows and columns.

5. **Make any changes you want to your Access data or create formulas to calculate new results based on your Access data.**

   (For more information about using Excel, see Part III of this book.) At this point you can print or save your Excel worksheet.

When you work with an Access database table in a Word document, Microsoft Office 2003 simply copies the data from Access and pastes it into Word. Any changes you make to your data in Word won't affect data stored in Access, and vice versa.

Part VII
The Part of Tens

The 5th Wave   By Rich Tennant

"I'm ordering our new PC. Do you want it left-brain or right-brain-oriented?"

In this part . . .

After spending your valuable time figuring out the many powers and puzzles of Microsoft Office 2003, flip through this part of the book to find out the secret shortcuts and hints that can make any of the programs in Microsoft Office 2003 even easier and more effective for your personal or business use.

Just make sure that your family, coworkers, or boss don't catch you reading this part of the book. They may stop thinking that you're an Office 2003 super-guru and realize you're just an ordinary person relying on a really great book. (Why not? Many of the best gurus do.)

Then again, why not buy extra copies of this book and give them to your friends, coworkers, and boss so they'll be able to figure out how to use Office 2003 on their own and leave you with enough time to actually do your own work for a change?

Chapter 20

Ten Tips for Using Office 2003

Microsoft Office contains so many features and commands that you should take some time to browse the tips in this chapter. See how quickly you can turn yourself from a computer novice to an Office 2003 guru (as long as you keep a copy of this book with you at all times).

Customizing the Microsoft Office 2003 User Interface

Microsoft tried to create the easiest, most intuitive collection of programs in the world. Yet chances are good that the programs are still too complicated for most mere mortals to use and understand. So rather than suffer in silence, take a few moments to customize the Microsoft Office 2003 user interface.

Changing icons on your toolbars

The toolbars in Office 2003 display the icons you use most often. However, toolbars only have a limited amount of space so you may want to choose which icons to appear on each toolbar by following these steps:

1. **Click on the Toolbar Options button on the toolbar that you want to customize.**

   To view a toolbar that may be hidden, choose View⇨Toolbars and then click on the toolbar you want to customize. When you click on the Toolbar Options button, a pull-down menu appears.

2. Click Add or Remove Buttons.

A pop-up menu appears that lists one or more toolbars such as Standard or Formatting.

3. Click on the name of the toolbar that you want to customize.

A pop-up menu appears that displays a check mark next to all the icons that currently appear in your toolbar as shown in Figure 20-1.

4. Click to the left of the icon that you want to appear in your toolbar.

If you want to hide an icon from view, click its check mark to make the check mark go away. Each time you display or hide an icon, Office 2003 changes the appearance of your toolbar so you can see what it looks like.

5. Click anywhere away from the pop-up menu of toolbar icons.

Congratulations! You've just modified your toolbars.

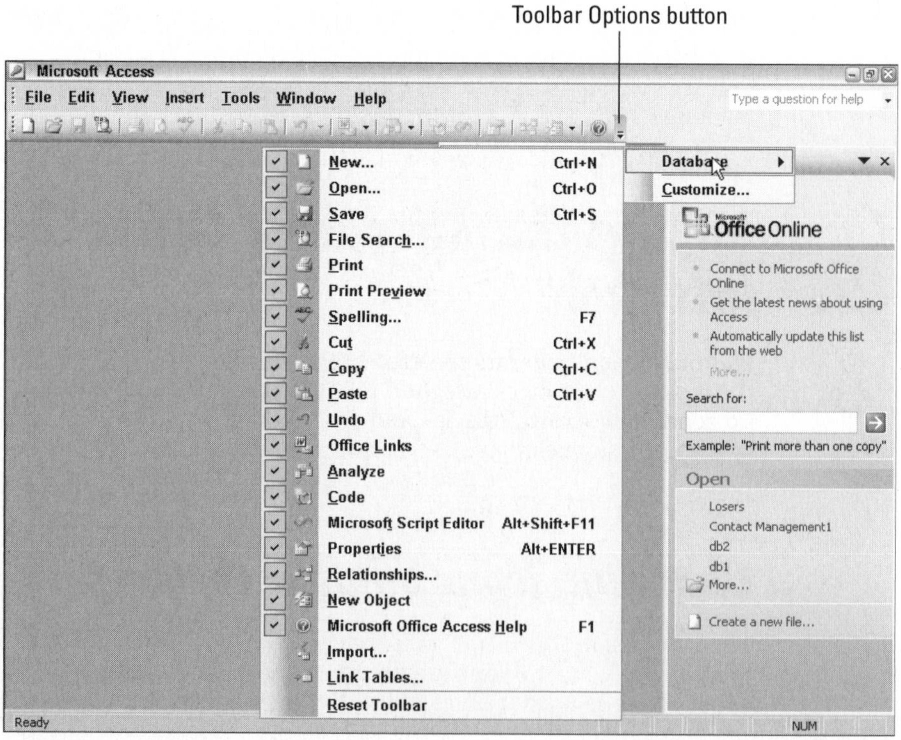

Toolbar Options button

Figure 20-1:
A check mark tells Office 2003 to display a particular icon on the toolbar.

In case you want to restore your toolbars to their original, factory-configuration, follow these steps:

1. **Click on the Toolbar Options button on the toolbar that you want to customize.**

   To view a toolbar that may be hidden, choose View⇨Toolbars and then click on the toolbar you want to customize. When you click on the Toolbar Options button, a pull-down menu appears.

2. **Click Add or Remove Buttons.**

   A pop-up menu appears that lists one or more toolbars such as Standard or Formatting.

3. **Click Customize.**

   A Customize dialog box appears.

4. **Click the Reset menu and toolbar usage data button and then click Close.**

   Office 2003 restores your menus and toolbars to their original condition before you started messing around with customizing them.

Zooming to avoid eye strain

To cram as much text on-screen as possible, Microsoft Office 2003 displays everything in a tiny font size. If you'd rather not strain your eyes, you can zoom in on your screen, blowing up your text so that the letters are easier to see.

Outlook doesn't offer a Zoom feature.

To zoom in (expand) or zoom out (shrink) the appearance of text on-screen, follow these steps:

1. **Choose View⇨Zoom.**

2. **Choose a magnification (such as 200% or 25%) and then click OK.**

   Your document appears at the desired magnification for your viewing pleasure.

If you own a mouse with a wheel stuck between the two buttons (such as the Microsoft IntelliMouse), you have another way to zoom in and out. Just hold down the Ctrl key and roll the wheel back and forth.

Enlarging your buttons

The Microsoft Office 2003 toolbar buttons can be cryptic but hard to see. Rather than squint and ruin your eyesight, you can enlarge the buttons. To make your toolbar buttons larger, follow these steps:

1. **Choose Tools⇨Customize.**

   The Customize dialog box appears.

2. **Click the Options tab.**

3. **Select the Large Icons check box.**

   Microsoft Office 2003 displays your buttons to make them look as if radiation mutated them to three times their normal size.

4. **Click Close.**

If you get sick of seeing large buttons staring back at you while you work, just repeat the preceding steps and clear the check mark from the Large Icons check box. Voilá — the buttons return to their normal size.

When in doubt, click the right mouse button

When you want to rename, edit, or modify anything in Office 2003, use the handy right mouse button pop-up menu. To use this pop-up menu, follow these steps:

1. **Highlight or click the item you want to edit.**

2. **Click the right mouse button.**

   The right mouse button pop-up menu appears.

3. **Click a command in the pop-up menu.**

Taking shortcuts with macros

Many people dream of the day they can give orders to a computer by talking to it; the current reality is that you still have to type on a keyboard if you hope to use your computer at all. Because most people would rather avoid typing, Microsoft Office 2003 offers a partial solution — *macros*.

Macros don't eliminate typing entirely, but they can reduce the number of keys you have to press to get something done. A *macro* is a mini-program that records your keystrokes as you type. After you record the keystrokes in a macro, whenever you need to use those exact same keystrokes again, you can tell Microsoft Office 2003 to "play back" your recorded keystrokes.

For example, suppose you find yourself typing the name of your company, The Mississippi Mudflat Corporation, over and over again. You can instead type it once and save it as a macro. Then, when you want the company name to appear in your document, Office 2003 can automatically type *The Mississippi Mudflat Corporation* for you.

You can create and run macros within Word, Excel, and PowerPoint.

When you create a macro in either Access or Outlook, you actually have to write a miniature program in a programming language known as Visual Basic for Applications (or VBA for short). The VBA language isn't difficult to learn, but it's way beyond the scope of this book. For more information about VBA, pick up a copy of *VBA For Dummies*, by Steve Cummings (Wiley Publishing, Inc.).

Recording macros in Word

To record a macro in Word, follow these steps:

1. **Choose Tools⇨Macro⇨Record New Macro.**

   A Record Macro dialog box appears, as shown in Figure 20-2.

2. **Type a name for your macro in the Macro name text box.**

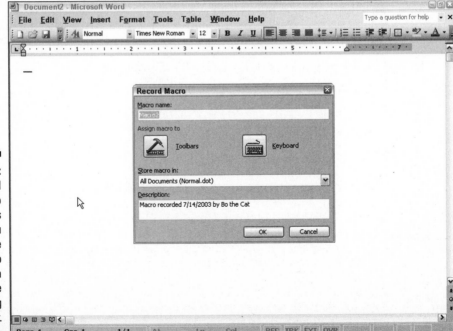

Figure 20-2: The Record Macro dialog box is where you can name your macro and assign a keystroke for running it later.

3. Click the Keyboard button.

A Customize Keyboard dialog box appears, as shown in Figure 20-3; it's where you assign a keystroke combination to your macro.

4. Press the keystroke that you want to represent your macro (such as Alt+F12).

You can repeat this step to assign multiple keystrokes to the same macro if you want.

5. Click the Assign button.

6. Click the Close button.

The mouse pointer turns into an arrow with an audiocassette icon; a Stop Recording toolbar appears, as shown in Figure 20-4, which you can use to pause or stop recording a macro.

7. Press the keystrokes that you want to record in your macro.

If you click the Pause Recording button, you can temporarily stop the recording of your macro.

8. Click the Stop Recording button when you finish recording the keystrokes.

To run your macro, press the keystroke combination that you chose in Step 4.

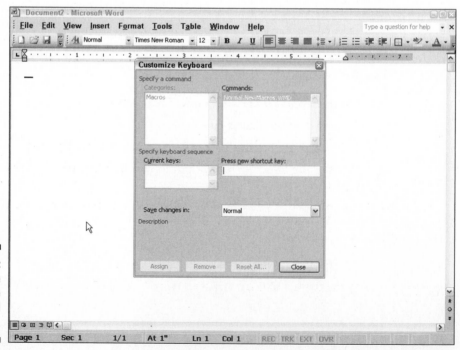

Figure 20-3:
The
Customize
Keyboard
dialog box.

Stop Recording button

Pause Recording button

Figure 20-4:
The Stop
Recording
toolbar.

Recording macros in Excel

To record a macro in Excel, follow these steps:

1. **Choose Tools⇨Macro⇨Record New Macro.**

   A Record Macro dialog box appears.

2. **Type a name for your macro in the Macro name text box.**

3. **Click in the Shortcut Key box (the one that has Ctrl+ to the left) and type a letter.**

   For example, if you want to replay your macro by pressing Ctrl+W, type **W** in the Shortcut Key box.

4. **Click OK.**

   A Stop Recording toolbar appears.

5. **Press the keystrokes that you want to record in your macro.**

6. **Click the Stop Recording button when you finish recording the keystrokes.**

To run a macro, press the keystroke combination that you chose in Step 3.

Recording macros in PowerPoint

To record a macro in PowerPoint, follow these steps:

1. **Choose Tools⇨Macro⇨Record New Macro.**

   A Record Macro dialog box appears.

2. **Type a name for your macro in the Macro name text box and click OK.**

   A Stop Recording toolbar appears.

3. **Press the keystrokes that you want to record in your macro.**

4. **Click the Stop Recording button when you finish recording the keystrokes.**

To run a macro in PowerPoint, follow these steps:

1. **Choose Tools⇨Macro⇨Macros (or press Alt+F8).**

   A macro dialog box appears.

2. **Click the name of the macro that you want to run.**

3. **Click Run.**

Protecting Your Microsoft Office 2003 Files

After you spend all your time learning how to use Microsoft Office 2003, the last thing you want to happen is to lose all your precious data that you sweated to create in the first place. So take steps now to protect yourself in the event of disaster, and you won't be sorry later.

Watching out for macro viruses

Microsoft Office 2003 gives you two ways to create a macro. The simplest way, as explained in the previous section, is to record your keystrokes and then play them back when you need them. The harder way to create a macro is to use the Microsoft special macro programming language (called Visual

Basic for Applications or *VBA*) to create more powerful and complicated macros.

Although the VBA programming language gives you the power to create a variety of different macros, it has also given mischievous programmers the opportunity to write computer viruses.

This new breed of computer viruses, dubbed *macro viruses*, can infect Word documents, Excel worksheets, PowerPoint presentations, and Access databases. When you give a copy of a document or worksheet that contains a virus to another person, you risk passing along the macro virus at the same time.

So to help prevent macro viruses from infecting and spreading through your Office 2003 files, Office 2003 offers a limited form of macro virus protection.

The most common macro viruses infect Word documents. The second most common macro viruses infect Excel worksheets; a handful of macro viruses attack PowerPoint or Access files. Buy an antivirus program and keep it updated regularly, to protect yourself from any future macro viruses that might attack your computer.

To turn on macro virus protection in Word, follow these steps:

1. **Choose File⇨Save or Save As.**

   A Save As dialog box appears.

2. **Click in the Tools menu that appears in the upper-right corner of the Save As dialog box.**

   A drop-down menu appears.

3. **Click Security Options.**

   A Security dialog box appears.

4. **Click Macro Security.**

   Another Security dialog box appears, as shown in Figure 20-5.

5. **Click the Security Level tab and click the High, Medium, or Low radio button.**

   Unless you have a good reason for choosing a lower security level, you should always choose the High radio button.

   If you choose the High Security Level, you may not be able to run macros created by someone else unless you set the security level to Medium or Low.

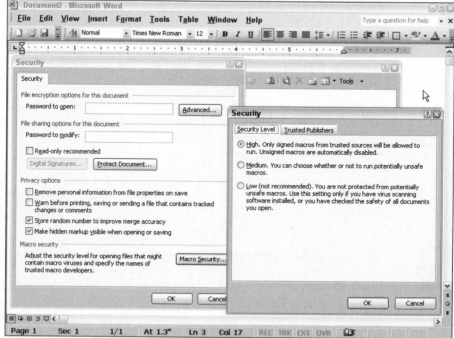

Figure 20-5:
The Security
dialog box
for changing
the macro
security
setting for
Word
documents.

The High Security Level helps prevent macro viruses from infecting your files, but some macro viruses are clever enough to shut this feature off. Don't rely on Office 2003's macro virus protection to keep your computer virus-free.

6. **Click OK twice.**

   The Save As dialog box appears again. Each time you save your document, Word uses your chosen security settings for this document.

7. **Click Save.**

If a macro virus has already infected your Word documents or Excel worksheets, turning on Office 2003's macro virus protection won't remove the virus. You should get an antivirus program, such as McAfee's VirusScan (www.mcafee.com) or Symantec's Norton AntiVirus (www.symantec.com), that can detect and remove macro and other types of viruses.

Encrypting your files

In case you want to keep your Office 2003 documents private, you can use Office 2003's built-in encryption program or buy an encryption program. Encryption scrambles your data so that no one but you (and anyone else who steals or figures out your password) can read it.

To turn on Office 2003, follow these steps:

1. **Choose File⇨Save or Save As.**

   A Save As dialog box appears.

2. **Click in the Tools menu that appears in the upper-right corner of the Save As dialog box.**

   A drop-down menu appears.

3. **Click Security Options. (Click General Options in Excel.)**

   A Security dialog box appears.

4. **Type a password in the Password to Open text box.**

   Your password appears as a series of asterisks to hide your password in case someone's peeking over your shoulder. (Quick! Turn around and look!).

   If you pick a simple password, people may be able to guess your password, which makes encryption as effective as locking a bank vault but taping the combination to the front of the door.

5. **Click the Advanced button.**

   An Encryption Type dialog box appears.

6. **Click the encryption method you want to use and click OK.**

   Office 2003 has three forms of built-in encryption:

   • Weak Encryption (XOR)

   • Office 97/2000 Compatible

   • Various versions of an encryption method dubbed RC4.

     If you choose RC4 encryption (which is the most secure of the three encryption methods), you can also click the up/down arrows in the Choose a key length text box. The higher the key number (such as 128), the more secure your document will be.

7. **(Optional) Type a password in the Password to Modify text box.**

   You can choose two different passwords in Steps 4 and 7 if you want. That way you can have one password that lets you open but not change a file (the password you chose in Step 4) and a second password that lets you open and edit that same file.

8. **Click OK.**

   A Confirm Password dialog box appears for each password you typed.

9. **Retype each password and click OK.**

   The Save As dialog box appears again.

10. **Click Save.**

Office 2003's encryption can stop most people from viewing your data, but determined thieves and spies will have little trouble opening Office 2003 encrypted files. For better protection, get a separate encryption program instead. Two popular encryption programs are Pretty Good Privacy (often called PGP and available from `www.pgp.com`) and GNU Privacy Guard (`www.gnupg.org`). Both of these programs allow you to encrypt individual files, entire folders, or complete hard drives so that only you can access your data (unless you forget your password).

Shredding your files

Encryption is one way to protect your data. However, when you encrypt a file, you usually wind up with two separate files: the newly encrypted file and the original unencrypted file. If you erase the original unencrypted file, someone can undelete that file and see your documents while avoiding your encrypted files altogether.

The problem stems from the way computers delete files. When you tell your computer to delete a file, it actually plays a trick on you. Instead of physically erasing the file, the computer simply pretends the file doesn't exist. That's why someone can use a utility program, such as The Norton Utilities, and unerase a file that you may have erased several hours, days, weeks, or even months ago.

If you want to delete a file, don't use the file deletion feature in Microsoft Windows. Get a special file-shredding program instead. These file-shredding programs delete a file, then overwrite that file several times with random bits of data. If someone tries to unerase that file at a later date, all they see is gibberish.

Two popular file-shredding programs are Eraser (`www.tolvanen.com/eraser`) and East-Tec Eraser (`www.east-tec.com/eraser`).

If you accidentally delete a file by using a file-shredding program, you can never retrieve that file again, so be careful!

Backing up your files

You should always keep extra copies of your files in case you accidentally mess up a file by mistake. If you lose or delete a file by mistake, a backup copy of your files enables you to continue working even though your original file may be history.

Word and Excel have a backup feature that creates a backup copy of your files each time you save a file. Unfortunately, using the Word or Excel backup feature won't protect you in case your entire hard drive crashes, so you may still have to store your backup copies on a floppy disk and keep them separate from your computer. To turn on this special backup feature in Word or Excel, follow these steps:

1. **Choose File⇨Save As.**

   The Save As dialog box appears.

2. **Click the Tools button.**

   A drop-down list appears.

3. **Click Save Options. (In Excel, click General Options.)**

   A Save dialog box appears.

4. **Select the Always Create Backup Copy check box.**

5. **Click OK.**

When you save a file with the backup feature turned on, your backup file has a name like `Backup of`. For example, if you saved a file called `Ransom note`, your backup copy would have a name of `Backup copy of Ransom note` and have a file extension of `.wbk` (for Word documents) or `.xlk` (for Excel worksheets).

Reduce Spam

Spam is unsolicited e-mail that often floods an e-mail account with phony "business opportunities" or invitations to look at pornography. Because unsolicited e-mail can make it hard to read your legitimate e-mail, you may be pleased to know that Outlook offers a way to either color or move spam out of your e-mail account.

Outlook filters out spam by looking for keywords usually found in spam. Unfortunately, Outlook's spam filters aren't 100 percent effective, but they can definitely help slow the flow of spam into your e-mail account.

Setting up Outlook's junk e-mail filter

To set up Outlook's junk e-mail filter, follow these steps:

1. **Choose Go➪Mail or press Ctrl+1.**

   Outlook displays the Mail and Inbox panels.

2. **Choose Tools➪Options.**

   The Options dialog box appears.

3. **Click the Preferences tab.**

   The Preferences tab appears.

4. **Click Junk E-Mail.**

   The Junk E-mail Options dialog box appears as shown in Figure 20-6.

5. **Click on one of the following options:**

   - **No protection**
   - **Low**
   - **High**
   - **Safe Lists only**

6. **Click OK.**

   The next time you receive junk e-mail, Outlook tries to identify it.

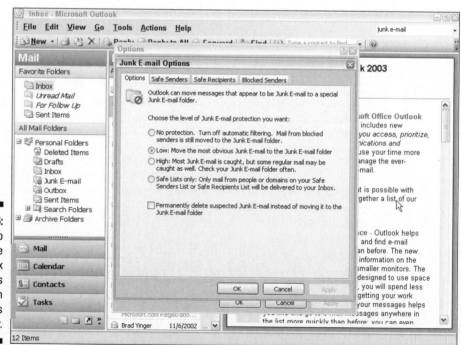

Figure 20-6:
The Ways to
Organize
Inbox
window lets
you turn on
Outlook's
spam filter.

Creating a list of trusted (safe) senders of e-mail

If you choose the Safe Lists only option, Outlook screens out all suspicious e-mail except those that come from your list of Safe Senders. To create a list of Safe Senders (people or companies you trust to receive e-mail from), follow these steps:

1. **Choose Go➪Mail or press Ctrl+1.**

   Outlook displays the Mail and Inbox panels.

2. **Choose Tools➪Options.**

   The Options dialog box appears.

3. **Click Junk E-Mail.**

   The Junk E-mail Options dialog box appears (refer to Figure 20-6).

4. **Click the Safe Senders tab.**

   The Safe Senders tab appears, as shown in Figure 20-7.

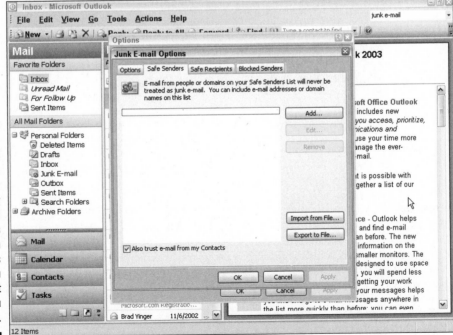

Figure 20-7: The Safe Senders tab lets you identify e-mail addresses or domain addresses that you trust won't send you junk e-mail.

5. **Click Add.**

   An Add address or domain dialog box appears.

6. **Type an e-mail address or a domain name and click OK.**

   If you type a domain name, Outlook automatically trusts any e-mail coming from that particular domain such as the Microsoft.com domain. By typing in a domain name, you won't have to type in everyone's specific e-mail address if all those e-mail addresses have the same domain name, such as bgates@microsoft.com or pallen@microsoft.com.

7. **Repeat Steps 5 and 6 for each e-mail address or domain name you want to store on your Safe Senders list.**

8. **Click OK.**

As an alternative (or in addition to) creating a Safe Senders list, you can create a Blocked Senders list, which contains e-mail addresses or domain names from people you absolutely know send you only junk e-mail. To create a Blocked Senders list, repeat Steps 1 – 8, above except in Step 4, click on the Blocked Senders tab.

Using Pocket Office

Laptop computers continue to drop in price and weight, yet increase in power. Some of the latest laptop computers weigh less than three pounds and have enough memory and processing power to run a full-blown copy of Microsoft Office 2003.

But rather than lug a laptop computer around the country, many people are opting for smaller, cheaper, and lighter handheld computers that run a slightly different operating system called PocketPC.

PocketPC comes with a version of Microsoft Office, dubbed Pocket Office, which includes Pocket Word, Pocket Excel, Pocket PowerPoint, and Pocket Access.

These pocket versions of Microsoft Office provide fewer features than the complete Microsoft Office 2003 suite. But Pocket Office can share data with your Microsoft Office 2003 programs, making it perfect for taking your data on the road and viewing or editing it on a handheld computer.

So if you travel frequently but dread breaking your back carrying a heavy and expensive laptop computer, consider buying a handheld PocketPC computer and using Pocket Office instead.

Chapter 21

Ten Common Microsoft Office 2003 Shortcuts

*W*ith each reincarnation of Microsoft Office, Microsoft tries to make all the different Office programs look and work more and more alike. Theoretically, after you learn how to use one Office program, you can master others fairly easily.

To help you master Microsoft Office 2003, this chapter lists the common keystrokes (shortcuts) that every Office 2003 program uses. That way, you spend less time figuring out how to use each program's commands and more time actually doing some work.

Creating a New File (Ctrl+N)

Anytime you want to create a new file in any Microsoft Office 2003 program, press Ctrl+N or click the New icon on the Standard toolbar. Office 2003 cheerfully responds by creating an empty file that you can use to start creating anything your heart desires.

Pressing Ctrl+N in Microsoft Outlook can create anything from a new e-mail message to a contact or appointment, depending on what you happen to be doing at the time.

Opening an Existing File (Ctrl+O)

You often need to open an existing file in order to make changes to it. Whenever you want to open a file, press Ctrl+O or click the Open button on the Standard toolbar to see an Open dialog box, where you can choose the specific file you want to open.

By default, Microsoft Office 2003 looks for existing files in the My Documents folder, which is usually `C:\My Documents`. Rather than lump all your files in the My Documents folder, create separate subfolders within the My Documents folder, which prevents files that belong to different projects or programs from getting mixed up.

To create a new folder:

1. **Choose File⇨Open.**

   An Open dialog box appears.

2. **Choose the drive and folder where you want to store your new folder.**

   For example, if you want to store a new folder inside you're my Documents folder, you'll have to switch to your my Documents folder first.

3. **Click the Create New Folder icon in the upper right corner of the Open dialog box.**

   The Create New Folder icon looks like a little folder with a spark in its upper right corner. A New Folder dialog box appears.

4. **Type a name for your folder in the Name text box and click OK.**

   Microsoft Office 2003 creates a new folder with your chosen name in the current displayed folder and drive.

By default, Word, Excel, PowerPoint, and Access always look in the My Documents folder whenever you try to open an existing file. To define a different folder for Word, Excel, PowerPoint, or Access to look in first:

1. **Start Word, Excel, PowerPoint, or Access.**

2. **Choose Tools⇨Options.**

   An Options dialog box appears.

3. **Follow the steps for the program you're using:**

   - **If you're using Access:** Click the General tab; click the Default Database Folder text box and then type a new directory name (such as `C:\My Documents\Secrets`).

   - **If you're using Excel:** Click the General tab; click the Default file location text box; and then type a new directory name (such as `C:\My Documents\Useless Work`).

   - **If you're using PowerPoint:** Click the Save tab; click the Default file location text box; and then type a new directory name (such as `C:\My Documents\Useless Work`).

   - **If you're using Word:** Click the File Locations tab; click Documents in the File Types box; click Modify; and then click a folder.

4. **Click OK.**

   Regardless of which Office 2003 program you're using, you're done. (Ah, simplicity. What a concept.)

If you open or save a file in a different directory, the next time you choose the Open command, your Office 2003 program looks in the directory where you last opened or saved a file. So, if you save a file to a directory called `A:\Stuff`, then the next time you open a file, Office 2003 first assumes that you want to look for a file stored in the `A:\Stuff` directory, regardless of the default directory you may have assigned.

Saving Your Work (Ctrl+S)

Save your work often — every ten minutes is good. That way, if the power suddenly goes out, you won't lose all the work you did over the past five hours. Whenever you take a break or walk away from your computer, press Ctrl+S or click the Save icon on the Standard toolbar to save your work. This advice is easy to remember after you lose an entire day's work because you forgot to save it to a disk.

Microsoft Word, Excel, and PowerPoint provide a special AutoRecover feature that automatically saves your work after a specified amount of time. To turn on the AutoRecover feature — and specify how often you want to save your work automatically — follow these steps:

1. **Choose Tools⇨Options.**

   The Options dialog box appears.

2. **Click the Save tab.**

3. **Click the Save AutoRecover Info Every check box.**

4. **Click the up or down arrow in the Minutes box to specify how often Word, Excel, or PowerPoint should save your file.**

5. **Click OK.**

Access automatically saves your data whether you like it or not, so it doesn't offer an AutoRecover feature that you can change or disable.

Printing Your Work (Ctrl+P)

No matter how often magazines tout the myth of the paperless office, your printer is one of the most important parts of your entire computer system. Whenever you want to print your files, just press Ctrl+P to make the Print dialog box appear. Specify which pages you want to print and how many copies you want, and then click the OK button.

If you're in a hurry to print, just click the Print icon on the Standard toolbar. Clicking the Print icon automatically sends your entire file to the printer, so make sure that you really do want to print every single page of that document.

Cutting (Ctrl+X), Copying (Ctrl+C), and Pasting (Ctrl+V)

If you want to move data from one place to another, cut and paste the data. If you want your data to appear in the original place as well as another place, copy and paste the data. To cut or copy data to another place:

1. **Select the data that you want to cut or copy.**

2. **Press Ctrl+X or click the Cut icon on the Standard toolbar to cut the data. Press Ctrl+C or click the Copy icon on the Standard toolbar to copy the data.**

3. **Move the cursor to the location where you want the data to appear.**

4. **Press Ctrl+V or click the Paste icon on the Standard toolbar.**

When you cut or copy anything from within any Microsoft Office 2003 program, the cut or copied object gets stored on the Windows Clipboard (which can only hold one item at a time) and the Office Clipboard, which can hold up to twenty-four items at a time. To view the Office Clipboard in Access, Excel, PowerPoint, or Word, choose Edit⇨Office Clipboard. The Windows Clipboard is used when copying or cutting data from an Office 2003 program to a non-Office 2003 program, such as WordPerfect or Quicken. Use the Office Clipboard to copy or cut data between two Office 2003 programs.

Finding a Word or Phrase (Ctrl+F)

Anytime you want to look for a specific word or number, you can use the fabulous Find command by pressing Ctrl+F and then clicking the More or Options button. When you use the Find command, Microsoft Office 2003 presents you with the Find dialog box, which gives you the following options:

- **Match case:** If you want to find *Bill* but don't want to waste time looking for *bill*.

- **Find whole words only:** If you want to find *cat* but not words like *catastrophic* and *catatonic*.

- **Use wildcards:** If you want to find parts of a sequence. For example, if you want to find all words that begin with *fail,* tell Microsoft Office 2003 to search for *fail**. (This option is only available in Word.)

- **Sounds like:** If you know what you want to find but don't know how to spell it, for example, searching for *elefant* when you really want *elephant.* (This option is only available in Word.)

- **Find all word forms:** If you want to find all uses of a word, such as *sing, singing,* and *sings.* (This option is only available in Word.)

Finding and Replacing a Word or Phrase (Ctrl+H)

The Find and Replace command lets you look for a word or number and replace it with a different word or number. For example, you may misspell your boss's name as *Frank the Jerk* when his real title should be *Frank the Imbecile.* Although you could manually search for *Frank the Jerk* and replace it with *Frank the Imbecile,* it's easier to leave such mindless, tedious, boring tasks to your computer and Microsoft Office 2003.

The Find and Replace command lets you search for specific strings. Unlike the Find command, the Find and Replace command can also automatically replace any text or numbers it finds with a new string of text or numbers.

When you press Ctrl+H to use the Find and Replace command, the Find and Replace dialog box appears and offers two buttons: Replace and Replace All.

The Replace button lets you review every string that Microsoft Office 2003 finds, so you can make sure that you really *want* to replace the string. The Replace All button doesn't give you the chance to review each string found; if you click the Replace All button, you may find Microsoft Office 2003 replacing words that you didn't really want to replace, so be careful.

Checking Your Spelling (F7)

Unfortunately, poor spelling can make even the most brilliantly written paper look amateurish and conceal its stellar quality. To prevent the raucous laughter of people who misconstrue such flaws as moronic, check your spelling before you let anyone see your files.

To check your spelling in a Microsoft Office 2003 document, press F7 or click the Spell Check icon on the Standard toolbar.

If you don't want Office 2003 to spell-check your entire file, highlight the text you want to spell-check and then press F7.

Using Undo (Ctrl+Z) and Redo (Ctrl+Y)

Microsoft Office 2003 is a forgiving chunk of software. If you make a mistake at any time, you can undo your last action by clicking the Undo button on the Standard toolbar or by pressing Ctrl+Z.

Not all actions can be undone. When you're about to do something that Microsoft Office 2003 can't undo, a dialog box pops up to warn you that your next action is irreversible.

If you made a mistake undoing an action, click the Redo icon on the Standard toolbar or press Ctrl+Y to redo your last undone action.

If you click the down arrow next to the Undo or Redo icons on the Standard toolbar, a drop-down list of your past actions appears. To undo or redo multiple actions, drag the mouse to highlight the actions you want and then click the left mouse button.

Index

● *E* ●

• **F** •

• *N* •

• R •

FOR DUMMIES®

The easy way to get more done and have more fun

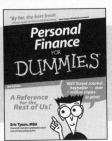

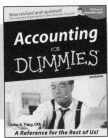

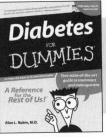

FOR DUMMIES®

A world of resources to help you grow

HOME, GARDEN & HOBBIES

0-7645-5295-3

0-7645-5130-2

0-7645-5106-X

Also available:

Auto Repair For Dummies
(0-7645-5089-6)

Chess For Dummies
(0-7645-5003-9)

Home Maintenance For
Dummies
(0-7645-5215-5)

Organizing For Dummies
(0-7645-5300-3)

Piano For Dummies
(0-7645-5105-1)

Poker For Dummies
(0-7645-5232-5)

Quilting For Dummies
(0-7645-5118-3)

Rock Guitar For Dummies
(0-7645-5356-9)

Roses For Dummies
(0-7645-5202-3)

Sewing For Dummies
(0-7645-5137-X)

FOOD & WINE

0-7645-5250-3

0-7645-5390-9

0-7645-5114-0

Also available:

Bartending For Dummies
(0-7645-5051-9)

Chinese Cooking For
Dummies
(0-7645-5247-3)

Christmas Cooking For
Dummies
(0-7645-5407-7)

Diabetes Cookbook For
Dummies
(0-7645-5230-9)

Grilling For Dummies
(0-7645-5076-4)

Low-Fat Cooking For
Dummies
(0-7645-5035-7)

Slow Cookers For Dummies
(0-7645-5240-6)

TRAVEL

0-7645-5453-0

0-7645-5438-7

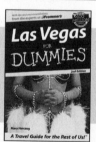

0-7645-5448-4

Also available:

America's National Parks For
Dummies
(0-7645-6204-5)

Caribbean For Dummies
(0-7645-5445-X)

Cruise Vacations For
Dummies 2003
(0-7645-5459-X)

Europe For Dummies
(0-7645-5456-5)

Ireland For Dummies
(0-7645-6199-5)

France For Dummies
(0-7645-6292-4)

London For Dummies
(0-7645-5416-6)

Mexico's Beach Resorts For
Dummies
(0-7645-6262-2)

Paris For Dummies
(0-7645-5494-8)

RV Vacations For Dummies
(0-7645-5443-3)

Walt Disney World & Orlando
For Dummies
(0-7645-5444-1)

Available wherever books are sold. Go to www.dummies.com or call 1-877-762-2974 to order direct.

FOR DUMMIES®

Plain-English solutions for everyday challenges

FOR DUMMIES®

The advice and explanations you need to succeed

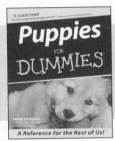

FOR DUMMIES®

We take the mystery out of complicated subjects